Analyzing Seniors' Housing Markets

Rick M. Jolson; courtesy AIA

At Brighton Gardens in Chevy Chase, Maryland, a 97,000-square-foot building complements the established mid-rise residential neighborhood and provides a variety of housing options and public spaces. The adjacent community center, shopping, and public transportation enable seniors to remain active in the community. Architect: Rick M. Jolson

1 Historical Perspective: The Emergence of Seniors' Housing

Early History

The origins of today's seniors' housing industry can be found in the communities developed by various church groups to care for elderly clergy and parishioners. When there was no such thing as Social Security and there were few pension programs, churches of various denominations began to respond to the increasing need to provide for the care of their elderly clergy as they retired from active service. This response addressed primarily the *housing* needs of aging clergy. Only within recent decades have sophisticated medical diagnostic and treatment modalities resulted in the need for long-term health care systems.

During this time, interest among older parishioners increased. Many elderly parishioners had reached an age when they no longer worked and similarly lacked an external economic support system that met their ongoing cost of living. Retirement homes that were originally open only to clergy began to extend their care to members of the church. Many early homes primarily served indigent widows. Frequently, such facilities offered housing and care for life in exchange for a nominal fee or an exchange of assets.

Trends Affecting the Development Of Seniors' Housing

Several factors substantially affected the creation of the seniors' housing industry as we know it today: demographics, medical care, the economics of aging, and the impact of working-couple households.

Demographics

The potential market for any product or service is driven, in large part, by the number of people in the market segment that it addresses. The increase in the population who might be considered to be of retirement age was one of the most dramatic demographic trends of the 20th century.

As illustrated in Figure 1-1, sheer numbers and the relative proportion of the older population to the total population have both increased. Between 1900 and 1990, the population age 65 and above grew from just over 4 percent to 12.5 percent of the total U.S. population. Before 2000, the fastest rate of growth occurred for those age 85 and older; that segment increased by approximately 40 percent between 1990 and 2000. Those age 75 to 84 years are expected to increase at about half the rate of their older counterparts. The baby boomers have begun to reach retirement age, doubling the number of persons age 65 to 74 between 2000 and 2030. This same phenomenon will drive the substantial increases among the older elderly groups (age 75 and older) during the period from 2030 to 2050. The significant increase in population for those 75 and older, representing the demographic market segment targeted by retirement housing, has formed a basis for the increase in the supply of communities designed to serve it.

The age 45 to 64 cohort represents the typical age of adult children who provide care and support to elderly parents as well as the future target market for seniors' housing. Trends for this age group, illustrated in Figure 1-2, show for the most part a steady increase between 1990 and 2050. While those age 45 to 54 represent the largest group, the age 55 to 59 group will experience the fastest rate of growth. Overall, the age 45 to 64 group is projected to increase by more than 40 million people during the 60-year period from 1990 to 2050.

Medical Care

In 1900, the average life expectancy at birth was 46.3 for an American male and 48.3 for an American female. By the middle of the decade, life expectancy had increased to 65.6 and 71.1 years, respectively. By 1990, life expectancy at birth had increased to 72.0 for men and 78.9 for women,[1] and it is projected that by 2020, the average life expectancy will reach 75.5 for men and 81.5 for women.[2]

The factor that contributed most directly to these extensions in life expectancy during the first half of the 20th century was the decrease in deaths of infants and children. The increases that have occurred since 1970, however, are the result of decreased mortality among the middle aged and elderly,[3] which reflects the substantial improvements that were made in medical diagnosis, treatment, and disease prevention during the 20th century. More particularly, the risks of dying from cardiovascular and cerebrovascular disease, two leading causes of death among the very old, have been substantially reduced. "The reasons for the sharp downturn in age-adjusted rates for the cardiovascular diseases include progress in controlling such risk factors as high saturated fat and cholesterol diets, cigarette smoking and hypertension, as well as positive developments in emergency, acute and long-term care for patients with coronary heart disease and stroke."[4]

It is not this book's intention to debate whether the quality of life of the elderly has improved significantly. Regardless, the increase in the number of those living to an older age and who experience decreasing capabilities in caring for themselves forms a market base for the provision of shelter and supportive and health care services. Chronic conditions such as arthritis, hypertensive diseases, and heart conditions are the more prevalent health problems for the older population. Such conditions frequently result in differing degrees of functional limitations in personal care or activities of daily living (ADLs)—defined as bathing, dressing, eating, getting in and out of bed and chairs, walking, going outside, and toiletting—which increase with a person's age. While these limitations vary widely from one individual to another, data indicate that increasing age frequently corresponds with increasing difficulties with ADLs. For example, according to data tabulated from the "1994–1995 National Health Interview Survey on Disability," 18.1 percent of individuals age 85 years and older have difficulties with two or more ADLs, compared with only 3.1 percent of those age 65 to 74. The overall population age 65 and older reflects a greater percentage of women (6.8 percent) than men (4.8 percent) experiencing this degree of functional impairment, which is at least partially attributed to the higher proportion of women in the upper age cohorts.[5] Among those 65 years and older, disability rates remained fairly constant throughout the 1970s and into the mid-1990s.[6] Difficulty in coping with routine personal care activities helps to create a market for services and environments to mitigate some of these conditions. Retirement communities in the various formats that exist today often encompass environments to provide such support.

Economics of Aging

A third and very important contribution to the market for seniors' housing has been the vast improvement in the economic condition of the elderly. In particular, four factors have contributed

Figure 1-1 **Actual and Projected Growth of Older Population (Thousands)**

Year	65–74		75–84		85+		65+	
	Number	Percent	Number	Percent	Number	Percent	Number	Percent
1900	2,187	2.9	772	1.0	122	0.2	3,080	4.1
1990	18,045	7.3	10,012	4.0	3,021	1.2	31,079	12.5
2000	18,391	6.5	12,361	4.4	4,240	1.5	34,992	12.4
2030	37,722	10.7	23,667	6.7	8,930	2.5	70,319	20.0
2050	36,014	8.9	26,632	6.6	19,352	4.8	81,998	20.3

Source: U.S. Census Bureau, Population Division, Population Projections Program, 2000.

Figure 1-2 **Actual and Projected Growth of Adult Offspring Population (Thousands)**

Year	45–54	55–59	60–64
1990	25,224	10,532	10,616
2000	37,678	13,469	10,805
2030	40,349	18,452	18,853
2050	45,445	22,445	21,199

Source: U.S. Census Bureau, Population Division, Population Projections Program, 2000.

to this improved economic picture: the passage of the Social Security Act, the increase in private and public pension fund enrollment (in terms of both people and dollars), the increase in asset values (particularly housing), and the development of federal health insurance (Medicare).

In 1935, the Roosevelt administration enacted the first Social Security Act (officially named Old-Age Survivors and Disability Insurance), providing for the payment of monthly benefits to qualified wage earners who were at least 65 years of age. A change in the act in 1939 provided separate benefits for secondary beneficiaries, such as wives, children, widows, and parents of wage earners. In 1950, Congress extended Social Security to self-employed individuals, most state and local government employees, household and farm workers, members of the armed forces, and the clergy.[7] Fewer than 1 percent of the elderly received Social Security benefits in 1940, compared with 93 percent in 1992 (with a mean income of $6,634).[8] The implementation of Social Security provided a base level of financial support for those who had reached retirement age.

This federal program was coupled with the emergence of private pensions for retired workers during the early part of the 20th century. By 1970, 3,312,000 individuals age 65 and older were enrolled in the private pension system, and by 1980, that number had more than doubled, to 6,767,000.[9] Enrollees in public pension funds (including civil service, military, and state and local governments) numbered 1,700,000 in 1970 and had increased to 3,960,000 by 1980.[10] Based on the 1999 Current Population Survey by the U.S. Census Bureau, 29,184,000 individuals age 65 and older were receiving Social Security benefits, and 10,501,000 individuals reported having a private pension.[11] While nearly all retirees older than 65 receive Social Security benefits, only about one-third are able to supplement this income with a private pension.

In 1966, 28.5 percent of individuals age 65 and older had incomes at or below the poverty level.[12] By 1999, only 9.7 percent of that age group was at or below the poverty level.[13] During the 1960s and early 1970s, the elderly realized significant gains in income resulting from specific improvements in Social Security and employer-sponsored pension benefits.

> Those retiring during the period also increasingly benefited from lengthening periods of coverage under Social Security between 1969 and 1972. Legislated cost of living increases from 1968 to 1971 raised benefits by 43 percent, while prices increased by only 27 percent. The 1972 Social Security Amendments mandated another 20 percent increase in benefits. The resulting improvement in the economic status of the elderly was significant.[14]

Overall, the ability of the elderly to afford retirement community living as an alternative to remaining in their own homes has increased substantially during the last several decades. For example, the median family income (in actual dollars) of families headed by an individual 65 or older in 1965 was $3,460[15] (the equivalent of $17,629 in 1997 dollars), compared with $20,761 in 1997.[16]

This is not to say that poverty is no longer a problem of the elderly, particularly single females. Historically, the proportion of nonelderly adults with incomes below the poverty level was significantly lower than for the elderly. Beginning in 1993, however, the trend reversed, and by 1999, nearly 9.7 percent of the elderly population age 65 and older had incomes that were below the poverty level, compared with 10 percent of those age 18 to 64.[17] Income differentiation is more pronounced among the elderly when one compares income for single individuals with that for couples and by age and gender. In 2000, 10.2 percent of the elderly age 65 and older had incomes below the poverty level. As Figure 1-3 illustrates, single women older than 65, particularly those 75 and older, are at a greater economic disadvantage than are men in the same age group (see Chapter 3).

Homeownership dominates this market segment. In 1997, about 79 percent of the elderly age 65 and older owned their own homes. Of that percentage, 77 percent owned them mortgage free.[18] Between 1980 and 2000, the extraordinary increases in housing values provided an asset base for many elderly, even those with relatively modest retirement incomes (Figure 1-4).

During the period from 1968 to 1999, median sale prices of existing single-family homes increased by 563 percent in the United States. These dramatic increases varied by region of the country, with the West significantly exceeding the national statistics.

In addition, the federal government played a role in the economic well-being of the elderly with the passage, in July 1967, of Medicare legislation, thereby providing federally funded insurance against many of the costs of acute medical care. In 1998, Medicare financed $216.6 billion for the health care of 38.8 million elderly and disabled beneficiaries, representing 19 percent of the nation's total spending for health care.[19] While programs such as Medicare provide substantial financial relief for the elderly from the rapidly accelerating costs of hospital and physician care, they have little impact on the costs of long-term care. Total health care spending for nursing home care in 1998 was $87.8 billion, with Medicare covering only $10.4 billion or 11.9 percent and Medicaid covering 46.3 percent. On the private side, almost all spending for nursing home care was paid for privately by patients or their families ($28.5 billion or 32.5 percent) in 1998.[20]

In fact, the cost of medical care for seniors continues to grow, despite federal programs. According to a study conducted by the Urban Institute, seniors pay approximately one-fifth of their income on out-of-pocket health care costs, such as premiums and prescription drugs. Average annual costs not covered by Medicare are $3,142, a figure that is projected to increase to $5,248 by 2025, when American seniors are expected to pay nearly one-third of their average incomes for health care.[21]

Figure 1-3 **Percentage of Elderly Population Below Poverty Level in 1999**

Age	Male	Female
65–74	7.1	10.3
75+	6.6	13.4

Source: U.S. Census Bureau, *Current Population Reports,* 1999.

Working-Couple Households

According to the U.S. Census Bureau, approximately 60 percent of married-couple households nationwide in 1998 were dual-income families where both the husband and wife worked. One of the results of dual-income families is the pressure on the traditional caregiver of elderly parents, the daughter or daughter-in-law. With women in the workforce, no one remains at home to care for frail, aging family members during the day. This situation does not, however, eliminate the need for informal caregiving or its availability. In 1997, a national survey indicated that more than 23 percent of all U.S. households with a telephone contained at least one caregiver,

Figure 1-4 **Median Sale Prices of Existing Single-Family Homes**

	United States	Northeast	Midwest	South	West
1968	$20,100	$21,400	$18,200	$19,000	$22,900
1999	$133,300	$139,000	$119,600	$120,300	$173,900
Change 1968–1999	563.2%	549.5%	557.1%	533.2%	659.4%

Source: National Association of Realtors®, unpublished data.

translating into an estimated 22,411,200 caregiving households.[22] Very few of the recipients of care resided in a nursing home, assisted living facility, or group home. The pressures created by having both members of the household in the workforce have undoubtedly contributed to the growth in the seniors' housing industry, particularly the assisted living segment described later in this chapter.

Product Emergence

Life Care or Continuing Care Retirement Communities

Some of the early retirement communities that still exist today—in particular, life care communities—were developed in the Pacific Southwest, North Central, and Northwest United States. For example, Hollenbeck Home opened its doors in Los Angeles in 1895. The early decades of the 20th century saw the opening of several other communities in California, including the Scripps Home in Altadena in 1913, Solheim Lutheran Homes in Los Angeles in 1923, and the Heritage in San Francisco in 1925. Early communities frequently combined housing and support services, offering residents the opportunity to reside and receive care for life. This care was frequently provided in exchange for personal assets. Those who moved to such communities enjoyed the security of knowing that they would not have to worry about how they would receive or pay for care as their needs increased. The life care or continuing care concept changed in the next few decades. In particular, as the need for long-term health care services increased and the nursing home became the institutional source for such care, retirement communities were developed with or added beds for such long-term care. For instance, Hollenbeck Home opened its skilled nursing facility in 1954, more than half a century after it originally opened the main facility.

The life care or continuing care retirement community (CCRC), as it has evolved during the last several decades, eventually offered its housing and services on a fee-for-service basis, which called for the payment of a specific upfront entrance fee and the ongoing payment of a monthly fee. This concept embodied a self-insured health care component that addressed the future need for nursing care among the residents. As the costs of providing increasing levels of health care accelerated, residents were assured that they would pay no more than a specified monthly fee tied to the cost of the fee for an independent living unit. For example, at Foulkeways, a Quaker life care community in the Philadelphia area, a resident who must move permanently from an apartment to the nursing home pays only the basic monthly fee for the studio apartment, the smallest unit offered by Foulkeways. With today's costs for long-term care and the average daily rates for semiprivate and private rooms in nursing homes in the same geographic area, it is a substantial cost savings for the resident. In 2000 in suburban Philadelphia, for example, one could expect to pay a minimum of $140 per day for a nursing home bed or $4,250 per month, compared with $1,622 per month paid by a resident of Foulkeways.

The insurance element inherent in the traditional life care concept has been compared with a pension plan. Similar to pension plans, life care communities receive revenues "in advance of the cash payments required for meeting promised benefits. . . . The payment of a CCRC entry fee plus recurring monthly fees is designed to advance-fund the cost of future health care for a CCRC resident."[23] Improperly han-

Definitions by Various Associations

Definitions of the terms used to describe different types of retirement communities are not uniformly agreed to, and uniform working definitions are made more difficult because of the variation in the regulatory definitions developed by states that regulate the various forms of retirement housing.

American Association of Homes and Services for the Aging

Continuing care retirement community. Provides for or arranges for the provision of housing and health-related services to an older person under an agreement(s) effective for the life of the person or for a specified period greater than one year. CCRCs employ a wide variety of contracts to specify the particular services and benefits afforded to residents in return for entrance and monthly fees. For various reasons, it is relatively common for a CCRC to offer several different contract types or variations of one type of contract.

All-inclusive (or extensive) contract. An upfront entry fee and monthly charges that remain the same regardless of the resident's level of care.

Modified contract. An upfront entry fee with monthly charges that remain the same regardless of the resident's level of care for only a specified period of time (e.g., 30 days per year), or increased monthly charges for the resident as the level of care increases but at a discount from the market value of the services (e.g., a 10 percent discount on the daily nursing rate for residents).

Rental contract. No upfront entry fee; resident's monthly charges increase directly with the level of care provided.

American Seniors Housing Association

Congregate housing/independent living units. Congregate or independent living units are designed for seniors who pay for some congregate services (housekeeping, transportation, meals) as part of a monthly fee or rental rate and who require little, if any, assistance with ADLs. Residents of congregate/independent living units may or may not receive some home health care services provided by in-house staff or an outside agency. Congregate or independent living units may be part of a congregate residence or part of a property that provides both congregate and assisted living services or part of a CCRC, but not part of a freestanding assisted living residence.

Assisted living. Assisted living beds are designed for frail seniors who need assistance with ADLs but who do not require continuous skilled nursing care. These beds can also be located in a separate wing or floor of a congregate residence or in a freestanding assisted living building. They typically have more stringent licensure requirements than congregate/independent living units.

Assisted Living Federation of America

Assisted living. A special combination of housing, supportive services, personalized assistance, and health care designed to respond to the individual needs of those who need help with ADLs and instrumental ADLs. Support services are available 24 hours a day to meet scheduled and unscheduled needs in a way that promotes maximum dignity and independence for each resident and involves the resident's family, neighbors, and friends.

Sources: Kathryn L. Brod, *The CCRC Industry 1997 Profile,* AAHSA, pp. 2 & 10; ASHA, *The State of Seniors Housing 1999,* p. 8.; and ALFA, "The Assisted Living Industry: An Overview, 2000," p. 4.

dled, this concept represents an area of substantial economic risk. Life care communities need to create a fee structure based on an assessment of future health care needs and costs of the pool of individuals residing in them. Some of the problems in this effort resulted in such shortcomings as the "practice of basing fees on the unit size (real estate basis) rather than an entrant's age or physical condition (actuarial basis) . . . despite industry-wide agreement that the product is the intangible, insurance-like concept of continuing care and not the living unit itself."[24] Other serious errors include the application of life expectancies to amortize entrance fees into the community's income stream and the lack of distinction made between mortality rates applicable to those living in apartments and those residing in health care centers.[25] These factors, combined with a lack of stringent health and economic admissions criteria, have created major financial and operational problems for some communities and will continue to do so for others in the future.

Partially in response to the concern over the ability to accurately predict future use and costs of long-term health care, some retirement communities began, in effect, to "unbundle" the costs of health care, thereby eliminating the insurance component from the life care community. Such communities may still include housing and health care in their services but do not attempt to include the future costs of health care in the entrance or monthly fees. Instead, when a resident has to make a permanent move (or in some cases, a temporary move) to the nursing home, the care provided in the nursing home is provided on a fee-for-service basis. Some communities offer various forms of discounted health care coverage, such as a specified number of free days in the health center or a daily rate for permanent transfers below the normal daily rate charged to those who entered the nursing home directly from outside the community rather than transferring from an independent living unit.

In its publication, *The Continuing Care Retirement Communities 1998 Profile,* the American Association of Homes and Services for the Aging (AAHSA) defined four different types of contracts in addition to the small number (6 percent) of communities offered under an ownership structure. Approximately 42 percent offered an "all-inclusive" contract, representing the traditional program under which residents would pay no additional cost for nursing care. Reflecting the changes in the market and consumers' preferences, nearly 41 percent offered either a modified (nursing care covered for a specified number of days) or fee-for-service (residents' monthly charges increase directly with level of care provided) contract. Interestingly, 11 percent of the respondents were rental communities that also charged for additional care as it was provided.[26]

Some evidence suggests, however, that there is strong continued interest in the classic all-inclusive contract, which AAHSA refers to as a *Type A* or *extensive* contract. In 1994, the AAHSA Development Corporation and Herbert J. Sims & Co. published a report on newer communities, focusing on those under construction or in operation for up to five years. The report included data from 51 communities (four of which were rental communities). Seventy-seven percent of the facilities charging entrance fees offered extensive (all-inclusive) coverage.[27]

The number of CCRCs has been variously estimated. In preparation for its 1997 study, AAHSA sent surveys to 2,106 communities that it felt met the definition of a CCRC. In what may represent the first comprehensive effort to estimate the supply of seniors' housing, the National Investment Center estimated that there were 1,900 CCRCs in 1999.[28]

Congregate Housing

During the last several decades, a major retirement community product type was developed that almost, if not entirely, eliminated the health care component. Such communities, frequently referred to as *congregate housing* or *adult congregate living facilities* (ACLFs), typically offer housing and support services such as meals, housekeeping, maintenance, transportation, and social and recreation programs. While these communities might include a wellness program and assistance with ADLs (either in the residential unit or in a separate section of the facility), they stop short of providing skilled or intermediate nursing care directly to the resident. Some ACLFs simply require that residents move when such care is needed. Other facilities have attempted to respond to the need for long-term care by facilitating such transfers through agreements with area nursing homes or through contracts or other referral arrangements with home health care agencies.

The development of congregate communities was encouraged to a certain extent in the 1980s by the Department of Housing and Urban Development's (HUD's) 221(d)(4) mortgage insurance program, known as the Retirement Service Center program. Between 1983 and 1989, this program built on HUD's existing 221(d)(4) insurance program to "cover the gap between the totally independent living arrangement of noncongregate housing for the elderly and the health-care-oriented nursing home."[29] In the HUD-proscribed basic program components, the Retirement Service Center program did not permit medical services to be part of the community's service package without prior approval, other than having a small number of infirmary beds. The program also prohibited the charging of "a founder's fee, initial admission fee, or similar charge beyond normal security deposits associated with standard rental projects."[30] The availability of this mortgage insurance, coupled with its favorable financing terms and the ultimate institution of a coinsurance program, resulted in the development of 190 projects designed to meet HUD's programmatic framework, such as rental projects that offered little or no health care. A large proportion of the communities financed in the 1980s under this program defaulted on their loans or were financially troubled. An audit report issued in April 1990 from the Office of the Inspector General pointed to "poor loan underwriting [and] inadequate program policies, procedures, controls, implementation, and design."[31]

In the 1990s, however, HUD began allowing rental seniors' housing communities to be covered under its 221(d)(3) and 221(d)(4) insurance program that had been largely revised since its predecessor, the Retirement Service Center program of the 1980s.

Several organizations have made efforts to estimate the supply of congregate housing units in the United States. The American Seniors Housing Association (ASHA) estimated a total of 5,500 professionally owned and managed properties comprising 660,000 units in 1999,[32] while the National Investment Center (NIC) estimated 5,964 properties with 705,376 units in that same year.[33]

Assisted Living

During the 1990s, assisted living facilities (ALFs) emerged as the dominant model in the seniors' housing continuum. Defined under various licensing categories, assisted living is defined by the Assisted Living Federation of America (ALFA) as:

> . . . a special combination of housing, supportive services, personalized assistance, and health care designed to respond to the individual needs of those who need help with activities of daily living and instrumental activities of daily living. Supportive services are available 24 hours a day, to meet scheduled and unscheduled needs, in a way that promotes maximum dignity and independence for each resident and involves the resident's family, neighbors, and friends.[34]

Assisted living has been positioned to respond to a need-driven market segment, but some have also described it as an alternative to nursing homes. Historically, assisted living could arguably be subdivided into two segments. The initial segment comprised the board-and-care industry and included many facilities that are privately owned and operated by a vast array of older not-for-profit organizations and mom-and-pop operators. In 1989, just before the start of the boom in assisted living, the National Association of Residential Care Facilities estimated that 41,000 board-and-care facilities housed 563,000 residents. These communities do not reflect the residential designs characterizing contemporary assisted living communities. Rooms offering one or more beds rather than apartments for residents are typical of these older facilities.

With the formation of ALFA and its success in focusing attention on the need for assisted living communities that met contemporary standards and consumer demand, the boom in assisted living development took off. Unlike CCRCs and congregate housing, assisted living became the focus of numerous large national companies, many of which went public during the 1990s. During that volatile period, the number of public companies actively involved in assisted living decreased through a variety of mergers and acquisitions. Nevertheless, Legg Mason estimated that the assisted living industry by 1999 had become a $15 billion industry, accounting for approximately 15 percent of the total long-term care industry.[35] The NIC estimated that a total of 27,277 properties offered assisted living services with a total of 585,735 units or 777,801 beds.[36] Because of the lack of uniform definitions, however, other estimates of the size of the industry vary. ASHA, for example, estimated that 6,500 professionally owned and managed ALFs in 1999 contained 550,000 beds,[37] whereas another national survey conducted in 1998 estimated a total of 11,459 facilities with approximately 611,300 beds.[38] And ALFA offered the highest estimate—30,000 to 40,000 facilities housing an estimated 1 million people—which includes everything from small, family-owned facilities to larger purpose-built ALFs.[39]

ALFs can be freestanding or part of a multilevel campus or community. The wide variations in ALFs are reflected in the different models. In a national study of ALFs issued in 1999, ALFs were characterized by levels of service and privacy. *High privacy* indicated that at least 80 percent of units were private. "*High service* was defined as having a full-time registered nurse on staff who provided nursing care, as needed, with facility staff, as well as [provided] help with at least two ADLs, 24-hour staff, housekeeping, and at least two meals a day."[40]

The study went on to estimate the national distribution of ALFs by category as follows:

Low privacy and low service	27%
Minimal privacy or service	32%
High privacy and low service	18%
High service and low privacy	12%
High privacy and high service	11%

Payment Mechanisms

Traditional Endowment Fees and Entrance Fees

Once the practice of offering care in exchange for assets was largely abandoned, the payment mechanism most widely used involved a combination of an upfront fee with an ongoing monthly fee. The upfront fee, variously referred to as an *entrance* or *endowment fee,* was designed to cover the development costs associated with the unit selected and, in the case of traditional life care communities, to provide a reserve for future health care costs. This entrance or endowment fee was generally nonrefundable. Different communities handled the issue of refundability in various ways. In some instances, such as Cadbury in Cherry Hill, New Jersey, the entrance fee was nonrefundable. In other cases, the entrance fee was, in effect, amortized over a period of time. For example, at Rydal Park, a life care community in Rydal, Pennsylvania, after an initial 90-day probationary period, residents who withdraw from the community during the first 50 months receive a prorated refund of their entrance fees. In addition, residents may specify a refund of one-half their entrance fee should they die during the first year of occupancy.

Monthly fees, on the other hand, are typically tied to the cost of operating the community and also depend on the type of unit selected and the number of people residing in the unit. In the early years of the industry, monthly fees were set at entrance and were never or rarely subsequently increased for a resident. The current practice, however, prompted by the economic realities of operating the community, is to increase monthly fees periodically (usually no more than once a year) and to tie these increases directly to inflation and the increased costs of operating the community.

Payment of the entrance or endowment fee and monthly fee is most often required only when a resident enters a community's independent living units. For those communities providing nursing care, two circumstances determine the fee for such care. Direct entry into a nursing home bed from outside the retirement community typically requires payment of a daily rate commensurate with the market rate for similar beds in the geographic area. Those who transfer to a nursing bed from the residential portion of the retirement community usually pay a specified monthly fee or a daily rate that, again, is likely to be similar to the local rates at area nursing homes.

For communities that incorporate health care coverage in their entrance/endowment and monthly fees, residents are able to declare a certain portion of the medical fees on their annual federal income tax statements as medical deductions. For instance, at the Quadrangle in Haverford, Pennsylvania, just under 30 percent of the monthly fee for a resident in an independent living unit is considered to be applicable to health care costs. In other communities, a dollar amount is specified for health care coverage.

Refundable Entrance Fees

During the 1980s, facilities were developed that offered fully (or nearly fully) refundable entrance fees. This concept was pioneered by Life Care Services (LCS), a company that had previously worked with not-for-profit sponsors on traditional endowment fee projects. Calling the new approach a return-of-capital program, LCS created an approach that, in effect, capitalized the project through the entrance fees. Basically structured as an interest-free loan to the nonprofit sponsor, the return-of-capital program refunded 90 percent of the entrance fees when the residents withdrew from the community (either voluntarily or through death). In its 1994 study, the AAHSA Development Corp./Herbert J. Sims & Co. reported that "less than half of the CCRCs in the *National Continuing Care Data Base* offer refunds of 90 percent or greater, while more than half of the emerging CCRCs offer these refunds."[41]

Other communities incorporated different approaches to refundability. Williamsburg Landing, in Williamsburg, Virginia, provided residents or their estates a full refund of the entrance fee, which was paid upon permanent transfer to the nursing center, death, or voluntary withdrawal from the community.

Today, the majority of retirement communities offer a choice of multiple entrance fee plans. For example, Adult Communities Total Services (ACTS), now Retirement-Life Communities, initially offered one entrance fee plan in which the fee was nonrefundable. It now offers a choice between a 50 percent refundable plan and the traditional nonrefundable plan. In Bloomfield, Connecticut, Duncaster offers residents a choice of three entrance fee programs with different terms for refundability.

Several major factors influenced the emergence of refundable entrance fees. One was consumer demand. Many seniors were interested in the concept of life care or continuing care but found the financial arrangements to be unacceptable. The influence of their family members—the future heirs—could also be felt in this resistance. Often, as entrance fees began to accelerate in relation to the increasing costs of real estate development, the upfront fees equaled a substantial proportion of an elderly household's assets. As elderly consumers became more sophisticated in evaluating options for retirement housing, their demands regarding the financial arrangements of continuing care reflected this sophistication. Although refundable entrance fees were typically 50 percent higher than their nonrefundable counterparts, many were willing to pay the extra cost to insure the integrity of their estate.

Another factor that influenced the introduction of the refundable entrance fee was the emergence of private, for-profit organizations. For such organizations, the nonrefundable entrance fee represented taxable income when received and would therefore produce substantial taxable income over a very short period of time. The refundable entrance fee, however, represented a loan or a form of debt, thereby lessening the chance of taxation to the company.

In addition, increasing competition contributed to the development of more substantial provisions for refundability. CCRCs found themselves competing for prospective residents who had a variety of choices in a given market, and offering various refund options provided a competitive edge.

Monthly Rental

Numerous communities eschew the entrance fee concept entirely, retaining only a monthly charge. Such communities, such as the Lafayette in Philadelphia, may offer a full range of care. The Lafayette includes 300 independent living units and a full 120-bed nursing unit. Frequently, however, rental communities embrace the congregate housing model described earlier in this chapter. In contrast to offering a contract that, for the most part, promises lifetime residency, rental communities may offer a yearly or even monthly lease. Rental communities cover both the entire cost of the debt financing and the operating expenses through their monthly fees, making these monthly fees quite a bit higher, in general, than the monthly fee required by a life care or continuing care community.

Payment of a monthly rental fee is typical of both congregate communities and assisted living facilities. In congregate communities, the monthly fee covers a basic service package that includes a specified number of meals per day, housekeeping services, scheduled transportation, maintenance and security, and an activities program. Frequently, linen service is also included. Residents may be able to purchase additional services for additional fees.

ALFs offer several different approaches. Some ALFs charge a monthly fee (sometimes quoted as a daily rate) that includes a full-service package: three daily meals, snacks, housekeeping and linen service, scheduled transportation, social and recreational programs, and assistance with activities of daily living or personal care services. Regardless of the extent of the assistance required, these communities do not vary the monthly or daily rate. It is much more typical for ALFs to charge a base fee plus incremental additional fees for higher levels of care, however. In many cases, communities that charge various levels of fees do not include any assistance with ADLs in the base fee. At Sunrise of Bath in Akron, Ohio, for example, prices vary based on the level of assistance with ADLs, and the base price excludes any assistance with ADLs.

Equity Models

Another less frequently used payment approach is the condominium or cooperative. While a few early examples of such communities exist, particularly in the Minneapolis area, most projects that offer residents equity opportunities were developed during the latter part of the 20th century. Condominium and co-op projects offer residents of independent living units an opportunity to share in the ownership of the community through shares in the corporation (a co-op) or by holding fee simple title (a condominium). Condo/co-op projects appear to offer an attractive option for those looking for the benefits of owning real estate, including tax benefits such as the deduction of mortgage interest, and not paying tax on the gain from the sale of a home because it is reinvested in a new home. In 1997, the laws pertaining to capital gains tax on the sale of a home changed to allow an exclusion of up to $250,000 of gain ($500,000 for certain married taxpayers filing a joint return), regardless of age for homes sold after May 6, 1997. Other benefits include the potential for appreciation of the unit's value. The condominium or cooperative payment approach has been applied to both continuing care or life care communities and congregate communities.

The Canterbury in West Hartford, Connecticut, does not have a nursing home; it offers residents shelter and services until they need to make a permanent move. In contrast, Beaumont at Bryn Mawr, Pennsylvania, offers its independent living units through purchase of certificates of membership in a nonprofit cooperative housing corporation. The certificate of membership, along with a proprietary lease agreement, entitles residents to occupy a villa or apartment in the community for life. The residents are provided a full continuum of care services, including independent living, assisted living, and nursing care, on one campus.

These two communities not only illustrate the difference in the condo or co-op structure but also reflect very different economic target markets. While the Canterbury, with purchase prices ranging from $30,000 to $70,000, targets the middle-income market, Beaumont at Bryn Mawr has intentionally targeted a very upscale market segment. Selling prices at Beaumont for cooperative units in 2000 ranged from $250,000 to $550,000, with monthly fees ranging from $2,523 to $3,408. The community reinforces this target market with its physical design. Beaumont at Bryn Mawr is built around a former estate and uses the estate as the central activity core. Residential units include villas ranging from 1,668 to 1,970 square feet of living space. Apartments are also quite large, ranging from 1,029 to 1,533 square feet of living space. Beaumont is currently the only equity model CCRC in Pennsylvania, and demand has been intense since it opened in 1988. In 2000, Beaumont's waiting list was eight to ten years for an apartment or villa.

Organizations Involved In the Industry

Not-for-Profit Organizations

Certain segments of the seniors' housing field have been dominated by nonprofit religious and fraternal organizations. Throughout the country, a large number of senior care facilities, particularly CCRCs and life care communities, are still owned and operated by religious denominations and private nonprofit groups. While many of the nonprofit retirement communities were developed originally with multiple levels of care, from independent living to nursing home, others grew out of a nursing home base. Recognizing and capitalizing on their knowledge and experience in this industry, nonprofit organizations have offered their expertise in development (either their own or in conjunction with a for-profit development firm), marketing, and/or management on a contract basis to others becoming involved in the industry.

For-Profit Organizations

For-profit organizations have come to play a significant role in the seniors' housing industry, particularly as assisted living emerged during the 1990s as the dominant development model. While for-profit organizations initially were more likely to provide contract development, marketing, and management services, ownership became a focal point for many. According to its *Seniors Housing Statistical Digest, 2000–2001,* ASHA estimated that as of June 2000, the ten largest seniors' housing owners, all of which were for-profit organizations, owned 1,381 properties containing 117,468 units.[42] The number of facilities owned more than doubled from the 52,719 reported in 1994. Although a great deal of the growth can be attributed to the emergence of assisted living during the decade, it was not limited to assisted living. A survey conducted by AAHSA shows that among a sample of 2,205 communities (not limited to CCRCs) nationwide, 26.6 percent are owned by for-profit providers.[43]

A particular trend during the 1990s was the creation of publicly held companies, primarily in the assisted living segment of the industry. In 1994, only two public assisted living companies existed: Assisted Living Concepts and Standish Care (no longer in business). By the latter part of the decade, about a dozen publicly held owner/operators existed. For-profit involvement was not limited to public companies. According to *Assisted Living Today*'s 2000 survey, 74 percent of the 50 largest assisted living providers were privately held companies, and an overwhelming 90 percent were for-profit providers.[44] Further, among the nation's 50 largest long-term care providers, 84 percent are for-profit organizations.[45]

Health Care Providers

Another major category of entrants in seniors' housing is health care providers, both those who focus primarily on long-term care and some whose traditional venue is acute care.

In 1983, *Modern Health Care,* a newsmagazine covering all aspects of the health care industry, began to include data on life care in its annual multiunit provider survey, reporting on both nursing home chains and multihospital systems that operated life care facilities. The data from survey respondents revealed that nine nursing home chains operated ten life care communities in 1981 and that 15 multihospital systems operated 37 such facilities. After 1983, the number of retirement facilities represented by the multifacility health care providers grew rapidly, as did the number of players. By the 1994 survey, 74 health care systems reported that they were operating 481 retirement communities. This number rose considerably, to 86 systems operating 573 retirement communities, by 1999.[46]

The interest and involvement of health care providers (both proprietary and nonprofit) were generated by several factors. Responding to the overall attention that seniors' housing received during the 1980s, many health care providers recognized this form of housing as a natural extension of their existing levels of care. In some cases, providers owned land that was vacant or underused, and the development of a seniors' housing community enabled them to increase the value of a non-income-producing asset. Another factor for hospitals was the desire to extend their business with older consumers, who otherwise were discharged after relatively short in-patient stays as a result of the pressures of the prospective payment system for Medicare reimbursement. For many providers, the operation of a seniors' housing facility furthered the mission to serve the elderly in a community while providing an opportunity to develop a revenue stream far less affected by changes in reimbursement.

Trade Associations

American Association of Homes and Services for the Aging

The not-for-profit retirement communities are represented, in large part, by AAHSA, a national organization based in Washington, D.C. As of January 2000, AAHSA had more than 5,600 member organizations, 93 percent of the membership consisting of retirement communities. AAHSA's member-sponsors include religious, fraternal, labor, civic, community-based, and government organizations. AAHSA provides its members with a broad variety of benefits, including representation in Congress and at federal agencies on issues affecting their constituents. In addition, AAHSA offers a national certification program for retirement housing professionals, a continuing care accreditation commission, and assistance to members in financing and development through the AAHSA Development Corporation.

Assisted Living Federation of America

In 1991, a new trade organization was formed for the specific purpose of representing issues and concerns of the emerging providers of assisted living. Initially called the Assisted Living Facilities Association of America (ALFAA), the association changed its name to the Assisted Living Federation of America in 1996, when it converted to a federation of state associations. This organization grew as rapidly as the assisted living segment of the industry during the 1990s, and in June 1999 ALFA combined its membership with NASLIE, the National Association of Senior Living Executives (formerly known as NASLI). Formed in 1985, NASLI was the first major trade association to focus primarily on serving the for-profit segment of the seniors' housing industry. At the time NASLIE was folded into ALFA, the latter organization had 6,400 members, including both for-profit and nonprofit providers.

American Seniors Housing Association

The American Seniors Housing Association emerged in 1991 to represent the interests of organizations participating in the seniors' housing industry in the areas of development, operations, construction, finance, and management. By early 2001, ASHA had approximately 260 corporate members. ASHA plays an integral role in seniors' housing advocacy by focusing on long-term care policy, state regulations, tax policy, building codes, property management, and finance. ASHA's founders established the association to help shape the legislative and regulatory agenda of the seniors' housing industry. In addition to emphasizing advocacy, ASHA is committed to expanding the scope of industry research. ASHA publishes a wide variety of definitive monographs and reports on financing seniors' housing, operations, fair housing, investment trends, construction, long-term care policy, building codes, corporate compliance, and other pertinent issues.

National Council on Seniors Housing

Another major organization that has targeted the retirement housing industry is the National Association of Home Builders (NAHB). NAHB is a national trade association representing approximately 200,000 members, with more than 800 state and local affiliates. In 1989, NAHB formed the National Council on Seniors Housing (NCOSH), which has grown steadily from its inception to an estimated 888 members in 2000. NCOSH membership provides informational and networking resources, updates on industry and legislative issues, a free subscription to NCOSH's quarterly newsletter, *Seniors Housing News,* educational opportunities, a nationally recognized annual conference, and numerous other services.

American Health Care Association

AHCA is a federation of 50 state health organizations representing nearly 12,000 nonprofit and for-profit health care organizations providing assisted living, nursing facilities, and subacute care. Founded in the 1950s as the American Association of Nursing Homes, the organization became the American Health Care Association in 1975. The National Center for Assisted Living (NCAL) is the AHCA's voice for assisted living, focusing on ensuring quality and access to assisted living services.

National Investment Center

Although not actually a trade association, NIC is an important organization serving the seniors' housing/long-term care industry. Founded in 1991, NIC, which is a not-for-profit educational forum, facilitates efficient capital formation for the seniors' housing and care industries through research, networking, and the provision of business and financial information. Since its creation, NIC has served as a valuable resource for lenders, investors, developers/operators, and others interested in meeting the housing and health care needs of America's seniors. In addition to the numerous studies sponsored and cosponsored by NIC, the organization sponsors an annual conference. In late 1999, NIC and the Johns Hopkins University formed the nation's first graduate business program for seniors' housing and care. The program is affiliated with the school's Real Estate Institute.

Accreditation

The only accrediting body for continuing care retirement communities, AAHSA's Continuing Care Accreditation Commission (CCAC) was founded in 1985. Accreditation is a voluntary process involving a year-long extensive self-evaluation by the retirement community's staff, residents, and board of directors and an on-site review by trained CCAC evaluators. The evaluators review three critical areas: resident life, health, and wellness; financial resources and disclosure; and governance and administration. While the CCAC is not a government agency or regulatory body, it does represent a "seal of approval" for retirement communities. As of August 2000, 293 retirement communities were accredited.

Two organizations emerged in 2000 to accredit and establish quality standards for assisted living: the Joint Commission on Accreditation of Healthcare Organizations (JCAHO) and the Rehabilitation Accreditation Commission (CARF). Both accreditation programs are voluntary yet demonstrate to consumers and regulatory bodies providers' intent to operate top-quality facilities through self-regulation. The accreditation movement responds, in part, to the concern about regulation in the assisted living industry, which varies significantly from state to state and has no overarching federal structure. JCAHO accreditation standards focus on a set of principals, including the rights of residents, individualized services, coordination of provider services, around-the-clock assistance, and supervision and advance notification of discharge and transfer assistance. A key goal of CARF's program is to develop standards that are oriented toward outcomes and focus on three major areas: leadership, outcomes management, and services. By embracing accreditation, the assisted living industry took a significant self-regulatory step, which could help to offset any efforts to create federal regulation.

Although JCAHO has been accrediting long-term care facilities since 1966, the organization more recently established standards for the voluntary accreditation of assisted living facilities. In May 2000, King-Bruwaert House in Burr Ridge, Illinois, became the first assisted living facility to be accredited by JCAHO. The JCAHO accreditation focuses on six functions that address the care of residents, including consumer protection and rights and assisted living community ethics, continuity of service, assessment and reassessment, resident services, resident education, and health and wellness promotion. In addition, six functions address the management of assisted living communities: improving performance, leadership, managing the environment of care, managing human resources, managing information, and preventing and controlling infection.

CARF has accredited approximately 25,000 programs or services in the areas of adult day services, behavioral health, employment and community services, and medical rehabilitation. Accreditation for assisted living facilities was instituted in 2000, with the first accreditation awarded to Learning Services in Gilroy, California, in April 2001. The accreditation process includes self-study as well as an onsite consultative survey by CARF surveyors. The consumer-focused standards were developed to help organizations measure and improve the quality of their programs and services.

ALFA endorses the CARF accreditation program, while AAHSA endorses the JCAHO program.

Financing Approaches

The financing of retirement communities was, for many years, dominated by tax-exempt bonds that had substantial advantages, particularly for the nonprofit sponsors dominating the industry. They offered a route to nearly 100 percent debt financing at long-term, favorable fixed-interest rates and allowed for the funding of capitalized development expenses. On the other hand, tax-exempt bonds for retirement facilities were typically unrated and involved substantial financing costs and high reserve requirements. For proprietary organizations, tax-exempt financing was more restrictive, limiting a project's capital costs.

As the industry, capital markets, and tax codes changed, however, financing mechanisms changed as well. The passage of the 1986 Tax Reform Act significantly impacted the means by which real estate was financed—and the retirement housing industry as well. The federal requirements associated with tax-exempt mortgage revenue bonds became more restrictive. An annual limit was placed on each state of $75 per individual or $250 million total. For proprietary developers, additional restrictions required that 20 or 40 percent of the residential units be occupied by tenants 50 or 60 percent below the area's median gross income. Nonprofit sponsors were still able to access the exempt bond market after the passage of the 1986 Tax Reform Act, however. True nonprofit corporations, as defined by Section 501(c)(3) of the Internal Revenue Code, had no limit on the amount of indebtedness and were not subject to state volume caps. Several limitations were placed on 501(c)(3) corporations using tax-exempt financing, however, including such things as a limitation of $150 million per exempt organization or related group of exempt organizations.

Ninety-five percent of the net proceeds of the bonds were used to provide facilities that are owned by a governmental unit or by a 501(c)(3) exempt organization and are for the organization's exempt function,[47] with no more than 2 percent of the proceeds to be used for issuance costs, limitations on the debt service reserves, advanced refunding, and the interest that could be earned on the bond proceeds.

Financing by commercial lenders, savings and loans associations, insurance companies, credit companies, real estate investment trusts (REITs), foreign companies, and individual investors (through limited partnerships) has broadened the base of capital available for the development of seniors' housing. Commercial banks and savings and loans typically have provided construction and mid-term loans for five- to ten-year periods with 20- to 25-year amortization. Insurance companies are more likely, on the other hand, to provide takeout financing for existing developments with an operating history. Credit companies typically provide construction financing dealing with tax-credit projects. REITs, which increased their activity during the early to middle 1990s but have played a significantly decreased role in the last few years, provide construction and acquisition funds with a mortgage loan or sale/leaseback option.

Fannie Mae (the Federal National Mortgage Association) and Freddie Mac (the Federal Home Loan Mortgage Corporation) are also involved in the seniors' housing industry. Fannie Mae purchases multifamily mortgages from specifically designated lenders, with a focus on completed projects. Freddie Mac also purchases mortgages from lenders and holds them in its portfolio or packages them into securities that are sold to investors. Like Fannie Mae, it looks for stabilized properties.

A number of private equity funds have also become involved in financing seniors' housing companies, particularly those in the assisted living and Alzheimer's care segment of the industry. Focusing primarily on organizations that have a long-term commitment to the industry, private equity funds tend to hold their portfolio companies for three to seven years and make corporate rather than project-specific development investments.

The U.S. government has a variety of programs designed to provide incentives and favorable financing terms to fund housing projects. Many federal programs are operated by HUD.[48] Federal programs used for the development or rehabilitation of seniors' housing include:

- *Section 221(d)*—Through the 221(d) Market Rate program, the Federal Housing Administration (FHA) insures mortgages for the new construction or substantial rehabilitation of multifamily rental properties for low- to moderate-income and displaced families. The program assists private industry by making capital more readily available and by reducing the risk of default for lenders. Nonprofit and cooperative sponsors use Section

221(d)(3), for-profit sponsors Section 221(d)(4); the difference is that a nonprofit sponsor can receive an insured amount equal to the full value of the HUD/FHA estimated replacement cost of the project, whereas the for-profit sponsor can receive a maximum of 90 percent of the estimate. In 1999, 198 projects or 32,264 units were insured under 221(d) programs. The 1980s program known as the Retirement Service Center program under Section 221(d) no longer exists; therefore, FHA still insures loans for apartments for the elderly but not those with central kitchens and the extensive amenities typical of retirement service centers.

- *Section 232*—HUD's Section 232 program insures mortgages that cover the construction or rehabilitation of nursing homes and assisted living facilities. The program allows the developer, either nonprofit or for-profit, to more easily secure financing through a HUD-approved lender by insuring the mortgage loan, thereby protecting the lender against the risk of default on the mortgage. In 1999, 131 loans for 13,425 units were insured under the Section 232 program.
- *Section 202*—Private nonprofit organizations with experience in housing or related social service activities are eligible for funding under HUD's Section 202 program. The program provides capital advances to finance the construction, rehabilitation, and other expenses associated with supportive housing for very-low-income elderly. If the project meets its obligation to serve very-low-income elderly persons for 40 years, the capital advance does not have to be repaid. As a minimum capital investment, the owner/developer is required to deposit 0.5 percent of the HUD-approved capital advance in a special escrow account, up to a maximum of $25,000 for a national sponsor or $10,000 for other sponsors. HUD's Rental Assistance program covers the difference between the approved operating cost per unit and the tenant's rent, which is 30 percent of his or her adjusted income. In 1996, nearly $394 million in capital advances for 5,554 units was allocated.
- *HOME*—The HOME program provides grants to state and local governments to create partnerships between nonprofit organizations and local communities to fund numerous types of activities to create affordable housing for low-income households. HOME is unique in that it allows local governments and groups to design and implement strategies specifically tailored to the needs of the local community. The flexibility of the program allows states and participating jurisdictions to use HOME funds for grants, direct loans, loan guarantees, or other forms of credit enhancement, or rental assistance or security deposits. States are automatically eligible for HOME funds, and local jurisdictions are allocated funds based on a formula that considers the "relative inadequacy of each jurisdiction's housing supply, its incidence of poverty, its fiscal distress, and other factors." In rental projects with more than five assisted units, at least 20 percent of the units must be occupied by families with incomes that do not exceed 50 percent of the HUD-adjusted median. More than $1.5 billion was allocated in 1999 in HOME funds.
- *Low-Income Housing Tax Credits*—Created by the Tax Reform Act of 1986, LIHTCs are administered by the Internal Revenue Service rather than HUD. They provide a dollar-for-dollar reduction in federal tax liability each year for a period of ten years in exchange for the production or rehabilitation of low-income rental housing. This program therefore does not provide a direct subsidy to tenants or developers but increases the amount of equity in the project, thereby reducing the level and cost of debt. To qualify, a project must have a minimum of 20 percent of units occupied by very-low-income households with incomes under 50 percent of the area median income or 40 percent of units occupied by low-income households with incomes under 60 percent of the area median income. The LIHTC program gives states more than $3 billion in annual budget authority to issue tax credits. An average of 1,300 projects and 56,000 units are placed in service each year.

Long-Term Care Insurance

One of the most notable trends during the 1980s was the emergence of long-term care insurance offered by commercial insurance companies. Depending on the particular policy, long-term care insurance covers a significant portion of long-term care costs, which may include skilled nursing care, in-home health care, adult daycare, assisted living, and dementia care, expenses often not covered by Medicare, Medicaid, and private health insurance. As retirees became more familiar with the concept, the number of long-term care insurance policies sold increased dramatically. According to the Health Insurance Association of America, the market grew an average of 21 percent each year between 1987 and 1997, and by June 1998, 119 companies had sold more than 5.8 million long-term care insurance policies.[49]

Long-term care policies were originally sold to individuals, but later group policies were sold to employers and to providers of seniors' housing. In the mid-1980s, several companies pioneered the use of group long-term care insurance in continuing care/life care communities, but by 2000, the majority of these companies had ceased offering group policies to retirement communities as a result of losses that were higher than anticipated. RegalCare (GoldenCare in the mid-1980s) was designed exclusively for CCRCs and is currently gaining momentum in the industry. Under RegalCare's plan, the community is the policyholder, and residents are required to participate. Although every participating community handles it differently, the policy costs are typically included in residents' monthly fees. For communities that do not offer life care contracts, RegalCare offers protection for incoming residents against future costs of long-term care, serving as a marketing advantage for communities.

Regulatory Environment

Continuing Care Retirement Communities

The rapid growth in the seniors' housing industry has resulted in an increasing amount of state regulatory legislation. Nearly all the legislation that has been passed addresses the life care or continuing care retirement communities that charge upfront entrance fees, and most of this legislation was passed during the 1980s. At the beginning of that decade, very few states had statutes in place. By 1999, 37 states had passed legislation (Figure 1-5).

Existing regulations vary with regard to the aspects of life care of the CCRCs they cover. Five major categories tend to be governed by regulation, however:

- *Preopening requirements*—The community may be required to have state certification and to disclose certain financial information to residents. Some states also require a minimum number of presales before granting a permit.
- *Contracts between the residents and the community*—Regulations may address the form and content of the residential contract, promotional materials, residents' rights, resident councils, liens, and terms of withdrawal from the community.
- *Health care requirements*—The community may be required to obtain a Certificate of Need to provide home health care, assisted living, or nursing home care and to meet life safety codes for medical facilities. Other requirements for the certificate may include admission of a certain number of nonresident Medicaid patients, a restriction on external marketing of the nursing home, or other state mandates for construction of a nursing home.
- *Financial requirements*—Regulations may require escrow deposits before and after occupancy, reserve requirements, performance bonding, and annual audits, and may govern fee adjustments and refunds.
- *Remedial procedures*—The steps taken if fraud, deception, or serious financial problems exist or the community refuses to disclose required information may be stipulated in the regulations.[50]

One of the most interesting pieces of legislation covering CCRCs was the amendment in August 1989 of New York State's insurance law establishing Article 46 permitting development of CCRCs. Until that time, New York law prohibited the development and operation of life care communities. In response to nursing home scandals that occurred in the early 1960s, New York State passed Chapter V of the Public Health Laws, Section 2803, prohibiting health-related facilities and nursing homes from requiring prepayment for basic residential health care services exceeding three months. This prohibition prevented any life care communities from being developed in New York. The environment that it created effec-

Figure 1-5 **States with CCRC Regulations**

State	Responsible Agency
Arizona	Department of Insurance
Arkansas	Insurance Commissioner
California	Department of Social Services
Colorado	Division of Financial Services
Connecticut	Department of Social Services
Delaware	Secretary of State
Florida	Department of Insurance
Georgia	Department of Insurance
Idaho	Department of Finance
Illinois	Department of Public Health
Indiana	Securities Commissioner
Iowa	Commissioner of Insurance
Kansas	Commissioner of Insurance
Louisiana	Department of Health and Hospitals
Maine	Superintendent of Insurance
Maryland	State Office on Aging
Massachusetts	No agency specified
Michigan	Corporation and Securities Bureau of the Consumer and Industry Services Department
Minnesota	No agency specified
Missouri	Department of Insurance
Nebraska	No agency specified
New Hampshire	Department of Insurance
New Jersey	Department of Community Affairs
New Mexico	State Agency on Aging
New York	Commissioner of Health
North Carolina	Department of Insurance
Ohio	No agency specified
Oklahoma	No agency specified
Oregon	Senior and Disabled Services Division
Pennsylvania	Department of Insurance
Rhode Island	Department of Health
South Carolina	Department of Consumer Affairs
Tennessee	Department of Commerce and Insurance
Texas	State Board of Insurance and Commissioner of the State Board of Insurance
Vermont	Department of Banking, Insurance, and Securities
Virginia	State Corporation Commission
Wisconsin	Commissioner of Insurance

Source: American Association of Homes and Services for the Aging, *Summary of State Continuing Care Retirement Regulations as of 2/12/99.*

tively slowed down the development of other non-insured models of retirement housing, resulting in a substantially undeveloped market in a state with one of the country's highest concentrations of elderly residents.

In 1994, several changes were made to the regulations. The first was to include what AAHSA refers to as *Type B* or *modified continuing care* contracts (see the feature box on page 8) under the regulations. Previously, only Type A communities or those offering extensive contracts were covered by the regulations. The second change permitted nonprofit organizations to access county industrial development agencies for financing. As of mid-2001, only four CCRCs that meet the above definitions had been opened, the first of which, Kendal at Ithaca, opened in 1995. Five others have received their certificate of authority and are in the presales, financing, or construction phases of development. A sixth has taken the first step in the process of being approved by the state.

Assisted Living

Assisted living is regulated in all 50 states, yet licensing varies widely from state to state (Figure 1-6). Some states have created a specific licensing category for assisted living, while others use the term loosely to cover the terms *personal care, residential care,* and *domiciliary care.* Just as licensing varies greatly among states, so does the definition of assisted living. Although state regulatory bodies are not likely to achieve a standard definition, states increasingly use the term *assisted living,* and there appears to be general consensus that assisted living provides personal and health care services in a residential environment. According to a 2000 study, 29 states used the term *assisted living* in licensing regulations, up from 15 states in 1996.[51] Regulations were being drafted or revised in 25 states, according to the survey.

The majority of assisted living facilities are regulated by states' departments of health. Regulations govern areas that include requirements for admission and discharge, level of services provided, unit characteristics, and administration and staff training and ratios.

While the assisted living industry has grown rapidly, it has targeted primarily the elderly with higher incomes. Developers and government agencies are now seeking ways to create more affordable assisted living. More and more states are opting to cover assisted living services under Medicaid to meet the needs of lower-income elderly who previously

Figure 1-6 **Regulations Covering Assisted Living, by State**

State	Responsible Agency	Classification
Alabama	Department of Public Health	Assisted living facilities
Alaska	Department of Administration	Assisted living homes
Arizona	Department of Health Services	Assisted living facilities
Arkansas	Department of Human Services	Residential care facilities
California	Department of Social Services	Residential care facilities for the elderly
Colorado	Department of Health	Alternative care facilities (personal care boarding homes)
Connecticut	Department of Public Health	Assisted living services agency
Delaware	Department of Health and Social Services	Assisted living agencies
Florida	Agency for Health Care Administration	Assisted living facilities
Georgia	Department of Human Resources	Personal care homes
Hawaii	Department of Health	Assisted living facilities
Idaho	Department of Health and Welfare	Residential care facilities
Illinois	Department on Aging	Assisted living establishments
Indiana	Department of Health	Residential care facilities
Iowa	Department of Elder Affairs	Assisted living program

Figure 1-6 (continued)

State	Responsible Agency	Classification
Kansas	Department of Health and Environment	Assisted living facilities
Kentucky	Department of Social Service and Kentucky Housing Corporation	Assisted living residences Personal care homes
Louisiana	Department of Social Services	Adult residential care facility
Maryland	Department of Health and Mental Hygiene	Assisted living programs
Maine	Department of Human Service	Assisted living services program
Massachusetts	Executive Office of Elder Affairs	Assisted living residences
Michigan	Department of Public Health	Homes for the aged
Minnesota	Department of Health	Elderly housing with services
Mississippi	Department of Health	Personal care homes
Missouri	Department of Social Services	Residential care facility
Montana	Department of Public Health and Human Services	Personal care homes
Nebraska	Department of Health and Human Services	Assisted living facilities
Nevada	Division of Health	Residential facilities for groups
New Hampshire	Department of Health and Human Services	Residential care home facilities
New Jersey	Department of Health and Senior Services	Assisted living residences Comprehensive personal care homes
New Mexico	Department of Health	Adult residential shelter care homes
New York	Department of Social Services	Assisted living program
North Carolina	Department of Human Resources	Assisted living residences
North Dakota	Department of Health	Basic care facilities
Ohio	Department of Health	Residential care facilities
Oklahoma	Department of Health	Assisted living centers
Oregon	Department of Human Resources	Residential care facilities Assisted living facilities
Pennsylvania	Department of Public Welfare	Personal care homes
Rhode Island	Department of Health	Residential care and assisted living facilities
South Carolina	Department of Health	Community residential care facilities
South Dakota	Department of Health	Assisted living centers
Tennessee	Division of Health Care Facilities	Assisted care living facilities
Texas	Department of Human Services	Personal care facilities
Utah	Department of Health	Assisted living facilities
Vermont	Department of Aging and Disabilities	Assisted living residences
Virginia	Department of Social Services	Adult care residences
Washington	Department of Health	Assisted living service facilities Enhanced adult residential care Adult residential care
West Virginia	Department of Health and Human Resources	Personal care homes
Wisconsin	Department of Health and Social Services	Residential care complexes
Wyoming	Department of Health	Assisted living facility

Sources: Murtha, Cullina, Richter, and Pinney, LLP, *Summary of Assisted Living Licensure Statutes and Regulations in the 50 States* (Washington, D.C.: American Seniors Housing Association, 1999); and American Seniors Housing Association, *Seniors Housing State Regulatory Handbook 2000* (Washington, D.C.: Author, 2000).

Figure 1-7 **States with Medicaid Waivers for Assisted Living**

Existing Medicaid Coverage	Alaska, Arizona, Arkansas, Colorado, Connecticut, Delaware, Florida, Georgia, Hawaii, Idaho, Illinois, Iowa, Kansas, Maine, Maryland, Massachusetts, Michigan, Minnesota, Missouri, Montana, Nebraska, Nevada, New Jersey, New Hampshire, New Mexico, New York, North Carolina, North Dakota, Oregon, Rhode Island, South Carolina, South Dakota, Texas, Utah, Vermont, Virginia, Washington, Wisconsin
Planned or Pending Medicaid Coverage	Indiana, Louisiana, Mississippi, Ohio, Pennsylvania

Source: Robert L. Mollica, *State Assisted Living Policy 2000* (Portland, Me.: National Academy for State Health Policy, July 2000).

had no alternatives to a nursing home. By mid-2000, 38 states reimbursed assisted living services through Medicaid, and five more states had plans to do so.[52] Although Medicaid coverage is expanding across the nation to meet the needs of the lower-income elderly, as of 2000 it served only about 58,500 beneficiaries nationwide.[53]

Notes

1. U.S. Census Bureau, *65+ in the United States,* Current Population Reports, Special Studies, P-23-190 (Washington, D.C.: U.S. Government Printing Office, 1996), p. 3-1.

2. Jennifer Cheeseman Day, *Population Projections of the United States by Age, Sex, Race, and Hispanic Origin: 1995 to 2050*, Current Population Reports, P-25-1130 (Washington, D.C.: U.S. Census Bureau, 1996).

3. National Center for Health Statistics, *Health, United States, 1986*, DHHS Pub. No. PHS 87-1232 (Washington, D.C.: U.S. Department of Health and Human Services, 1987).

4. I. Rosenwaike, N. Yaffe, and P.C. Sagi, "The Recent Decline in Mortality of the Extreme Aged: An Analysis of Statistical Data," *American Journal of Public Health,* October 1980, p. 1074.

5. National Center for Health Statistics, Centers for Disease Control, and U.S. Department of Health and Human Services, "1994–1995 National Health Interview Survey on Disability (Phase I)."

6. H.S. Kaye, M.P. LaPlante, D. Carlson, and B.L. Wenger, "Trends in Disability Rates in the United States, 1970–1994," Disability Statistics Abstract 17 (Washington, D.C.: U.S. Department of Education, National Institute on Disability and Rehabilitation Research, November 1996).

7. *The Guide to American Law,* Vol. 9 (New York: West Publishing Co., 1984), p. 286.

8. U.S. Census Bureau, *65+ in the United States,* p. 4-14.

9. "National Institute on Aging Macroeconomic-Demographic Model" (Washington, D.C.: U.S. Department of Health and Human Services, 1984) in *America's Elderly: A Sourcebook,* ed. E.E. Duensing (New Brunswick, N.J.: Center for Urban Policy Research, 1988), p. 75.

10. Ibid., p. 77.

11. U.S. Department of Commerce, Economics and Statistics Administration, and U.S. Census Bureau, *Money Income in the United States, 1999,* Current Population Reports, September 2000, Table 12.

12. National Center for Health Statistics, *Health, United States.* Reproduced in *Aging America: Trends and Projections,* 1987–88 ed., p. 57.

13. U.S. Census Bureau, Current Population Reports, CPS Annual Demographic Survey, March supplement, 1999.

14. U.S. Census Bureau, data tabulated from Current Population Surveys of 1967 to 1987. Reproduced in *Aging America,* p. 56.

15. *Aging America,* p. 158.

16. U.S. Census Bureau, *Money Income and Poverty Status of Families and Persons in the United States: 1986,* Current Population Reports Series P-60, No. 157 (July 1987). Reproduced in *Aging America,* p. 39.

17. U.S. Census Bureau, Current Population Report, CPS Annual Demographic Survey, March supplement, 1999.

18. Ibid.

19. K. Levi, C. Cowan, H. Lazenby, A. Sensenig, P. McDonnell, J. Stiller, and A. Martin, "Health Spending in 1998: Signals of Change," Health Care Financing Administration.

20. Ibid.

21. S. Maxwell, M. Moon, and M. Segal, *Growth in Medicare and Out-of-Pocket Spending: Impact on Vulnerable Beneficiaries* (Washington, D.C.: Urban Institute, 2001), pp. vi–x.

22. National Alliance for Caregiving and American Association of Retired Persons, "Family Caregiving in the U.S.: Findings from a National Survey," June 1997, p. 8.

23. H. Winklevoss and A. Powell, *Continuing Care Retirement Communities: An Empirical, Financial, and Legal Analysis* (Homewood, Ill.: Irwin, 1984), p. 77. Published for the Pension Research Council, Wharton School, University of Pennsylvania.

24. Ibid., p. 34.

25. Ibid., pp. 292–293.

26. PricewaterhouseCoopers, "Continuing Care Retirement Communities, 1998," p. 15.

27. AAHSA Development Corp. and Herbert J. Sims & Co., *Emerging Continuing Care Retirement Communities: An Analysis of Key Statistics* (Washington, D.C.: Author, 1994), p. 13.

28. National Investment Center, "NIC National Supply Estimate of Seniors Housing and Care Properties," 2000, p. 3.

29. See HUD Notice H83-58.

30. Ibid.

31. Office of the Inspector General, "Multiregional Audit of the Insured Retirement Services Centers Program," 90-TS-111/112-0008, April 6, 1990, p. ii.

32. American Seniors Housing Association, *Seniors Housing Statistical Digest, 1999–2000* (Washington, D.C.: Author, 1999), p. 8.

33. National Investment Center, "NIC National Supply Estimate," p.10.

34. ALFA, "The Assisted Living Industry: An Overview, 1999."

35. Kirsten H. Jensen, "The Assisted Living Industry: What a Difference a Year Makes" (Baltimore: Legg Mason Wo od Walker, Inc., January 1999), p. 8.

36. National Investment Center, "NIC National Supply Estimate," p.10.

37. Ibid.

38. Catherine Hawes, Miriam Rose, and Charles D. Phillips, *A National Study of Assisted Living for the Frail Elderly* (Beachwood, Ohio: Myers Research Institute, 1999), p. E-3.

39. Assisted Living Facilities Association of America, "An Overview of the Assisted Living Industry, 1993," Washington, D.C., 1993.

40. Hawes, Rose, and Phillips, *A National Study of Assisted Living for the Frail Elderly,* p. E-7.

41. AAHSA Development Corp. and Sims, *Emerging Continuing Care Retirement Communities,* p. 14.

42. American Seniors Housing Association, *Seniors Housing Statistical Digest, 2000–2001* (Washington, D.C.: Author, 1999), p. 17.

43. Kathryn L. Brod, *The CCRC Industry 1997 Profile* (Washington, D.C.: American Association of Homes and Services for the Aging, 1997), p. 3.

44. Elizabeth A. Bartlett and David Divaker, "Largest Providers 2001," *Assisted Living Today,* September 2001, pp. 25–28.

45. "The CLTC 50+," *Contemporary Long Term Care Magazine,* May 2000, pp. 45–50.

46. "Multi-Unit Provider Survey." *Modern Healthcare Magazine,* May 22, 1995, and May 24, 1999.

47. Internal Revenue Code §145(e) as cited in Michael W. Peregrine and Lauren K. McNulty, "Tax Exempt Financing Faces an Uncertain Future," *Retirement Housing Report,* August 1988.

48. http://www.hud.gov.

49. Susan A. Coronel, "Long Term Care Insurance in 1997–1998" (Washington, D.C.: Health Insurance Association of America, 2000), p. 3.

50. J.W. Parrillo and H.K. Bertelsman, "Regulation in the Retirement Housing Industry," in *1987 Retirement Industry Study*, Laventhol & Horwath.

51. Robert L. Mollica, "State Assisted Living Policy 2000" (Portland, Me.: National Academy for State Health Policy, July 2000).

52. Ibid.

53. Ibid.

Edward Jacoby; courtesy AIA

The Goddard House in Brookline, Massachusetts, provides a noninstitutional residential environment. Many of the interior spaces resemble those of an independent home. Architect: Alfred Wojciechowski, Childs Bertman Tseckares, Inc.

2 Components of Market Analysis for Seniors' Housing

Historical Role of Feasibility Studies

Feasibility studies have long been a component of project financing in both the health care and real estate industries. In particular, feasibility studies have been an intrinsic part of the documentation necessary for tax-exempt bond financing, which has historically been a major financing vehicle for the development of health care facilities, including life care, continuing care, and assisted living communities.

Feasibility studies traditionally were conducted primarily by the major accounting firms because of the mandate of independence that characterized their position with regard to their clients and the standards by which they conducted their work. Although all the major firms became involved to some extent in the seniors' housing field, only a few chose to specialize in this industry. Three of the largest national public accounting firms that have dedicated significant resources to the seniors' housing industry are BDO Seidman, LLC; KPMG Peat Marwick, LLC; and PricewaterhouseCoopers, LLP. In addition, investment banking firms accept studies done by a variety of smaller regional firms with significant experience in seniors' housing.

In certain ways, traditional feasibility studies resembled audits, the major purview of accounting firms. Conducted just before financing, studies typically contained two principal sections, one on demographics (in effect, an analysis of supply and demand) and one on financial information. The client provided assumptions for review to the firm conducting the feasibility study. The accounting firm conducted a set of procedures that involved the review of those assumptions, and the opinion letter that accompanied the resulting feasibility study attested to the reasonableness of key assumptions, including market area definition, depth of income-qualified households, proposed rate structure, forecasts of use, and financial assumptions such as operating expenses, staffing, reimbursement, and debt service coverage ratios. Financial feasibility studies were incorporated or referred to in the text of the offering statements for the bonds. They provided an independent opinion on the reasonableness of the underlying assumptions for prospective bond purchasers.

As the industry has developed and matured, feasibility studies and their role also have changed. Although many feasibility studies are still conducted at the point of project financing, the feasibility process has also been modified for use in project planning. Feasibility studies, particularly the demographic portion (referred to hereafter as *market studies*), have become a common and useful tool for developing and/or refining planning assumptions. Whereas studies that are commissioned for use in financing are conducted when the planning has been completed, recognition of the value of the market study has shifted its use to earlier stages in the development process. A market study conducted when planning for a facility is initiated enables the user to make the most fundamental decision, that is, whether or not to proceed with the development. Assuming the decision is positive, market analysis can yield guidance and insights with regard to project features and characteristics, market niche opportunities, and market strategy and positioning.

Key Components of Market Analysis

One of the first steps that should be undertaken when considering the development of a seniors' housing community is an analysis of local market conditions. Market analysis is sometimes carried out directly by the development team or project sponsor, using in-house staff to evaluate a variety of market-related issues to determine whether or not to proceed with development plans. It is particularly true for national providers that are constantly expanding their portfolios. The highly specialized nature of analyzing the seniors' housing market, however, has resulted in the delegation of much of the market analysis to outside consulting firms. Some firms have developed specific expertise in this field. Sometimes, however, analysis is conducted by organizations and individuals with expertise in other types of real estate development or health care services but with little specific experience in the seniors' housing field.

The format and methodologies employed to conduct market analysis for seniors' housing have been influenced by feasibility analyses conducted in the more traditional health care and real estate industries. The underlying framework for all such analysis is the evaluation of supply and demand. On the most basic level, such studies attempt to assess the size of the potential market for a specific product or service and the extent to which that market must be penetrated for the undertaking that is being evaluated to be successful.

On a much more sophisticated level, a market analysis can be used to go well beyond a go/no go decision. Market studies are also valuable planning tools. Organizations often use market analysis to identify and describe the target market and to define the type of seniors' housing community that will best meet its needs. The ways in which the components of market analysis can be used to help plan a project are discussed throughout this chapter.

In addition to the quantification of potential market depth and demand, market studies for seniors' housing projects typically include a number of key elements:

- Site analysis
- Market area definition
- Socioeconomic trends and characteristics
- Quantification of demographic information about the elderly
- Attitudes, perceptions, and familiarity with seniors' housing
- Analysis of the competition.

This chapter describes these elements in detail. Information on different approaches to each element of market feasibility is referenced throughout this chapter. The quantification of potential market depth and demand, fill rate, and absorption are discussed in Chapter 3. In addition, an increasing number of market studies now include direct consumer research resulting from focus groups and surveys. The consumer research component of market analysis is discussed in Chapter 4. Certain norms or benchmarks have emerged in assessing the potential for success in a market, for instance, draw from the geographic market area, demographic characteristics of residents, and market penetration. Those benchmarks are discussed throughout this book, but particularly in this chapter and in Chapter 3.

Site Analysis

The site chosen for a seniors' housing community must be evaluated from several perspectives, including the suitability of the location for the contemplated use, particularly with regard to surrounding land uses; accessibility to transportation; and proximity to selected services. The size, configuration, and topographical nature of the site may dictate the project's overall size, configuration, and cost.

A report published in 2000 emphasizes the importance of the site as an occupancy driver: Fitch, Duff & Phelps, the major bond-rating agency involved in the seniors' housing industry, considers proximity to services and places of interest, ease of accessibility, and degree of visibility the key factors in site assessment.[1] Site selection also influences the delineation of the geographic area from which prospective residents will be drawn and the character of the socioeconomic target market attracted to the project.

Compatibility of Surrounding Land Use

Many retirement communities that were developed in the 1960s and 1970s (as well as those developed earlier) were on large tracts of land selected not so much for their suitability but because of their availability. Some communities have been developed on sites donated to nonprofit sponsors, thereby dictating where they are located. For example, Foulkeways at Gwynedd, in Gwynedd, Pennsylvania, was a former farm donated to the Gwynedd Yearly Meeting. At the time of Foulkeways's development in 1967, Gwynedd was a comparatively undeveloped suburb of Philadelphia. The site was not well served by public transportation, and very little shopping was available near the community. Since that time, Gwynedd has experienced significant development activity. Now the closest shopping is at a shopping plaza one mile from the site. Perhaps more significant has been the growth of population in Gwynedd and the surrounding towns. In 1960, the population was 9,207; by 1990, it had increased about 140 percent, to 22,155. Because of the considerable changes over time that occurred in the area surrounding Foulkeways, the problem of the site's original isolation was corrected. But this situation does not always apply. In fact, availability still affects site selection today. On more than one occasion, developers have controlled sites that may have been considered originally for residential, commercial, or other uses. In some cases, when other land uses have turned out to be not viable, the developer has turned to seniors' housing. This lapse of judgment about the importance of location for a community can have as deleterious an effect on the marketability of a seniors' housing community as it would on a tract for single-family houses. Only rarely does an organization determined to develop seniors' housing actually engage in a market analysis designed specifically to identify the best site for the project.

In today's seniors' housing market, however, assessment of the compatibility of surrounding land uses is critical in choosing a site. This evaluation must consider what types of land uses characterize the immediate neighborhood where the facility is to be developed. The surrounding area must support the image and market being targeted for the community. An upscale target market, for instance, will be drawn to a location that reflects the values and lifestyle to which those residents are accustomed. The "if you build it, they will come" syndrome does not work for seniors' housing. The availability of an increased number of options, as well as the most popular option—remaining at home—will prevail over a poorly located facility.

Access to Transportation

The site for seniors' housing projects should permit easy access to transportation systems, including both public transportation and highway or road transportation. The site should be easy to locate for residents and their family members, and it should be easily accessible to the staff who will work at the community. In areas where public transportation systems are good, it is ideal for a seniors' housing site to have reasonable access to commuter trains and public bus service, particularly because they facilitate staff members' access during working hours. In rural and many suburban markets, public transportation is not readily accessible. In those cases, local residents are more accustomed to relying on cars and driving to find shopping and services. Communities located in these markets should provide adequate transportation services to meet the needs of their residents.

Proximity to Services

Elderly residents of independent living units maintain reasonably active lifestyles for as long as they are able. Most residents shun isolation and prefer to take part easily in social, cultural, and recreational activities. Proximity to shopping, primarily convenience shopping such as grocery stores, dry cleaners, and pharmacies, is an important criterion in site selection. The site should be located in an area that also is well served by religious institutions and health care providers such as hospitals and physicians. Access to the same types of services is important as well for assisted living communities. While residents may not venture out on their own, organized trips to shopping, church services, and outside entertainment are an important element of the activities planned, and the service is enhanced if the activities are close by.

There appear to be two schools of thought with regard to the nature of access to such services, particularly convenience shopping. Some industry experts advocate that sites be chosen based on residents' ability to walk to a selected number of services. They suggest that many residents prefer to be in such a location. Other experts disagree and do not emphasize the importance of choosing a site that allows pedestrian access to these services. To a certain extent, the importance of this issue is influenced by the project's geographic area. In suburban areas that require driving and do not readily permit walking to services, for example, a site that affords pedestrian access is not as significant a consideration. Moreover, the majority of communities provide transportation to appointments and scheduled shopping trips, removing the burden of driving and need for services within walking distance.

Site Configuration and Topography

Although some market feasibility consultants consider the relationship of the site's topography and configuration a factor in feasibility, it is more typically part of the architect's services. Early in the planning stage, the site's overall potential for development must be evaluated and determined, given the buildable land it encompasses, the grade of the parcel, and other development constraints that might be present. It may be possible to overcome certain constraints, but the cost of overcoming them must be assessed to determine whether the changes will fit within the overall development budget or whether the impact on the budget will result in resident fees that may not be affordable for the targeted market segment.

Visibility

A site's visibility also affects whether a particular location is appropriate for seniors' housing. For example, a facility with good visibility to passing traffic has a marketing advantage, particularly for assisted living communities. According to ALFA's provider survey in 1999, nearly 11 percent of residents first became aware of the assisted living community by driving past it. Many consultants feel that visibility is somewhat more important for assisted living than for independent living communities, partly because it is an adult child who most frequently initiates the search for an assisted living community for an older relative. The decision is usually more crisis driven for assisted living, so factors such as driving by a facility regularly can enhance marketability. In comparison, the same ALFA study revealed that 8.2 percent of respondents in independent living communities first became aware of the community by driving by it, although the percentage differed substantially between communities located in metropolitan areas (10.5 percent), where it was nearly the same as for assisted living communities, versus those located in nonmetropolitan markets (4.3 percent).[2]

The impact of visibility is illustrated by the experience of a community in Oxford, Mississippi, called Azalea Gardens. Azalea Gardens, which offers both independent and assisted living, is located at the rear of the site on which it was developed. Moreover, its location is not on the route that goes to the local hospital or provides access to shopping and recreational amenities in Oxford. For these reasons, it is not visible to passing traffic. Although many people from the outlying areas come to Oxford to shop and take advantages of its other amenities, awareness of Azalea Gardens drops precipitously for residents living outside Oxford. According to the developer, awareness of Azalea Gardens, based on specific consumer research, was 96 percent among those surveyed in Oxford but dropped off to 10 to 30 percent in the immediately surrounding area, a factor that directly affected the community's absorption.

Zoning

Few sites where seniors' housing communities are developed have the necessary zoning in place when they are optioned or acquired. The fact that seniors' housing may be treated as a residential or institutional land use frequently results in the need for amendments to existing zoning codes. And attitudes toward permitting this land use vary widely. In some areas, the development of seniors' housing is encouraged by municipalities through such approaches as zoning density bonuses and other favorable treatments given to developers seeking zoning approvals for large mixed-use projects. In other cases, the concerns raised, particularly by neighbors, about increased density and associated potential traffic have resulted in difficulty in obtaining zoning. In some areas in the Northeast such as the New York City metropolitan area and parts of Massachusetts, obtaining the necessary zoning has been particularly difficult. An evaluation of a site's suitability for use as a seniors' housing community must consider whether appropriate zoning is already in place and, if not, the likelihood of being able to obtain zoning approvals. During negotiations for an option to purchase land for retirement housing, a contingency for the purchase frequently is the ability to obtain the appropriate zoning.

Market Area Draw and Socioeconomic Characteristics

The specific location chosen for a seniors' housing community usually directly influences the geographic areas from which the project will draw the majority of its residents. Most seniors prefer to live in an area relatively close to where they reside before the move, remaining close to their familiar neighborhood and network of family and friends. While wanting to remain close to home, seniors also want to relocate to a neighborhood that conveys their lifestyle and socioeconomic stature. As indicated, the selection of seniors' housing, whether a lifestyle choice or need driven, still has some of the fundamental characteristics of a real estate decision. In particular, the nature of the neighborhood where the site is located dictates the nature of the target market. A site in a working-class neighborhood attracts a moderate-income, working-class market, not an affluent one. One cannot assume that because options for seniors' housing in an area are limited, people will move to any site where a facility is located. The most compelling alternative that older people have, and most frequently choose, is to simply stay where they are and not move at all.

Market Area Definition

Defining the market area is one of the most critical components of market analysis for seniors' housing communities. The analyst's decisions about how to define the market area form a geographic framework for the remainder of the analysis. Defining geographic market area involves determining the boundaries from which most residents can be expected to move. Analysts typically consider that approximately 70 percent or more of a community's potential residents can be expected to move from within the market area defined for the project. Both ALFA and AAHSA have published information on geographic draw;[3] a comparison of the results is shown in Figure 2-1. The responses shown in Figure 2-1 for the AAHSA study reflect statistics for both levels of care located in a single facility. The ALFA sample represents both freestanding independent and assisted living communities as well as those offering both levels of care.

A comparison of independent living with assisted living in the two studies makes it clear that assisted living units draw a larger proportion of residents from within ten miles than do independent living units. The results for assisted living probably reflect, in part, the influence of adult children who persuade elder family members to move to assisted living communities close to the adult child. In fact, a follow-up question in the ALFA survey about the distance from the facility that family members live supports this notion, although the proportion of family members within ten miles of the independent living facilities is still significant when compared with assisted living facilities (see Figure 2-2).

Moreover, at the same time assisted living development became relatively ubiquitous during the 1990s, a comparative slowdown occurred in the development of communities offering or stressing independent living. As such, those seeking assisted living arguably have more choices and are able to stay closer to home than those who wish to move to independent living. Further, independent living residents, particularly those who may be influenced by sponsorship, may be willing to travel a slightly greater distance to move than need-driven assisted living residents.

Figure 2-1 **Percentage of Residents Who Relocated, by Distance Moved**

	AAHSA Study		ALFA Study	
	Independent Living	Assisted Living	Independent Living	Assisted Living
<5 Miles	25%	55%	21.8%	28.5%
5–10 Miles	21%	15%	17.9%	24.4%
10–15 Miles	11%	8%	15.9%	16.9%
15–25 Miles	10%	8%	20.1%	14.2%
>25 Miles	35%	14%	24.3%	16.0%

Figure 2-2 **Distance from Facility to Family Members**

Distance	Independent Living	Assisted Living
<5 Miles	25.2%	28.7%
5–10 Miles	23.3%	27.9%
10–20 Miles	24.0%	21.4%
20–50 Miles	11.9%	10.5%
>50 Miles	15.6%	11.5%

In addition to this local market area draw, communities often find that a number of residents move from outside the area or from out of state for a variety of reasons. AAHSA's survey in 1998 showed that 35 percent of incoming independent living residents moved from beyond 25 miles of the CCRC,[4] while ALFA's 2000 study (which reflects 1999 data) of independent living communities showed that 24.3 percent came from beyond 25 miles.[5] ALFA's 2000 study indicated that 16 percent of assisted living residents moved from distances greater than 25 miles. The reasons cited most often include moving to be closer to family and adult children and relocating to a destination market or warmer climate. Having family members nearby is a major influence in the selection of an assisted living community. Based on an ALFA study, an overwhelming 78 percent of assisted living residents have family members living within 20 miles of the facility; only 11.5 percent have relatives more than 50 miles away.[6]

Based on the market area definition reached, the remainder of the study elements—demographics, analysis of the competition, and market penetration—focus on that specific geographic area. Defining the geographic market area also is a tool for defining the limitations of the area to be studied. Several approaches, including the following techniques, have been used to reach decisions about the geographic market area for seniors' housing communities.

Defining Market Area Based on Presales

Achieving a significant (typically at least 50 percent, but more frequently 60 to 70 percent) level of presales of independent living units is commonly required with the development of a CCRC that involves the payment of a substantial entrance fee. Presales involve the reservation of an independent living unit with a deposit, usually 10 percent of the entrance fee. Presale requirements are always linked to the financing of the CCRC but are also sometimes related to the release of escrow funds, as specified in state regulations governing this type of retirement community. Presales or preleasing is more difficult to attain with rental independent living communities and even more so for assisted living, where the decision to move occurs much closer to the move itself. In a study published by ASHA in 2000, the average period reported for preleasing assisted living communities was 5.4 months and for congregate seniors' housing communities was 8.4 months, in contrast to 33.6 months for CCRCs.[7] While most providers offering rental independent living and assisted living begin marketing before construction is completed, few do so before financing; therefore, little or no preleasing information exists for the feasibility consultant to use in defining the market area. As such, the comments in this section apply to communities requiring entrance fees.

When a market study is conducted during the period when a retirement community is being marketed, the market area may be defined based on the geographic origin of those who have placed a deposit to reserve a unit. Defining market area boundaries based on presales is most typically used for studies prepared for financing purposes (most often for tax-exempt bond financing). In response to some state regulations and the requirements of most underwriters and a growing number of other direct lenders, project financing does not take place until a certain percentage of the residential independent living units have been reserved. Studies conducted for inclusion in the financing package therefore have a demonstrated pattern of market area draw based on the place of origin of those individuals who have made deposits. In most feasibility studies incorporated in tax-exempt bond offering statements, for instance, the section that describes the market area definition bases that definition on management's data regarding the current addresses of presales. The market area can then be determined based on the towns or ZIP codes where most presales have originated. This information may be translated into a radius, a city, a county, a portion of one or more counties, or any other geographic area supported by the presales data. Presales are usually confirmed in writing by the feasibility firm to secure the documentation necessary to satisfy the due diligence process.

A variation of this technique is used in studies conducted for the expansion of existing communities, including rental independent living and assisted living. The information about residents' origin for those already living in the facility can be used to determine the likely area from which new residents will be drawn. Frequently, such communities also have waiting lists, particularly for independent living units, from which some, if not most, new residents may be drawn. The data from the waiting list further substantiate the definition of the market area for the new expansion. Waiting list and resident origin data can be used for market analyses that are designed to determine the initial feasibility of an expansion and can also be used to supplement presales data (in the case of a CCRC) for the feasibility study used for financing the expansion.

The means by which market areas are defined is substantially facilitated for projects that are structured with an entrance fee or equity contribution. Based on a survey conducted by the AAHSA of nonprofit CCRCs opened between 1994 and 1999, 78 percent of communities with entrance fees required a 10 percent deposit to reserve a unit. Moreover, an average of 71 percent of independent living units were presold at the time of financing.[8] For the many rental communities, however, evidence of preleasing is much more difficult to obtain to the extent that it occurs at all before financing. Given the absence of a large upfront fee, the demonstration of preleasing is limited to the payment of at least one month's rent in advance. These sums are typically far less than the deposit based on an entrance fee and often are refundable. The result is less persuasive to lenders, in particular because it is more uncertain that preleasing will be converted to actual move-ins. It also appears that many organizations have had greater difficulty obtaining advance commitments from prospective residents for rental communities than for those requiring entrance fees or equity. Similarly, while assisted living facilities do not rely on presales, marketing begins, on average, six months before a new facility opens, according to ALFA's 2000 survey.[9]

Radius Analysis

Choosing a radius from the site, such as five or ten miles, or even 20 or 25 miles, is another approach used to define the market area from which residents might be expected to be drawn. This approach is based primarily on the assumption that most residents come from within a relatively proximate geographic area, one that might be defined as within an hour's drive of the site. The radius analysis is a relatively simple way of creating a market area definition that facilitates obtaining and analyzing demographic data. Most commercial information vendors, such as CACI Marketing Systems and Claritas, provide data on the basis of radius definitions.

Using a radius, however, has potential serious shortcomings. The radius defines geographic boundaries without regard to factors that influence people's patterns of movement. Real physical, jurisdictional, and psychological boundary lines can easily be missed by using a radius to define market area boundaries, resulting in an incorrect and potentially misleading demographic profile of the market being analyzed. For example, a market area definition using a radius of five miles for a project in Camden, New Jersey, would include the more affluent suburban community of Cherry Hill, New Jersey. The socioeconomics of the city of Camden would make it highly unlikely for a senior living in Cherry Hill to consider moving there. The socioeconomic distinctions between the city and the nearby suburban area would be overlooked with a simple radius analysis, potentially misrepresenting the project's target market and overstating the market's size and depth.

County Analysis

Many studies have been conducted using the county where the seniors' housing community is to be located as the defined geographic market area. Some studies include the subject county as well as one or more bordering counties. This method permits easy access to data and actually facilitates the use of existing census data (rather than purchased data from commercial information vendors) and projections prepared by government planning agencies that are typically done countywide. This approach has the same potential for misrepresentation as the radius analysis.

Neither a radius nor a county is an intrinsically incorrect approach to market area definition, however. They often provide a good starting point for an organization that is considering whether it makes sense to undertake a serious effort to develop a seniors' housing community. In some cases, the geographic area contained within the radius or the county may represent the true geographic market area, but this finding should be tested and corroborated through detailed market and consumer research.

Municipalities, ZIP Codes, Census Tracts

For all market studies, particularly those being carried out to help plan a seniors' housing community, the most exacting way of defining a geographic market area for further study is to develop boundary lines that reflect the best estimate of the specific area from which residents are expected to be drawn. This approach may result in an irregularly shaped boundary rather than one that fits comfortably into a radius or conforms to a county. The use of a radius or county allows the analyst to conduct the study from the office. Without the benefit of presales data or data about existing residents or those on a waiting list (in the case of an expansion of an existing facility), however, the creation of a geographic market area definition that attempts to reflect likely patterns of movement requires that considerable time and effort be spent in the field. Through a series of interviews with key informants, including local planning agencies, residential realtors, health service providers, representatives of other local competitive facilities, and others who know the area well, a reasonably accurate determination of a facility's market area can often be made.

The introduction of geographical information software (GIS) has proven to be an asset for market feasibility analysts in determining market areas. GIS technology is a blending of computerized mapping with database systems. Demographic and competitive data can be layered onto geographic maps to create a visual image that can help analysts better define a market area. Any data tied to location, for example by longitude and latitude, street address, or ZIP code, can be mapped using GIS software. As the GIS industry continues to advance, analysts will increasingly recognize it as a cost-effective and user-friendly tool that can help define a market area more accurately.

The effort to define a market area specifically tied to the proposed seniors' housing community should take into consideration a variety of factors, as follows.

Natural Geographic and Jurisdictional Boundaries. The first level of scrutiny in preparing to develop a set of boundary lines for the market area is geographic. Once the subject site is located on an area map, the analyst should review the map to determine whether the site is proximate to state or county borders. If the site is located very close to the border between states or counties in a state, key informants must be selected who can respond to questions regarding whether such lines create barriers, either physical or psychological, to movement. Because natural barriers such as rivers and mountains frequently affect patterns of movement, this possibility must be investigated. For instance, DuBois Village is a 60-bed assisted living community that opened in 1996. The community is located in the town of DuBois in Clearfield County in central Pennsylvania. The town is in the northwest portion of the county and is separated from the town of Clearfield, the county seat, by Clearfield Mountain, which is a significant natural barrier to movement throughout the region. The mountain results in a psychological boundary that has been reinforced by the way industrial, commercial, and residential neighborhoods have formed, primarily on the eastern side of the mountain near the town of Clearfield. DuBois Village traditionally draws 90 percent of its residents from local areas to the west of Clearfield Mountain. Only 5 percent of residents reportedly move from the other side of Clearfield Mountain. Had the market analysis for this project considered the whole county the primary market area, it would have substantially overestimated the pool of households from which the project could expect to draw residents.

Studies conducted for seniors' housing communities being developed by existing providers of health care services such as hospitals and nursing homes can use an additional valuable tool in the market area analysis. Patient origin data and the institution's existing service area provide some guidance in determining where the provider's sphere of influence extends. This analysis is particularly useful for providers who are planning to develop a community that will be located adjacent or proximate to their existing facilities. For example, a feasibility study for the addition of independent and assisted living to the Jefferson House nursing home campus in Newington, Connecticut, analyzed origin data for nursing home residents; data revealed that 80 percent of residents moved from within the defined market area. Before opening, the new independent living community, Cedar Mountain Commons, was over half sold, with 84 percent of sales coming from the defined market area.

Although existing patient origin data for health care facilities do not necessarily represent the exact defined market area for a seniors' housing community, they represent an element that should be considered. One must remember that a nursing home typically has a narrower geographic draw than a CCRC or rental retirement community, and, in the case of a hospital, attention must be focused on the nature of the institution. For instance, a primary care facility tends to serve the local market, whereas a tertiary care facility that offers highly specialized and sophisticated care is likely to draw from a much wider region.

Major Highways. Road systems can also significantly affect the definition of market area. Major highways can segment markets and serve as boundaries to a market area. At first glance, a detailed map can give the analyst insight into the patterns of movement in an area and highlight issues that require further investigation. Some sites may be located in a heavily populated area where highways appear to converge and intersect from every direction close to the site, while others might be in a region where roads run primarily north/south or east/west. These routes can shape the market area based on how they connect the region and form orientation patterns.

The ease and convenience of travel form driving habits among those seeking services, shopping, and amenities, thereby creating a comfort zone or familiar territory for local residents. Highways that carve out patterns of orientation for shopping and services often have the same effect on seniors' housing markets. In some cases, a major highway may be the actual boundary of the market area, because local residents tend not to cross the highway to reach services. This factor was evident during a study in Ewing Township, New Jersey, adjacent to the city of Trenton. Route 1, a major local thoroughfare from Trenton to Princeton, is lined with commercial properties, including shopping malls, movie theaters, and restaurants. Residents from points east of Route 1 (Hamilton, West Windsor, East Windsor, and Washington townships) readily travel to use services along Route 1, but they do not often venture farther west, across Route 1. Likewise, residents from points west of Route 1 (Ewing, Lawrence, Hopewell, and Princeton townships) also use services along Route 1 but rarely cross Route 1 to reach the more eastern portions of Mercer County.

What may seem reasonable on the map in terms of mileage from a given area to the site may actually not be within a comfortable driving distance for seniors and their families. Rural, suburban, and urban markets behave differently in terms of how far residents can be expected to move and whether the site is perceived to be conveniently located to one's family and familiar network of services. Traffic congestion and other roadway problems can render a site "too far." Interviews with key informants and spending time in the field driving are crucial to understanding these issues.

Influence of the Site on Market Area. Although seniors' housing communities differ in many ways from other kinds of residential real estate developments, they are similar in their dependence on location in influencing prospective residents to consider a move. During the early days of developing retirement communities, when few were available, the site where a community was located may not have been a very influential factor, given that individuals had few choices if they wished to reside in such a community. The appeal of the sponsor, frequently a nonprofit religious organization, helped to draw people to some communities.

As the number and types of seniors' housing communities increased, however, the value of a good site location has increased in importance—although in some respects the move to a seniors' housing community is need driven. Particularly for independent living, the move still retains many of the discretionary aspects of other residential real estate. Most people choose to live in an area that reflects their socioeconomic status and values and allows them to continue to participate in the community and networks they have created. To the extent that a location satisfies those desires and aspirations, it will pass a certain test of acceptability.

In some cases, particularly for assisted living, the move is being made to enable residents to be closer to their children. In these instances, the location becomes important in terms of accessibility to younger family members and suitability in terms of image.

Many lessons have been learned about the unwillingness of older people to move to locations that do not reflect their status, lifestyle, and values. For example, the feasibility study done for Fiddler's Woods in Philadelphia assumed that it was appropriate to define the primary market area as the Philadelphia metropolitan statistical area (MSA).[10] The study further focused its analysis on the Jewish population living in the defined area. The delineation of this rather extensive market area was based in part on the fact that it would be one of only two life care facilities in the Philadelphia metropolitan area that specifically targeted elderly Jewish residents. Fiddler's Woods was located in the northeast portion of Philadelphia, a part of the city characterized for the most part by working middle- and lower-middle-income residents. Although some elderly residents living in the northeast portion of the city certainly could have qualified to reside at Fiddler's Woods, those living in more affluent neighboring suburban Montgomery County were much less likely to choose to move to Fiddler's urbanized, less affluent location. Thus, the geographic and, in fact, economic target market that was assumed to be attracted to this facility was considerably smaller than predicted. For a variety of reasons not limited to this inaccurate assumption, few units were sold during the preopening marketing period, and Fiddler's Woods failed to make a required interest payment to the trustee for the bondholders, Fidelity Bank. The facility went into bankruptcy and never opened. Forum Group, Inc., eventually acquired the property, opening it as a rental community called the Lafayette (which subsequently was sold to Holy Redeemer Health System). The favorable terms of the acquisition allowed the owners to offer a reasonably priced rental facility, well priced for the local market. A substantial number of the residents were drawn from the nearby neighborhoods in Philadelphia rather than from the surrounding suburbs.

Psychological Boundaries. The Clearfield County, Pennsylvania, example cited earlier illustrates how a natural boundary (Clearfield Mountain) can also become a psychological boundary. Psychological boundaries can be tied to other natural, economic, or perceptual barriers, some more obvious than others. The best way to assess whether individuals resist or outright reject a site is to test its acceptability through direct consumer research (see Chapter 4). Once again, however, the implementation of carefully planned field research can reveal psychological or perceptual barriers that may not be evident because they are not tied to natural landmarks. Interviews with planners, realtors, and other key informants who know a local area well should yield insights of this sort. A tour of a location that appears to be an acceptable site does not reveal how people in the area perceive that location. For instance, without interviewing and asking key informants the right questions, an analyst might miss the fact that Fiddler's Woods would not attract a substantial number of residents from suburbs located only a few miles from the site. The barrier was a psychological one, reflecting the fact that this area may actually have been where some of those now-affluent suburban elderly had grown up but been able to leave behind. "Going home," in this case, would have represented a visible indication of a loss of status.

Influence of Sponsorship. One factor that can significantly affect the distance people will move to a seniors' housing community is the potential influence of a project sponsor. Communities associated with and/or sponsored by religious or fraternal organizations, particularly those with a focus on independent living, often draw from wider geographic areas than other projects because of the influence or policies of that sponsor. For example, Cornwall Manor, a multilevel continuing care community in Lebanon, Pennsylvania, was founded in 1949 by a group of Methodist clergy and laymen from the now Eastern Pennsylvania Conference of the United Methodist Church. The community was originally called the Methodist Church Home at Cornwall and was known later as Cornwall Manor of the United Methodist Church. This historic affiliation with the church attracted residents from throughout Pennsylvania and the entire East Coast. In 2000, approximately 65 percent of residents moved from outside the local area, with a large percentage moving from Philadelphia and nearby suburbs (more than 50 miles away) and 30 percent moving from out of state.

Urban/Suburban/Rural Influence. The distances people will travel to move to a retirement community may differ based on whether the site is in an urban, suburban, or rural area. This differentiation is based primarily on anecdotal evidence, although it does appear that the more urban the location, the smaller the reach of its geographic draw, and that rural sites may extend their draw farther than other types of locations. Several factors affect this issue. For instance, facilities located in highly urban areas may have difficulty drawing residents from suburban areas. In downtown Philadelphia at Logan Square East, a life care facility, for example, most residents lived in downtown Philadelphia immediately before they moved to this facility. Those who may have been living in the suburbs when they raised their families had already moved into the city as empty nesters. Logan Square East, however, has been much less successful at drawing residents directly from the suburbs. Not only are many competitive facilities available in those suburbs, but many suburbanites will not even consider moving to the city. Once again, the psychological barrier is a factor in this decision. For many suburbanites, the city represents a dangerous, undesirable place, one they rarely visit for shopping and cultural activities and one they would not consider moving to. City dwellers have similar biases against suburban—and certainly rural—locations, where they lose the mobility and independence of city living, its cultural and other amenities, and existing social ties.

On the other hand, facilities built in rural settings may enjoy a much larger geographic draw than their suburban counterparts, perhaps partly because people in rural areas are more accustomed to traveling greater distances to find the services they need. It may also reflect the fact that competitive facilities are sparsely located, increasing the geographic size of the competitive market area. Density of population frequently is inversely proportional to the size of the market area.

Primary and Secondary Market Areas. Market feasibility studies for seniors' housing communities frequently specify a primary and a secondary area from which the project is expected to draw residents. The primary area typically represents locations close to the community from which the project may expect to draw the largest share of its residents; the secondary area represents locations that are somewhat more distant or difficult to reach.

The use of primary and secondary market areas is often found coupled with a radius analysis. Studies using the radius method may incorporate the area within the closest ring (five, ten, or 15 miles) as the primary market and an area representing a more distant ring (20, 25, or even 50 miles) as the secondary market. As noted, the proportion of residents drawn to a community falls off as distance increases, even within a relatively localized area. As with all market analyses, the distinctions between primary and secondary markets are most valuable if they reflect an area from which residents can reasonably and actually be expected to move to the project. For facilities that have conducted presales, the primary market area is typically that geographic area where the majority of future residents currently live. If a concentrated but smaller proportion of sales appears to be coming from a more distant defined geographic area, it is the secondary market area.

Some studies appear to refer to primary and secondary markets without actually attending to the meaning or implications of the words. Although distinctions may be made in the description of each area, they are not carried through in the analysis.

Socioeconomic Trends and Characteristics

Most market studies include a description of the characteristics of the geographic market area and, in some cases, the larger region where the seniors' housing community is to be located. This description broadens the analytical context for the project from the elderly market itself to the overall market where a facility will operate. Descriptions of market area characteristics range from the very brief to an overdone, frequently indiscriminate collection of data with little or no interpretation.

Information most frequently found in market studies includes population and household trends and projections, economic indicators, and development trends.

Population and Household Trends and Projections

The overall and elderly population trends for the facility's market area are important considerations. The statistics should indicate historical trends as well as forecasts into the future. Most frequently, these analyses focus on a ten- to 15-year period dating from the most recent decennial census to estimates of the present to forecasts approximately five years into the future. Companies such as CACI Marketing Systems and Claritas do not provide demographic forecasts beyond a five-year period from the estimated current year. Their forecasts are based, among other things, on extrapolations of the historical demographic trends formed by the base census year and their estimates of the current year. Concern about the validity of projecting beyond a five-year horizon limits all data vendors from projecting beyond that time period. Historical data are typically based on the U.S. census for the defined geographic area, whereas projections or forecasts are prepared by commercial data vendors or by state, regional, or local planning offices. Changes in the overall population allow those planning, evaluating, or investing in the project to determine whether the area where it is to be located is characterized by growth, stability, or decline.

The U.S. Census Bureau is implementing a new approach for collecting information, the American Community Survey. In the past, the Census Bureau collected demographic information through the decennial census by asking one in six households to fill out a long form. The American Community Survey will replace this form with an ongoing survey that will provide "estimates of demographic, housing, social, and economic characteristics every year for all states, as well as for cities, counties, metropolitan areas, and population centers of 65,000 people or more."[11] Every three to five years, the data will be available for smaller areas. This change in the collection of census data is a vastly improved resource for market analysts, enabling them access to more reliable and timely information.

While trends among the overall population are important to understanding a market, the data and projections of specific market segments are vital elements of the study. Elderly population and household data can be obtained in five-year increments from ages 65 to 69, 70 to 74, 75 to 79, 80 to 84, and 85 and over (Figure 2-3). Population and household trends by age cohort provide the analyst a greater level of detail to evaluate the market. Some studies, particularly those for assisted living, also include figures on households with adult children age 45 to 64 to illustrate the trends among this group, which is considered influential in selecting seniors' housing for their aging parents. These characteristics can be compared with regional or national statistics to provide a more meaningful profile of the local market. In 2000, for example, a national average of 5.9 percent of the total population was 75 or older. Comparing this statistic with one local market consisting of a portion of Ocean County, New Jersey, where 11.5 percent of the total population is older than 75, for example, reveals the unusually high percentage of the target market in the general population.

Demographic data are frequently presented in the form of tables and in some studies are described in the text of the report, with comments on the rates of change over the period examined.

Figure 2-3 **Elderly Population in the State of Connecticut, 2000**

Age	Population
65–69	117,556
70–74	114,009
75–79	101,096
80–84	73,249
85+	64,273
Total Population	3,405,565

Source: U.S. Census Bureau, *Census 2000.*

Economic Indicators

Some studies include general (that is, non-age-specific) information on the economic characteristics of the area, particularly regarding income and housing values. Income data may reflect median or mean household or family income for the overall market area or for specific municipalities in it. Many studies show income levels by age cohort for both the elderly and adult children, enabling further understanding of the local market. Such income data are typically derived from the most recent decennial census. In some cases, studies also include information on effective buying income overall and per household and/or retail sales for the metropolitan area. These data may be compared for the locality, state, and/or nation to provide a context for local characteristics. This information is rarely interpreted but is provided as background information for users to draw their own conclusions about the economic character of the area.

Information about housing values is extremely useful and important in studies of all types of seniors' housing projects. In particular, studies that contain an analysis of the average selling price of homes and the average length of time required for homes to sell provide pertinent information. The ability of prospective residents of seniors' housing communities to sell their homes and the values of those homes directly affect affordability and the project's absorption. For projects charging an entrance or purchase fee, average home sale prices are a point of reference for the ability of local residents to afford the upfront fees. Frequently, elderly homeowners have paid off their mortgages, and proceeds from the sale of the home provide a source of capital used to pay the upfront fees charged by many retirement facilities. The interest income earned from the proceeds of the sale of a home can also be used to offset the monthly fees at a seniors' housing community that does not charge upfront fees. In some cases, the principal accumulated from the sale of a home is drawn on each month and used to pay a portion of the monthly fee. This spending down of assets is most often the case when assisted living or nursing care is required and monthly fees become higher than monthly income. According to ALFA's study, 18.5 percent of assisted living residents were spending down assets to supplement income to pay for services in 1999.[12] Studies by NIC of residents of assisted living facilities also concluded that elderly residents are drawing on their assets to pay monthly fees. Assets were reported to decrease in relation to the length of stay in assisted living facilities[13] and were found to be an important factor in contributing to a person's ability to pay for health care and other needs.[14]

Although many projects target those who have above-average assets and income, this information still provides a good yardstick with which to compare potential pricing schemes. Because a market study represents a snapshot of a particular period of time, information on housing values and home sales provides an indicator, at the time of the study, of the viability of the housing market and its potential impact on the project's affordability and absorption period. This information can be obtained from local realtors or representatives of the area board of realtors, who can access the database represented by the multiple listing service. The Internet is also a good source for accessing current information about home values: the National Association of Realtors® *(www.nar.org)* provides national and regional current sales data, and *www.dataquick.com* allows users to search for median housing values by ZIP code.

Another economic indicator frequently presented in market studies relates to employment and unemployment. Many studies, both those used for financing and those used for planning, present statistical data on unemployment levels over a period of time for the area being studied as well as the composition of the employment base for the region. Frequently, a list of major employers is presented, with the number of people they employ. These data are typically found in market studies for a wide variety of real estate and health care uses; however, most studies contain no commentary about or interpretation of the data. These data rarely if ever are tied directly to the issue of the market for the seniors' housing community. Seniors' housing communities, particularly those offering assisted living, however, frequently draw residents because they are convenient to adult children, who may influence the decision to move. Thus, consideration of employment opportunities and job growth may have a direct tie to the market for the planned community. Not only may it be an indicator of the strength of the secondary market—that is, adult children—but it may also provide insights into the extent to which a community might expect to draw from outside the typical local market area.

A good example is Charlotte, North Carolina. Economic growth there, particularly in the banking industry, brought significant in-migration of adult children moving to join the burgeoning Charlotte workforce. Many moved from outside the metropolitan area and even from out of state. This nonindigenous workforce reflects itself in the extent to which seniors' housing communities in the Charlotte area have drawn from outside their local market area. Many have reported that 40 to 50 percent of their residents do not come from the Charlotte area or even, in many cases, from North Carolina. The relationship of the economy, the character of the workforce, and the seniors' housing industry creates a significant issue when assessing market demand in the Charlotte area. As such, an examination of certain aspects of the employment base in an area may be helpful in evaluating the market for a seniors' housing community. Rather than compiling a simple list of employers, however, it may be more instructive to interview the appropriate human resources personnel for major employers to determine whether they are receiving inquiries for assistance from employees who are trying to relocate aging parents.

Development Trends

Market analysis may encompass a review of major development trends in an area. This analysis takes into consideration such activities as residential and commercial development; the attraction, expansion, and/or relocation of major employers in an area; and new infrastructure (e.g., highway expansion). Development can have an impact on the viability of a proposed seniors' housing community. The strength of the housing market affects the ability of elderly residents to sell their homes and raise the necessary capital to afford entrance into many seniors' housing communities. The development of new shopping centers and malls may be perceived as a desirable improvement to the area's retail market and services. The location of major employers represents an indirect market base for seniors' housing communities, as middle managers and executives seek housing to relocate aging relatives. Finally, the accessibility of sites for retirement communities can be altered through the development of new or expanded road and highway systems.

Quantification of Demographic Information about the Elderly

In addition to general population statistics, the demographics study typically presents specific information about the elderly population. The focus of the demographic analysis in market studies for seniors' housing communities is on statistics that characterize the elderly in the defined market area.

This analysis focuses on the characteristics of the area's elderly in terms of the size of the senior population, the number of households headed by an elderly person, their economic characteristics, and, in some cases, their housing tenure, household size, and household makeup. This analysis also is done in preparation for the penetration or "demand" analysis, which attempts to quantify the pool of households eligible for market-rate seniors' housing.

Some studies include information on the population age 65 and older. Most seniors' housing communities, however, draw from an older segment of the population, typically at least age 70 and more likely age 75 and above. As expected, independent living settings attract the youngest elderly, and assisted living communities are on average home to the oldest elderly. According to AAHSA's survey conducted in 1998, the average age at entry to independent living in CCRCs was 78.[15] In its 2000–2001 "Seniors Housing Statistical Digest," the American Seniors Housing Association reported that the average age of residents who moved into CCRCs in its sample was 77.2 years, into congregate housing was 81.7 years, and into assisted living housing was 83.1 years.[16] As the assisted living industry has evolved, the average age is even higher than in independent living settings. According to ALFA's study, the average age of residents in 1999 was 83.8 in assisted living communities.[17] Feasibility studies for assisted living communities most often include those over the age of 75, although some studies consider the elderly market to be those over the age of 80. Thus, studies now include analyses of elderly population and elderly households by age group, with some showing two breakdowns, those age 65 to 74 and those age 75 and older. As with analysis of the general population, the analysis of the elderly population is typically presented to show a trend from the past to the near future. The analysis of population data about the elderly typically presents statistics indicating both the rate of growth and the proportion of the general population represented by each elderly age group. In some studies, these proportions are compared with a larger area, such as the state where the project is located or even the United States. The comparison allows the user to evaluate whether the geographic area where the project is located has a typical or atypical proportion of elderly population. Similar data are frequently presented to quantify the number of elderly households in the market area.

A profile of household income for the elderly may be presented, providing data on the number of households by income distribution. These data typically are provided over a similar period (e.g., base census year, current year, and five years in the future) as other data included in the study to indicate trends. Data vendors such as Claritas and CACI Marketing Systems provide information on income of elderly households based on the most recent decennial census, estimates for the current year, and projections five years ahead. These data are segmented by age group and frequently are presented for households headed by someone age 65 to 74 or by someone age 75 or older. The income distribution data provide a way of determining how many households will qualify for potential residency in the project being evaluated as well as other competitive projects in the market area. These data ultimately are used to quantify the qualified pool of households that forms the basis of the demand analysis or penetration calculations.

Adult Children

Market studies frequently include descriptive data on adult children (those age 45 to 64), including information on the number of people and households in this age cohort and the income characteristics of households in this segment. People in this age group are frequently involved in an older family member's decision to move to seniors' housing. As the level of care increases, so does the responsibility of this group for actually making or significantly influencing the decision to move. According to ALFA, family members are the largest single source of referrals to assisted living communities (20.3 percent of residents reported families as a referral source in the 2000 study).[18] The study by the National Investment Center indicated that nearly 84 percent of residents in assisted living said that their daughter or son was involved in their decision to move; 55 percent said they were the most influential person in their decision to move.[19]

In fact, many adult children live close to the seniors' housing communities where their parent or parents reside. ALFA reported that in 1999, 55.4 percent lived within ten miles of the assisted living facilities surveyed (in comparison, 48.5 percent of families lived within ten miles of the independent living communities surveyed).[20] NIC reported an even higher proportion of family members (59.7 percent) living within ten miles of assisted living communities.[21]

Attitudes, Perceptions, and Familiarity With Seniors' Housing

Attitudes, perceptions, and familiarity with seniors' housing are best evaluated through direct consumer research (see Chapter 4). It also is possible, however, to gain some insights through interviews with nonelderly key informants. Possible contacts include social service staff in hospitals, home health agencies, area offices on aging, senior centers, adult daycare centers, caregiver support groups, estate planners, lawyers whose clients are the elderly, and clergy from the major religious denominations. Together, these groups were responsible for referring approximately 25 percent of incoming assisted living residents in 1999.[22] Appropriate questions posed to those who deal with an elderly constituency and questions posed during interviews with representatives from competitive facilities can provide information about attitudes and perceptions. Respondents typically are willing to share opinions regarding the need for additional seniors' housing, perceptions of the site and location, characteristics of the local elderly market, suitability of pricing, and services and amenities desired. Through interviews with key informants, the analyst can often uncover issues that should be further explored and tested through consumer research.

Unfortunately, very few market studies that do not include consumer research address these issues. In some cases, this information has been obtained from interviews, but it simply is not contained in the actual market study. Although the absence of this information may be justifiable in studies being prepared for use in financing documents, it should be much more routinely included in studies being done for planning purposes.

Competitor Analysis

Competitor analysis addresses the supply side of the market study's supply and demand framework. It can accomplish several goals, depending on the nature of the study. Studies prepared for financing purposes incorporate competitor analyses to provide lenders and/or investors with information on the extent of competition for the facility being financed and how well it is doing. Fitch, for example, considers occupancy levels an important method for determining demand, "because [they show] actual usage of services at all providers in the market. . . . 'Hard' occupancies, defined as 90 percent and above, are viewed favorably as indicators of adequate demand. 'Soft' occupancies, less than 90 percent, are viewed as concerns."[23] Information on competitors is also used in evaluating market depth and whether it is sufficient to fill the subject and competitive facilities. The competitor analysis also provides an indicator of the extent of competition as well as the extent to which a given market might be exposed to and educated about seniors' housing. For instance, in an analysis that identifies few or no existing competitive facilities, one can assume that the market for the project being financed will need to be more educated about the concept than in an area with numerous facilities, particularly if the latter have been developed during a comparatively extended period of time. This analysis can also provide insights into how active the competitive environment will be during the project's initial absorption period. Information on occupancy levels at existing facilities and about other projects that are under construction or being planned is necessary for lenders and investors to be better informed about how competitive the market will be during this period.

Market studies conducted to help plan communities can offer even more extensive benefits through a well-conducted competitor analysis. The information obtained about competitive properties can shed a great deal of light on which types of facilities are doing well in a given market and which ones may be having more difficulty. Data about competitors can be used to help determine programmatic features and pricing that meet the needs of the specific market where the project will operate. When the analysis provides information on which types of units at competitive facilities are and are not doing well, the analyst is able to assist the client in making decisions about the appropriate unit mix. In general, a highly detailed competitor analysis allows the analyst and client to reach decisions about how to design and position the project to compete directly with other facilities in the area or perhaps to find a market niche that is not being addressed. In the Philadelphia area, for example, where traditional life care has been the dominant concept, Bellingham opened in 1990 in Chester County as the first rental community in the area. The market study and consumer research conducted in planning this project indicated that an affordable rental project would be attractive to older residents of this area whose primary alternatives were to pay high entrance fees to enter a continuing care or life care community. The community has proved to be a success in this market: it is fully occupied and has a waiting list of up to one year for independent living. At the time this book was written, Bellingham was constructing an additional 50 assisted living units, and plans are to add a wing for those with dementia and a skilled nursing facility within the next five years.

Data about competitors can be gathered in several ways. The most extensive information and the best insights regarding competitors are obtained by visiting the facility and meeting with a member of the management team, such as a marketing director. A visit enables the analyst to engage the informant in a lengthier, somewhat more informal dialogue, which often leads to obtaining much more information than provided by a brochure or a telephone interview. It also provides the analyst an opportunity to see the physical plant and surrounding area. When time and consulting budgets are limited, however, data about competitors can usually be obtained over the telephone and through the facility's brochures. In addition, many communities now have Web sites that provide detailed information, and some even offer virtual tours of the facility.

Defining the Competition

Defining what constitutes a competitive facility varies widely. Distinctions between what is and what is not competitive might be based on geographic location, pricing, program format, and ownership and sponsorship.

Geographic Location. Most studies look at competitive facilities in the geographic area that has been defined as the project's market area (primary and/or secondary). The analyst might or might not consider facilities close to or on the perimeter of the market area competitive. A key to determining whether nearby facilities are competitive is to understand whether those facilities attract residents from the project's market area. Studies may or may not attempt to quantify the amount of overlap in geographic area between a competitor and the project being analyzed. This type of quantification can be difficult, because it is somewhat subjective and relies on anecdotal data or approximations obtained from interviews with competitors about the specific geographic parameters of that facility's market area. As the industry has evolved, however, marketing representatives have become more savvy and are aware of critical data, including understanding their facility's primary market area and knowing precisely where residents have moved from. In many markets, interviews with competitors are enlightening and, coupled with knowledge of the local market's characteristics and orientation patterns, can lead to a fairly accurate assumption regarding the percentage of market area overlap with the project's market.

Program and Pricing. Some studies consider only facilities with similar approaches to pricing and program as competitors. For example, studies for a continuing care retirement facility may consider only other continuing care/life care communities competitive. Congregate communities that do not offer health care services similar to the considered project may not be mentioned in the study or may be described but dismissed as noncompetitive. In other studies, projects that offer similar services but lower fees may not be considered direct competitors. This decision may be reflected simply by a comment in the text or by a reduction in the number of units from such facilities that are included in the penetration analysis.

Ownership and Sponsorship. Some studies distinguish between facilities that are owned and sponsored by religious or fraternal nonprofit organizations and other nonprofit or proprietary owned facilities in the market area. Occasionally, facilities sponsored by a religious group are dismissed or discounted because they cater to or are perceived to cater to only the affinity group represented by the sponsoring denomination, or because they draw residents from that denomination or fraternal order from a much wider geographic area than that defined for the project. In fact, denominationally sponsored facilities frequently draw residents from many religious denominations.

Level of Care. Independent living and assisted living most often target seniors needing different levels of care. Independent living, as implied by the name, targets those seniors who are still able to live without significant assistance and who are more interested in a hospitality-oriented service program. Assisted living, on the other hand, primarily targets and serves more frail and dependent residents requiring some level of assistance with ADLs. In some cases, such as CCRCs, both levels of care are present, but in other cases communities do not include both. This approach is more common for assisted living, which during the 1990s emerged as a standalone product that might include a specialized section for those with memory impairment but did not include a dedicated independent living component. Some assisted living communities do serve residents who do not require assistance with ADLs, but they usually constitute a very small proportion. Studies for seniors' housing communities incorporating a single level of care most often place their primary focus on communities offering a similar level of care, whether freestanding or in a continuum of care. Such studies may also include reference to the less competitive level of care not being offered.

Defining competition for the purpose of sizing the potential pool of eligible households in a market area is an exercise in quantification that nearly all market studies encompass. In reality, however, when the time comes to market and sell a project, not all seniors' housing facilities that may have been counted in this quantification will in fact be seen as competitive by the marketing staff or the ultimate arbiters of competition, the consumers (see Chapter 4).

Status of the Competition

Analyses of the competition are divided into at least two components: those facilities that are already operational and those that have not yet opened. Operational facilities allow one to determine how the market has responded to the housing concepts embodied by those facilities. The latter component is instrumental in determining the extent to which the project will compete with and try to fill up at the same time as new facilities that will open in a similar time frame. Planned facilities may include new facilities as well as expansions of existing ones. Discussions of planned facilities may encompass everything from those that are certain to be built (such as those under construction at the time the analysis is conducted) to those that are rumored but have not gained final approvals from local or state agencies. Planned projects also include facilities that are in the process of gaining or have gained zoning approval, those that are not yet financed, and those that are financed but not yet constructed. How these planned projects are treated in the final market sizing and penetration analysis varies greatly (see Chapter 3).

Data about the Competition

The information gathered on competitive facilities is often summarized in tables (see Figure 2-4) and may be discussed in narrative form. Competition also may be shown on a map of the market area, giving a graphic depiction of where facilities are located, whether they are clustered in any specific part(s) of the market area, and how far they are from the proposed facility. In addition to the facility's name, location, ownership and/or sponsorship, and year of opening, the following information may be provided for each competitive facility.

Facility Description. The information on the physical plant usually indicates the total number of units or beds for each level provided, including independent living, assisted living/personal care, and/or nursing. In addition, the information may include the number of units or beds by type (e.g., studio, one-bedroom, and two-bedroom units). This information may be coupled with the average or specific range of sizes (i.e., square feet) for each unit type.

Figure 2-4 **Existing Competitive CCRCs**

Facility	Number of IL Units	Number of AL Beds	Number of NH Beds	Entrance Fee for IL Units	Second Person Entrance Fee	Refund Policy	Monthly Service Fee	Second Person Service Fee	Services	Occu-pancy
A	91	19	62	$54,900–112,900	$10,000	Plan A: Refundable less 1% monthly, no refund after 4 months upon death. Plan B: 50% refundable plan for those under age 89; first 50% is refundable less 2% per month.	IL: $1,080–1,424	$987	2 meals daily or 30 meals monthly reduces fee $45. Services: 1, 2, 3, 4, 5	IL: 100% AL: 90% NH: 95%
B	245	32	54	$40,000–219,000	$16,000–27,000	Fully refundable in first 6 months, then less 2% monthly up to 5 years. No refund upon death.	IL: $1,493–3,359 AL: $2,200	$750–1,200	3 meals, 1 meal plan available for reduced fee. Services: 1, 2, 3, 4, 5	IL: 93% AL: 90% NH: 93%
C	238	0	60	$38,400–82,500	None	Refundable less 1.25% monthly.	$1,039–1,926	$597	1 meal. Services: 1, 2, 3, 4, 5	IL: 85% NH: 75%
D	359	51	120	$36,100–205,600	$12,500–37,100	Plan A: Refundable up to 50 months less 2% per month. Plan B: 90% refundable plan available for 2-bedroom units only for age-qualified applicants. Must be under 80 for single occupancy and under 85 for double occupancy (one must be under 80).	$1,546–2,928	$995–1,312	3 meals (monthly meal credits available). Services: 1, 2, 3, 4, 5	IL: 98% AL: 92% NH: 90%
E	219	120	82	$77,400–86,300	$20,000	Fully refundable in first 3 months, then less 2% per month up to 50 months.	$1,302–2,334	$682–699	1 meal. Services: 1, 2, 3, 4, 5	IL: 93% AL: 90% NH: 90%
F	150	0	0	NA (rental)	NA	NA	$1,338–3,364	$738	1 meal. Services: 1, 2, 3, 5	97%

Key

IL = Independent Living	1 = Recreational facilities	4 = Linen services
AL = Assisted Living	2 = Transportation	5 = Maintenance
NH = Nursing Home	3 = Housekeeping	NA = Not applicable

The facility description may also incorporate a description of the overall design and construction characteristics of the community, indicating how many stories it is, what size land parcel it occupies, and what type of construction it represents. It may also list the types of common space provided. In addition, a more subjective description of the decor of the common space and the design features of the units may be provided, although it is rarely contained in market studies, particularly for those prepared for financing purposes.

Pricing. The approach to pricing (entrance fee, rental, condominium, cooperative) and the actual fees charged to reside in the facility are described. The pricing information may also indicate whether the facility offers a refund program if entrance fees are charged and whether more than one pricing program is available. For instance, some CCRCs offer two entrance fee programs, a lower nonrefundable fee and a higher refundable fee.

Pricing structures for assisted living can be very complex and difficult to compare. Assisted living communities charge for assistance with ADLs in a number of ways. Some communities offer an all-inclusive monthly fee that incorporates an unlimited number of personal care services (within regulations), while others charge additional fees according to the level of service provided. The most popular fee structure for assisted living is tiered pricing, which allows a facility to categorize residents according to the amount of care needed. Typically, a resident assessment establishes the appropriate level. Communities usually offer three to five tiers, which can be grouped based on the amount of time, number of ADLs, or specific services required. Among the responding properties to ALFA's 2000 survey, 40.5 percent relied on a tiered pricing formula for services, 14.9 percent included assistance with ADLs in the monthly fee, 13 percent charged a flat fee for each service provided, 6.5 percent charged an additional hourly fee for each ADL service, and 25.1 percent provided a different billing option.[24] The analysis should clearly identify the type of fee structure before attempting any comparisons.

The information provided about fees may be presented in ranges or by unit type. Entrance fees, condominium or cooperative purchase prices, and monthly fees are included. Because these fee ranges typically reflect single occupancy, usually fees for second persons residing in a unit are also included in the presentation.

Gathering and analyzing information on pricing approaches and fee levels make it possible to evaluate whether any approach appears to dominate the market area. In addition, the analyst and client can see which economic segments have already been targeted and whether demand still exists among those segments—or whether other economic niches should be explored. Finally, the analysis permits a determination regarding the relative acceptability of different pricing approaches and fee levels and further enhances the ability to plan to emulate what has already been done or to find unmet opportunities. Before preparing a financial analysis, the analyst can use the competition's pricing as a guideline for establishing prospective fee ranges for the facility being studied. Fees established to fall within the parameters set by competitive facilities, however, must be tested through financial analysis to ascertain whether market-based fees will be sufficient to cover the cost of developing, financing, and operating the facility.

Services. The programs and services offered by a facility may be included in the fees paid by everybody or in some cases offered on a fee-for-service basis.

In CCRCs, it is important to specify the amount of health and nursing care covered by the basic fee structure because of the many different types of contracts—from the all-inclusive life care approach to the unbundled fee-for-service structure. As noted, many communities offer a tiered pricing structure, requiring a clear description of what is included in base fees and for each different level of care.

For assisted living communities, services are usually regulated by the state department that issues the license. Minimum and frequently maximum limits on the types of services that can and must be provided are described in the regulations and vary from state to state. Those variations can be substantial. For example, the regulations for assisted living residences in New Jersey allow intermittent nursing care to be provided to residents, while the regulations in Pennsylvania for its version of assisted living (personal care homes) do not permit such care. Both states mandate that the facility arrange health-related services and that transportation be provided or secured, whereas Massachusetts mandates neither.

Tables presenting data about competitors frequently include a key that enables the user to see which services are included in the fees. In addition, information may be provided regarding optional services offered at additional cost to the resident. Services include such items as meals, housekeeping, linens, an emergency call system, maintenance, transportation, personal care, and social programs. In addition, if nursing home care and health care services are available, the study indicates the extent to which they are included in the fees or offered on a fee-for-service basis.

Occupancy Levels, Waiting Lists, and Absorption. Data about competitors should include information on the occupancy level each facility had achieved at the time the survey was conducted.

A number of facilities incorporating independent living units, assisted living units, and nursing beds maintain policies limiting the use of assisted living and nursing care to individuals already residing in the community's independent living units. For such facilities, particularly those that have been in operation for five years or more, the occupancy levels of the higher care (assisted living and nursing) do not therefore actually reflect the demand or need in the open market. At facilities that do accept nonresidents into assisted living and nursing care units, however, occupancy and waiting list information is an important indicator of market conditions.

Frequently, waiting lists vary by unit type and by level of care, a factor that can be an important clue to what is doing well in the market and what may be less marketable. For communities that have opened relatively recently and/or have not yet reached full occupancy, it is increasingly important to learn when marketing efforts began and when the operators started taking deposits, and to calculate the length of time required to absorb those units that are full. Calculations of absorption are an important element of judging feasibility and projecting fill rates, particularly in markets where the competition is hot.

The length of a waiting list may be described as length of time or number of people. Information on waiting lists can be misleading for several reasons. For independent living units, some individuals place their names on lists well in advance of being ready to move to ensure a place when they are ready. It is particularly the case for facilities that are experiencing significantly more demand than they can accommodate. In addition, in some areas, people place their names on more than one waiting list, especially when the cost to do so is modest. For assisted living facilities, because of their need-driven nature, waiting lists may be short because of high turnover rates. Information on waiting lists provided during an interview is not always reliable.

Residents' Demographics. Data delineating the average age of residents at entry, their distribution by gender, and their status as singles or couples are not consistently obtained in market studies. Information on age at entry is extremely helpful in targeting the market and calculating the size of the age-eligible pool in the area at the time of the study. For studies done to help plan a new community, information on age and household type (i.e., singles versus couples) can be instrumental in refining the community's design and service program. Although the information is not necessarily quantified or made available in a systematic way, most market analysts attempt to learn where residents lived immediately before moving to competitive facilities. This information is a critical component in supporting and refining the definition of the market area for the project. It can also facilitate determining the amount of geographic overlap between the competitive facilities and the subject property.

Description of the Location. The location of competitive facilities is an important factor in determining the desirability of the facility and whom it attracts. During fieldwork, the analyst should evaluate the location of competitive facilities, which can be compared with the subject's location to identify competitive advantages and disadvantages. Some of the same principles apply as for a real estate decision. Is it convenient to shopping, services, churches, and amenities in the community? Can family members and visitors easily reach the facility? Is the site aesthetically pleasing in an attractive setting or is it adjacent to a poorly maintained property or unappealing area?

Positioning. While planning studies typically are not included in a study being used for financing, their value can be increased by incorporating information about how different communities position themselves (see Chapter 6). That information may focus on sponsorship (nonprofit fraternal or religious organizations) or branding (for example, Marriott and Sunrise are brand names in assisted living), economic target market, type of resident, proximity to amenities, or the community's overall philosophy. Positioning statements may be reflected in collateral materials such as brochures, newsletters, or advertisements and may also be reflected by marketing personnel.

Perceived Competition. Asking the competition whom they consider to be their major competitors provides an insider's view of the marketplace and reveals the niche the facility serves. It also facilitates a discussion of what advantages and disadvantages are perceived among competitive facilities. Marketing representatives are usually willing to share feedback from consumers who compare facilities based on their likes and dislikes. Marketing studies intended for planning purposes may include this anecdotal information to create a more thorough understanding of the competitive environment and to make recommendations based on consumers' preferences.

Plans for Expansion and Change. Future plans to expand or make changes affecting the unit mix of a seniors' housing community should be incorporated in the competitive profile in a market study. Highlighting these changes serves two purposes, qualitative and quantitative. First, it indicates market demand and preferences, and second, the changes can be factored into the market depth analysis calculating future demand. For example, a facility may plan to combine ten studio units and replace the space with five one-bedroom units because the facility cannot fill the studio units but has a significant waiting list for one-bedroom units. This change would reduce the overall number of independent living units while creating a more marketable product. Changes in the market provide clues about what the target market desires.

Identifying Competitive Facilities

Competitive facilities can be identified through several means. Existing facilities may be listed in the local telephone directory's yellow pages under headings such as Retirement Communities and Homes, Assisted Living, or even Continuing Care Retirement Communities. The area agency on aging—or a similar agency—should maintain a list of the various types of seniors' housing communities in its geographic jurisdiction. Several directories, such as the *National Continuing Care Directory*, the *Directory of Retirement Facilities* published by HCIA Sachs, and the American Association of Homes and Services for the Aging's membership directory, list retirement communities. Numerous sites on the Internet provide search mechanisms for retirement and assisted living communities.

State agencies are also good sources of information about planned retirement communities that meet their regulatory definitions. Facilities that have initiated or even completed the state's approval process but have not yet been built can be identified through this source. Other state government sources of information include the health department if a planned facility is to include a licensed assisted living and/or health care component (see Chapter 1 for a list of state agencies that regulate CCRCs and assisted living communities). Because assisted living and nursing beds in many cases are subject to some form of approval related to determination of need, letters of intent or full applications help to identify planned new construction and expansion of existing facilities.

The local municipal or county zoning and/or planning boards also may provide information on planned facilities. The staff at these organizations are aware of projects at their earliest planning stages and when they have reached the point of seeking the necessary approvals. The F.W. Dodge Construction Report provides detailed information about planned seniors' housing projects, including key contacts, status, valuation, and location.

Notes

1. R.C. Wetzler and R. Lageman, "Measuring Demand for Seniors' Housing," Fitch, Duff & Phelps, 2000, p. 2.

2. Assisted Living Federation of America, National Investment Council, and PricewaterhouseCoopers, "Overview of the Assisted Living Industry, 2000," pp. 17 & 21.

3. PricewaterhouseCoopers, "The Continuing Care Retirement Communities 1998 Profile" (Washington, D.C.: American Association of Homes and Services for the Aging, 1999), p. 26; and ALFA, PricewaterhouseCoopers, and NIC, "Overview of the Assisted Living Industry, 2000," pp. 18 & 22.

4. PricewaterhouseCoopers, "Continuing Care Retirement Communities 1998 Profile," p. 26.

5. ALFA, PricewaterhouseCoopers, and NIC, "Overview of the Assisted Living Industry, 2000," Table 24, p. 22.

6. Ibid., Table 14, p. 18.

7. American Seniors Housing Association and PricewaterhouseCoopers, "Seniors Housing Absorption Trends, 2000," p. 6.

8. Herbert J. Sims & Co. and American Association of Homes and Services for the Aging, "From Start-Up to Success: A Statistical Analysis of Emerging Continuing Care Retirement Communities," 1999, p. 25.

9. ALFA, PricewaterhouseCoopers, and NIC, "Overview of the Assisted Living Industry, 2000," Table 1, p. 11.

10. Price Waterhouse & Co., "Official Statement for Jewish Retirement Homes, Inc.—Fiddler's Woods," Appendix A, Financial Forecast, Exhibit I. Prepared for issuance of $35,155,000 in first mortgage gross revenue bonds.

11. http://www.census.gov/acs/www/About/What.htm.

12. ALFA, PricewaterhouseCoopers, and NIC, "Overview of the Assisted Living Industry, 2000," Table 9, p. 17.

13. ALFA and NIC, "National Survey of Assisted Living Residents: Who Is the Customer?" 1998, p. 246.

14. NIC, "Income Confirmation Study of Assisted Living Residents and the Age 75+ Population," 1999, p. 20.

15. PricewaterhouseCoopers, "Continuing Care Retirement Communities 1998 Profile," p. 24.

16. ASHA, "Seniors Housing Statistical Digest, 2000–2001," 2000, p. 24.

17. ALFA, PricewaterhouseCoopers, and NIC, "Overview of the Assisted Living Industry, 2000," Table 7, p. 16.

18. PricewaterhouseCoopers, "Continuing Care Retirement Communities 1998 Profile," Table 10, p. 17.

19. ALFA and NIC, "National Survey of Assisted Living Residents: Who Is the Customer?" Tables 23 & 24, pp. 131–132.

20. ALFA, PricewaterhouseCoopers, and NIC, "Overview of the Assisted Living Industry, 2000," Table 14, p. 18, & Table 25, p. 22.

21. ALFA and NIC, "National Survey of Assisted Living Residents: Who Is the Customer?" p. 150.

22. ALFA, PricewaterhouseCoopers, and NIC, "Overview of the Assisted Living Industry, 2000," Table 10, p. 17.

23. Wetzler and Lageman, "Measuring Demand for Seniors Housing," p. 3.

24. ALFA, PricewaterhouseCoopers, and NIC, "Overview of the Assisted Living Industry, 2000," Table 2, p. 12.

The Amsterdam Nursing Home in upper Manhattan was established in the late 1800s. The current building marries modern facilities with homey touches like antique furnishings. Architect: The Geddis Partnership

3 Analysis of Market Depth and Absorption

Quantifying Market Depth

A major component of the market study is the quantification of the depth of the market and therefore the level of risk associated with proceeding with a project. This component draws on all the elements introduced in Chapter 2. It takes into consideration the potential demand by using the demographic profile of the elderly market segments to size the potential market and the supply by using the competitor analysis. For independent living projects, the final result is a market penetration analysis that, appropriately or not, has become a focal point for measuring and evaluating potential demand. A market penetration analysis, although traditionally referred to as a *demand* analysis, in fact does not represent demand, per se. Rather, it is a tool that leads to the development of certain benchmarks that are thought to assess risk. For assisted living projects, establishing market penetration standards has been much more elusive, largely because of the lack of standardization in criteria used to size the market. Where applicable, the differences between demand analyses for independent living and assisted living are highlighted and discussed throughout this chapter.

This chapter also presents a comparison of market feasibility studies for seniors' housing communities conducted by most of the major accounting and other firms involved in this industry. While professionals such as feasibility consultants, investment bankers, and other lenders generally agree about most benchmarks for evaluating independent living, there is significantly less agreement on benchmarks for assisted living. Areas of similarity and differences between the analysis of independent and assisted living, and significant differences in key elements of the methodologies used to evaluate assisted living are highlighted throughout this chapter. In fact, industry-wide benchmarks for methods to quantify the qualified market and determine appropriate penetration rates for assisted living are still not available.

In addition to these elements, the chapter assesses regulatory impacts with regard to the potential for developing nursing home beds and in some cases assisted living components as project components. At the end of 1998, 37 states had passed legislation governing continuing care and life care communities. Many states require the submission of market or full financial feasibility studies for approval of the development of a CCRC or life care community. (Information on states regulating retirement communities that require feasibility studies is presented later in this chapter.)

Sizing the Market

The demographic aspects of the demand analysis estimate the size of the pool of elderly households within the defined market area by making a series of qualifying assumptions related to the characteristics of the project being evaluated. The primary elements considered include the anticipated age of the residents likely to move to the facility, the annual income necessary to support that residency, housing tenure (i.e., whether the elderly householder is currently an owner or renter), and type of household (i.e., primarily single individuals living alone or couples). The latter two elements are not incorporated in all analyses (typically, they are not part of the analyses for independent living), whereas the former two are always present. When prepared correctly, these analyses are always based on elderly households rather than the elderly population, because it is a household unit (even if that unit represents a single individual) that makes the move.

Age

Independent Living. Most retirement communities draw households headed by someone age 75 or older into independent living units. One rarely sees a study conducted by an experienced firm that considers the population under 70 years of age in calculating market depth or demand. Some studies, particularly those that include cottages and/or townhouses, begin with those age 70 and above, whereas others consider only households headed by someone age 75 and above. Studies done for financing purposes where substantial presales have taken place are able to draw inferences about age from the data collected about prospective residents.

Studies that do not have the benefit of using profile data about depositors should make assumptions on the proper qualifying age based on what can be learned about the experience of local competitive facilities. Although there are exceptions, most retirement communities throughout the country find the average age of entrants in the upper 70s (one study reported that for CCRCs, the average age of entry to independent living units was 78),[1] with 20 to 30 percent of residents between 70 and 75. Based on this information, some analysts assume that a portion of the planned facility's units will be filled by residents under 75 and adjust the qualified household pool to reflect this assumption.

Anecdotal data suggest that the average age at entry has increased since the early 1990s. The risks in selecting an inappropriately low age for this analysis are clear. It not only leads to oversizing because of the proportionately larger number of households in the younger age groups but also is misleading in other ways (see Figure 3-1). For instance, income tends to decrease with age. The assumption of 65 as a minimum age therefore not only inflates the overall size of the pool of households being considered but also further inflates its size by including a greater number of income-qualifying households.

Assisted Living. Although the typical age at entry for assisted living is the low 80s, most studies use 75 as the minimum age (others use 80). In "Guide for Content and Format of a Market Analysis for Residential Care Facilities" for the 232 Mortgage Insurance program, HUD specifies that age 75 be

Figure 3-1 **Elderly Household Income (Estimated), State of Connecticut, 2000**

Household Income Range	Total Households by Age of Householder			
	65–74	Percent	75+	Percent
Total Households	147,241	100.0	129,579	100.0
$0–14,999	25,839	17.5	42,929	33.1
$15,000–24,999	21,865	14.8	23,085	17.8
$25,000–34,999	19,599	13.3	15,995	12.3
$35,000–49,999	21,632	14.7	13,894	10.7
$50,000–74,999	23,499	16.0	13,968	10.8
$75,000+	34,807	23.6	19,708	15.2

Source: Claritas, "Senior Life Report," October 2000.

used as the minimum age for demand analysis for assisted living communities.[2] Fitch, Duff & Phelps, in "Measuring Demand for Seniors Housing," also uses 75+ as the minimum age for assisted living.[3]

Income

Independent Living. Numerous methods have been employed to determine the minimum annual income used to qualify the pool of households considered in the demand analysis. Feasibility studies used for financing frequently use data from the annual *Consumer Expenditure Survey* published by the U.S. Department of Labor's Bureau of Labor Statistics (BLS). The data reflect estimates of the average annual expenditure by age group (65 to 74, 75 and older) for goods and services, including food, apparel, services, transportation, housing, medical care, and miscellaneous items such as recreation, gifts, and insurance. The qualities and quantities of goods and services vary by age. Moreover, estimates can reflect differences in regional costs as well as differences in urban, suburban, and rural expenditures.

Estimated expenditures are adjusted in certain categories affected by the facility's services covered by the payment of monthly fees, including housing costs, food, transportation, and, when appropriate, medical costs. Typically, the housing component is replaced by the annualized weighted average monthly fee or the fee for the most predominant unit type, such as a one-bedroom apartment. Depending on the number of meals included in the fee, food costs are adjusted accordingly. If a retirement community plans to offer transportation, the transportation budget is adjusted to reflect the assumption that the residents will have less need for public transportation or their own cars. Finally, for life care and continuing care retirement communities that provide substantial coverage for nursing and, in some cases, other medical costs, the medical care component of the budget is adjusted.

Based on the historical use of these data, patterns or standards begin to emerge regarding the relationship of annual income to the amount of affordable fees. Organizations in the business of operating retirement communities have developed fee-to-income ratios that they believe are necessary to qualify for residency in the community. The development of income requirements for screening residents was in part a response to the difficulties in which many early communities found themselves because residents, particularly those who had resided there for a lengthy period, were no longer able to afford the monthly fees. The problem resulted from the combination of minimal or no income screening before accepting a resident and some of the flawed actuarial analyses conducted.

Studies that use fee-to-income ratios to qualify the pool of eligible households may reflect the policy of the facility's management (typically the case in studies done for financing) or the best judgment and experience of the firm conducting the study. No actual standards have been developed, but fee-to-income ratios ranging from 60 to 70 percent (depending on the services covered by the monthly fee) have been used. Among the methodologies presented later in this section, ratios for independent living range from 60 percent to 67 percent.

These ratios typically are based on information available regarding household income. Households typically are qualified based on whether they can afford to pay the monthly fees charged by the facility. If pricing is known by unit type for the planned project, a weighted average monthly fee is typically used to calculate required annual income.

Planning studies done before setting fees may simply select an appropriate minimum income based on the likely economic target market for the project. Some earlier studies tended to estimate on the low side, using $15,000 to $20,000. Most analysts assume, however, that unless a low-income group is being targeted, a minimum of $25,000 to $30,000 is usually a starting point.

Whether or not a community charges a substantial entrance fee can affect the minimum income level calculated. Most seniors are homeowners (depending on the market), and the vast majority of those who own homes have paid off the mortgage by the time they reach their late 70s. According to the 1999 *Consumer Expenditure Survey,* for example, 77 percent of households age 75 and older were homeowners.[4] Of those homeowners, 12 percent were still paying a mortgage, and 88 percent owned their homes mortgage free. For communities that charge an entrance fee, studies usually assume that the equity in the home when sold will be used to pay the entrance fee and, therefore, the fee-to-income ratio is not affected by home values. For rental communities, on the other hand, because homeowners will be able to invest the proceeds from sale of the home and supplement their incomes based on interest earnings, some analyses factor home values into calculating the minimum income for owners. Assumptions are made regarding the proportion of the proceeds that will be kept by the seller (usually 90 percent) and the interest rate that will be applied to those proceeds (usually a conservative rate not exceeding 6 percent), and this information is used to adjust the minimum income (see Figure 3-2).

Figure 3-2 **Calculation of Impact of Home Value on Minimum Income for Rental Units**

Average Monthly Fee	$2,000
Annual Income Required for Monthly Fee	$24,000
Minimum Income Assuming 60% Fee-to-Income Ratio	$40,000
Average Home Value	$150,000
Interest Income from Investing Proceeds	$8,100 ($150,000 × 90% × 6%)
Net Income Required after Applying Interest Income	$31,900

Because the income information provided by data vendors is before taxes, some analysts further adjust it by converting the analysis to an after-tax basis. Analysts disagree about the tax issue. For example, some apply an average 20 percent tax rate to senior households' income in an analysis like the one in Figure 3-2. This approach may be too aggressive, however, given the composition of the income base, and it varies as well based on income level. For example, in the 1999 *Consumer Expenditure Survey,* income after taxes for consumers 75 and older was only 5 percent lower than income before taxes.[5]

For projects charging entrance fees, some analysts establish a higher minimum income for renters to qualify than for homeowners. This approach is designed to indicate that the renter may have to liquidate certain income-producing assets to come up with the fee to enter the facility. In fact, for many facilities that target residents with annual incomes of $25,000 and above, overstating the market size by including renters is not a significant problem. In many areas, the pool of elderly renters does not demonstrate income distribution similar to elderly homeowners. Renters tend to be more highly concentrated in the lower end of the income ranges (those below $25,000). Figure 3-3 presents income distribution for four actual markets based on Senior Market Reports (SMRs). The SMR is a sophisticated demographic segmentation system that was created by Project Market Decisions; it uses Public Use Microdata Sample (PUMS) data, other decennial census data, current estimates of households and income, and original research on home values. The SMR presents data that cross-tabulate income by age, household type, and housing tenure.

Assisted Living. Because assisted living typically incorporates a more significant service package, a higher fee-to-income ratio than for independent living is typically used. Ratios ranging from 75 percent up to 100 percent have been observed in studies done by various firms involved in the industry. A variety of factors, however, can influence the calculation of minimum income for assisted living communities. In addition to the use of invested home proceeds described in the previous section, the level of service included in the fee influences the ratio. A blended fee combining both unit types and different levels of care might be used, or the average fee might simply be based on a single level of care. Differences in this type of assumption can lead to a significant difference in the income level used in the analysis.

An extremely provocative finding emerged from a study of 1,023 assisted living residents.[6] Sixty-four percent of residents had incomes below $25,000, while the average annual fee charged by participating communities was just over $24,000. These findings were supported by NIC's 1999 "Income Confirmation Study."[7] Some analysts have speculated that respondents purposely underreport these incomes, reflecting concern about fee hikes or tax consequences, or that underreporting is unintentional because respondents do not know their true income. In an article published in the *Seniors Housing and Care Journal,*

Figure 3-3 **Owner/Renter Income Analysis**

	Owners		Renters	
	Number	Percent	Number	Percent
75+ Households (Income $25,000+)				
Market A	4,925	83.2	993	16.8
Market B	2,773	66.8	1,378	33.2
Market C	505	76.5	155	23.5
Market D	3,222	69.5	1,417	30.5
65+ Households (Income $35,000+)				
Market A	10,362	89.9	1,160	10.1
Market B	6,286	80.4	1,530	19.6
Market C	885	86.5	138	13.5
Market D	9,178	85.3	1,580	14.7

Source: Project Market Decisions, selected Senior Market Reports.

however, Margaret Wylde (the principal investigator of the NIC studies) and her coauthors combine these data with other findings related to net worth and family support to suggest that "income and net worth in a market area should not be used as the sole estimates to project demand for an assisted living community."[8]

The heated debate about the use of income to qualify assisted living residents has contributed to the dilution of the meaning and value of a market penetration rate analysis for assisted living.

Household Type and Tenure for Independent And Assisted Living

Although many studies use only age and income to qualify and size the total pool of households qualified to reside in a project, some have made an effort to further refine that pool based on household type and housing tenure. One difficulty in conducting such an analysis is related to the sources of available data that cross-reference income by age of household and by housing tenure and/or household type.

The Census Bureau typically describes households as *family* households (which implies more than one person lives in the household) or *nonfamily* households (which includes householders who live alone). Although the difference between these two types has not been of particular importance for analyses of independent living, it is important for the analysis of assisted living communities, as 95 percent or more of the residents are single individuals. Reports provided by national vendors such as Claritas provide a breakdown of population age 65 and older by household type that reflects only the base year of the census. Additionally, information from the base census year is provided on poverty status by household type. No information is available from sources such as Claritas that cross tabulates household type by income distribution. Household income distribution is affected by household type (nonfamily households, particularly those living alone, tend to cluster more heavily in the lower-income levels than do family households). The general lack of availability of good data on household income by household type makes it difficult to accurately size the number of age- and income-qualified single-person households, which make up the majority of the market for assisted living.

The publicly available source for this type of data is the Public Use Microdata Sample prepared by the Census Bureau. PUMS consists of computer tapes containing complete census records obtained in the decennial census for a sample of housing units and the people living in them. The standard PUMS products, based on each decennial census, are the 5 percent and 1 percent samples for the United States and Puerto Rico and a special 3 percent sample dealing specifically with the elderly population. The 5 percent and 1 percent samples have been stratified and weighted to accurately reflect the total population. (They are similar in content to the A and B files made available in 1980.) These samples vary with regard to the geographic boundaries used. The Public Use Microdata Area (PUMA) is the lowest level of geography identified on any PUMS file. The 5 percent sample is basically a county-level file, if that area had more than 200,000 persons. The 1 percent sample is basically a metropolitan area file.

PUMS permits the development of special cross tabulations because of the level of detail represented in the data. For example, cross-tabulations by age of householder with information on housing tenure, household type, income, and home value or rents can be created.

Housing tenure—whether one owns or rents a primary residence—is another factor incorporated in some market studies to more accurately size the market for a retirement community. The data, which are made available through most commercial vendors, provide a breakdown of elderly owners and renters in the year of the decennial census on which the data are based (in 2001, for example, household tenure in these reports still reflected 1990 data, because the 2000 Census data on tenure by age had not yet been published). In reports provided by commercial lenders, this information is not cross referenced to household income. Some consulting firms have used the PUMS files or American Housing Survey for the closest geographic approximation of the market area to estimate household income by housing tenure for the elderly.

The American Housing Survey (formerly the Annual Housing Survey) publishes data that cross reference household composition by age of householder with income for owners and renters. The data reflect all householders age 65 and older. The drawback of the survey, published by the U.S. Census Bureau for HUD, is that the survey is now conducted for only 47 MSAs throughout the United States. These 47 are divided into groups of approximately 12 each; the groups are interviewed and their information reported on a rotating basis about every four years. The usefulness of the American Housing Survey is therefore limited to projects located in those MSAs. Moreover, because the data are aggregated on the basis of such large geographical areas, their application to smaller subsets of the MSA can misrepresent the characteristics of those smaller areas.

The separation of owners from renters becomes particularly important for facilities structured on the entrance fee or equity basis (typically only for independent living). Residents of retirement communities that charge substantial upfront fees most often raise the money for that payment through the proceeds from the sale of their residence. Some firms therefore prefer to limit the pool of eligible households to homeowners if the project being analyzed is not a rental facility. Although elderly renters may in fact have a substantial asset base on which to draw, there is no way to ascertain whether it is the case. Therefore, to be more conservative, analysts choose to omit renters. This approach may be overly conservative, however, given that in many areas, households residing in competitive retirement facilities may actually be included in the renter pool.

In the 2000 Census, the characteristics of renter-occupied units paying cash rent broke out a specific category of housing units with meals included in the rent. Although this question was intended to identify congregate facilities offering services, the extent to which the census actually captured existing congregate communities and categorized CCRC units in this group varies; without getting down to the level of census tracts, one cannot be sure that those numbers included in this category correspond to the existing competitive communities.

Housing Values for Independent Living And Assisted Living

The aspect of financial qualification in market analysis that has been far more elusive than income is household assets. It has been documented that the primary asset held by the elderly is their home (for those who own a home). Because of the relative absence of regional, and particularly local, data on ranges of overall asset value for elderly households, to the extent that assets are considered at all, analyses are limited to home values.

While efforts to quantify market potential using housing tenure reflect the increasing sophistication in demographic market segmentation, for the most part, they make a certain leap of faith with regard to housing values. Several studies that separated owners from renters simply assumed that all owners who qualified by virtue of income would also have a home with enough value to cover the cost of the entrance fee or purchase price. Many available data sources include housing value distribution data for elderly homeowners but do not cross-reference them to household income. The associated problem is that, in many areas where housing values have escalated dramatically, individuals have in effect become house-rich, but their annual incomes have not kept pace with the increased values of their homes. Therefore, when one looks at housing value distribution without correlating it to income, one can overstate the number of homeowners who have both income and home value to support a facility's fees.

Project Market Decisions's data system does tie housing values to income. In its SMR, the homeowner data indicate the median and mean home value for households by income range. The data in the SMR are presented in the current year.

Household Type

Independent Living. Seniors' housing appears to be less attractive to couples than to single individuals. Although couples may express interest during the premarketing of a retirement community, the ratio of couples to singles substantially favors singles by the time the facility fills for the first time. The ratio of couples to singles also reflects both the type of facility and the characteristics of the community being designed. Facilities with a substantial number of large units (e.g., two-bedroom apartments or cottages) might expect to attract more couples than a facility dominated by small units. ASHA reports that 22 percent of those moving into CCRCs were couples, compared with 9.6 percent moving to congregate communities and 6.2 percent to assisted living communities.[9]

Knowing this fact makes the equal treatment of all elderly households subject to question. Some studies have attempted to address this issue. One approach has been to break down householders into two categories: single-person households and two-person households (or couples) and to assume that each household segment is drawn to different units based on size and affordability. For example, singles may be assumed to be interested only in studios and one-bedroom apartments, couples to be interested only in one-bedroom and larger units. Separate market penetration calculations may be made based on unit and household type.

One problem encountered in carrying out such an analysis is the appropriateness of the data source used. The American Housing Survey provides data by housing tenure that profiles elderly households (65 and over only) by household size and type. The drawback to this data source, as indicated earlier, is that it reflects larger regional areas than the smaller localized markets typically delineated for retirement communities. Therefore, it is possible to misrepresent the characteristics of specific submarkets in the region covered by the American Housing Survey. National data vendors provide information on household types by age 65 and older and 75 and older but only for the census year, and they do not correlate household type by income.

Project Market Decisions's SMR presents cross tabulations by housing tenure, age of householder, household type, and income in the current year. Studies that have been completed using these data have modified the pool of eligible households by using this specific localized data on household types. The SMR breaks down all data by four household types: one-person male, one-person female, married couples, and others. *Others* represents households made of more than one person other than married-couple households, for example, siblings living together or a couple living with children. Discount rates can be applied to any of the household types to more accurately reflect the pool of households that are likely to make up the target market for the project being analyzed.

Assisted Living. With regard to assisted living, it has become a common practice to exclude all if not most of the married-couple households when sizing the market. Financing sources such as the HUD 232 Mortgage Insurance program and some state housing finance agencies that have established underwriting standards for assisted living require that the analysis focus on single-person households. "HUD's approach to estimating demand for assisted living typically focuses on the number of single-person (one-person) households."[10] As described above, various sources are used to estimate household distribution. Consultants frequently use the

1990 Household Type and Relationship data set reported by Claritas in its "Senior Life Report" (see Figure 3-4). A major drawback associated with using these data is that the data are broken out into only two income categories: above the poverty level and below it.

As shown in this figure, the distribution of households by type is strongly influenced by income. Using such a gross income indicator as poverty level, however, does not offer much refinement. Specialized data products such as Project Market Decisions's SMRs provide much more refined breakdowns on households by age, income, household type, and tenure.

Clearly, if the analysis is based on single householders, the depth of the market is significantly altered based on the income level being applied to the analysis, yet the methodology used in many studies frequently does not recognize this factor.

Frailty

Independent Living. Because most residents who move into the independent living units found in various types of retirement communities are initially expected to function at a fairly high level, studies for this level of care do not apply measures of frailty to screen qualified households.

Assisted Living. Understanding levels of frailty can be key to evaluating the need for assisted living. Respondents to ALFA's "Overview of the Assisted Living Industry, 2000" reported that residents required help with an average of 3.1 ADLs in 1999,[11] a finding consistent with studies conducted by ALFA in previous years. Most feasibility studies attempt to qualify the market not only by age and income but also by those who are frail and need assistance. Many different approaches can be used to determine the number of frailty-qualified households.

The U.S. Census Bureau, for example, reports the population requiring and seeking assistance with ADLs. Of those age 75 to 79 in 1991, 19.5 percent needed assistance, while 31.2 percent of those 80 to 84 and 49.5 percent of those 85 did.[12]

Another source that has been used in market studies comes from the U.S. Department of Health and Human Services National Center for Health Statistics's National Health Interview Survey, which reported that 39.7 percent of persons age 75 and older required assistance.

In addition, the U.S. Census Bureau, in the 1990 and the 2000 Census, asked respondents whether they had a health condition lasting six months or more that resulted in difficulty in going outside the home alone to go shopping or visit a doctor's office or difficulty in taking care of their own personal needs such as bathing, dressing, or getting around inside the home. These questions directly address ADLs. Results of this question for specified geographic areas are included in the Claritas "Senior Life Report" and are sometimes used to approximate the size of the market needing help with ADLs (see Figure 3-5). One benefit of these data is that they are geography specific.

Other measures have been published of the need for assistance with ADLs and IADLs (instru-

Figure 3-4 **Poverty Status by Household Type for Age 75+ Householders**

	Above Poverty Level		Below Poverty Level	
Household Type	**Number**	**Percent**	**Number**	**Percent**
Total	9,337	87.3	1,356	12.7
Married-Couple Family	3,484	32.6	159	1.5
Other Family	911	8.5	47	0.4
Male Householder	206	1.9	11	0.1
Female Householder	705	6.6	36	0.3
Nonfamily	4,942	46.2	1,150	10.8
Householder Living Alone	4,853	45.4	1,143	10.7
Householder Not Living Alone	89	0.8	7	0.1

Sources: U.S. Census Bureau and Claritas, "Senior Life Report," 1990.

Figure 3-5 **Number and Percentage of People Needing Help with ADLs**

	Age 65+		Age 75+	
	Number	Percent	Number	Percent
Persons	11,396	100.0	4,146	100.0
Mobility or Care Limits	2,031	17.8	1,217	29.4
Mobility Limits Only	776	6.8	505	12.2
Self-Care Limits	409	3.6	134	3.2
Both Limits	846	7.4	578	13.9
No Mobility or Care Limits	9,365	82.2	2,929	70.6

Sources: U.S. Census Bureau and Claritas, "Senior Life Report," 1990.

mental activities of daily living) besides those delineated in this chapter. Some would argue that, in fact, the need for assistance with IADLs rather than ADLs is a better measure of those who are likely candidates for assisted living. The variety of measures used and the differences among these measures produce different results, contributing to the difficulty in establishing clear standards for measuring market depth and risk in assisted living (see "Standards and Benchmarks").

In trying to assess the target market for a facility that serves those with Alzheimer's disease (AD) or related disorders, some feasibility studies use prevalence of Alzheimer's by age cohort. While various studies present estimates of prevalence, they can range significantly from an estimated 2 percent to 12 percent of the total population age 65 and older. A 1998 study by the U.S. General Accounting Office presents a meta-analysis developed from 18 studies that estimate prevalence rates. All the studies reviewed in that report estimate prevalence rates for populations that are considered relevant to the United States and that use widely accepted diagnostic criteria for finding cases of Alzheimer's and dementia (see Figure 3-6).[13]

Figure 3-6 **Percentage of Elderly Population with Alzheimer's Disease, by Age**

Age Cohort	All AD (Mild, Moderate, Severe)	Moderate or Severe AD
65–69	1.1%	0.6%
70–74	2.2%	1.3%
75–79	4.6%	2.5%
80–84	9.2%	5.1%
85–89	17.8%	10.0%
90–94	31.5%	18.7%
95+	52.5%	34.9%

Source: U.S. General Accounting Office, *Alzheimer's Disease: Estimates of Prevalence Rates in the United States,* Report to the Secretary of Health and Human Services, January 1998.

Quantifying the Competition

Independent and Assisted Living

The second major component of the formulas that assess demand or risk based on quantitative measures addresses the competitive environment or the *supply* side of the equation. Once again, various approaches are used to quantify supply. These variations occur in determining which facilities should be accounted for, what geographic area should be encompassed, and what proportion of competitive units should be considered.

In many markets, communities offering independent living may include continuing care or life care, congregate, entrance fee, rental, and equity-based projects. A market may have some facilities in operation, others under construction, and more in the planning stages. For a market analyst, the question becomes which communities should be considered in conducting a quantitative demand analysis. Some take into consideration all existing market-rate facilities, regardless of whether they are for profit or nonprofit, full service or limited service, or for rent or purchase requiring an upfront fee or equity. This approach reflects a primarily quantitative, analytical process. It assumes that those households making up the pool of eligible prospects may choose to consider a variety of alternatives offered in the market. Given that it is difficult if not impossible demographically to forecast which households will consistently be drawn to a certain type of product, the assumption that all competitive projects may draw from the same qualified pool is the most conservative approach.

Another method is to consider only those facilities with a service program directly comparable with that planned for the project being analyzed. In particular, this approach has been used for full-service continuing care communities offering assisted living and nursing care. What to include as competition varies greatly among firms that specialize in market studies in the seniors' housing industry. Some analysts attempt to recognize the differences among types of programs by applying discounts to communities that offer a different level of care (for example, discounting rental units in a standalone congregate community with no assisted living or nursing care available when conducting a study for a CCRC). In some cases, the amount of competition is taken into consideration when making a decision to determine what competitive units are counted in the analysis. In markets that are heavily developed, noncomparable communities may not be included or may be discounted, whereas in markets where there are few competitors, all forms of seniors' housing may be included.

Even more complex is the issue of what to count as competition, taking into account the level of care being evaluated (independent versus assisted living). At one time, it may have been appropriate to create firm lines between these two levels of care, but doing so would be inadvisable in the current market, where the lines between levels of care have blurred. For example, numerous retirement communities that focus primarily or exclusively on independent living allow residents to receive chronic assistance with personal care needs in their units through outside home health care agencies or through their own home care agency. The total number of independent living units in such a community should arguably be categorized into two groups, independent living and assisted living (albeit unlicensed). On the other hand, some assisted living providers, intentionally or not, serve residents who are relatively independent and require no assistance with ADLs. This practice is supported by tiered pricing levels that offer lower rates for those who do not need such help. The proportion of units occupied by residents who do not require assistance with ADLs might then be excluded in an assisted living demand analysis (and included in an independent living analysis), as the residents of such units would not meet the ADL screening criteria, if applied, when sizing the market.

Finally, a decision must be made regarding how to treat future competition. This decision is based mainly on what status facilities have achieved at the time of the analysis. At any given time in nearly every market, planned facilities range from those under construction to those existing merely as rumors. Depending on the use of the study, determining which to include can be handled in several ways. For those studies being completed for planning, a sensitivity analysis might be conducted that considers several what-if scenarios from the best case—only those planned communities actually financed and/or under construction—to the worst case—all planned facilities, even those still in the early planning stages.

Other relevant methodological questions involve whether to include only those facilities located in the defined geographic market area or to also consider those that border it, and how much of the competitive supply to include. To the extent that facilities immediately outside the defined market area are considered, some level of discounting frequently is applied to total units considered to be a drain on the market. In some cases, anecdotal information regarding the origin of residents may be used to determine the percentage of units drawing residents from the market area (also known as *market area overlap).* Some analysts attribute market area overlap to individual facilities or to the total number of competitive units in a market, while others assume that all units are filled from residents in the market area. Only in a few instances is a gravity model employed that relates distance of competitors from the project being analyzed to quantify the competitive drain from the market.

In another variation, some analyses remove all existing competitive units from the pool of qualified households, while others remove only units considered unoccupied or vacant. Most factor in the turnover of existing units (that is, the number of units expected to be refilled annually), assuming an annual turnover rate of approximately 20 percent.

Assisted Living

Because most studies estimate market size and demand based on households, some analysts distinguish between *group quarters* and *households,* as the population living in each is mutually exclusive. The rationale is that those individuals living in nursing care beds and boarding homes are no longer counted in the pool of households that had been quantified earlier. According to the Census Bureau, individuals living in facilities such as nursing homes are counted among those in group quarters rather than among general households. The census of 1990 and years prior also included assisted living beds or room and boarding care homes in the group quarters category. The 2000 Census, however, recognized the distinction of assisted living, and residents are counted as renter households rather than group quarters residents. Room and boarding care homes are no longer counted as group quarters and were counted as renter households in the 2000 Census.

Quantitative Market Depth Analysis

Once the estimates have been prepared of the qualified pool of households and the competition, a market penetration analysis is undertaken. The market penetration analysis has become a way of assessing risk that most lenders have come to rely on. The market penetration percentage is not actually an indicator of market demand. Taken in the context of other factors, it helps to evaluate the level of risk associated with the project.

> The penetration rate calculates the relationship between the number of independent living units (ILUs) at the CCRC (i.e., the subject property) and the number of households with age and income qualified individuals within the CCRC's primary target region who are eligible for residency at the community. The calculation also reduces the number of eligible households for competitive ILUs available at other communities within the primary target region.[14]

This definition clearly indicates that the penetration rate is for the subject property only, once competitive units have been subtracted from the pool of age- and income-qualified households (see Scenario A below). The public finance group of Fitch, Duff & Phelps, the major bond-rating agency, presented its own example of a penetration rate calculation in a Health Care Special Report that calculates penetration rates based on an age- and income-qualified pool of households that is net of occupied existing competition.[15] Fitch's recommendation for penetration rates presents two different calculations. The first is for units that are expected to turn over per year, adjusted for the proportion expected to be filled from the market area. The second is for filling of new units, after a 95 percent occupancy and market area draw percentage are applied.

An alternative approach (see Scenario B below) uses penetration calculations based on all competitive units. A comparison of the specific approaches to market penetration analyses reflecting the specific techniques used by several major feasibility firms is presented later in this chapter.

Scenario A	
Qualified Households	10,000
Competitive Units	500
Net Qualified Households	9,500
Project Units	200
Market Penetration	2.1%

Scenario B	
Qualified Households	10,000
Competitive and Project Units	700
Market Penetration	7%

Scenario A presents market penetration for the subject project only. For this approach, the pool of eligible households is reduced by the number of units in competitive facilities. Market penetration using Scenario A is the percentage that the project must capture of the remaining (net pool of) households once the competitive units have been subtracted from this pool. Scenario B calculates penetration for all facilities determined to be competitive and includes the units in the project that is the subject of the study. This approach results in a market penetration that reflects how much of the total eligible market must be captured to fill all the competitive communities in the market area. Some, including Fitch, refer to this rate as the *saturation rate,* a term that by its nature has an inherently negative bias.

When both approaches are used together, the analysis enables the user to place the penetration rate required to fill the project's units in the context of the overall competitive market environment. This result is particularly useful and instructive in comparatively deep markets where the market penetration for the project alone may be low (say below 2 to 3 percent). Although a low market penetration rate calculated for the subject property can be interpreted as a positive indicator of market potential, it can take on a different meaning once the calculation is done, including the subject and existing and planned competitors. The same market that yielded a low penetration rate for an individual project may reflect a high saturation rate if numerous projects are in operation (particularly with unfilled units) and/or are planned. The market share or saturation analysis provides an additional measure of the percentage of households that will be required to meet stabilized occupancy. "A penetration rate calculation is only useful in conjunction with a saturation rate calculation. Alone, each calculation has little meaning."[16] Another way of evaluating the additional absorption burden that will be placed on a market is to compare market penetration rates using existing competitive facilities only with rates that result from adding planned completions. Doing so allows the analyst to evaluate how much more absorption during a short period of time will be required for new facilities to fill.

Other terminology deriving from market penetration, which in some cases also demonstrates variances in the approach described above, shows up in studies conducted by major national firms. The following definitions further demonstrate the lack of standardization in terminology in the seniors' housing industry.

- *Net estimated market penetration*—For some firms, a calculation of market penetration rate that does not subtract all existing and planned competitive units from the pool of age- and income-qualified households. Instead, it estimates the number of planned units (including the subject and competition), the number of unoccupied units (subject and competition), and annual turnover in competitive properties to reach a subtotal of units to be occupied by market area households who are 75 and older and income qualified. That unit count is adjusted downward by the percentage of units expected to be filled from the market area and the percentage expected to be occupied by those age 75 and older. The resulting number of units is divided by the number of age- and income-qualified households. In studies conducted by other firms, it refers to the percentage of age- and income-qualified households that the subject's units will require to be full, once existing and planned competition has been subtracted from the pool of qualified households.
- *Current supply penetration*—A calculation that divides the estimated number of existing competitive units operating at their occupancy rates in the current year and existing and planned competitive units in the year in which the subject property is to open by the estimated age- and income-qualified households in each year.
- *Project penetration*—The methodology described above under *market penetration,* coupled with a market penetration calculation that includes all competitive units plus the subject.
- *Required market penetration*—A methodology in which the total unoccupied competitive units in the market area plus an assumed 20 percent average annual turnover of existing occupied units plus the total number of planned units (including the subject) are divided by the total age- and income-qualified households.
- *Market share*—In some cases, used in calculating the percentage of age- and income-qualified households that must be captured to fill all competitive (existing and planned) units. In others, used to measure the percentage of total units filled from the market area that the subject must have to fill its units.
- *Capture rate*—Used by some analysts to reflect the same calculation defined as the *penetration rate.*

There are several alternatives to conducting a market penetration/share analysis that include all independent living units in all competitive retirement communities. Although this approach is the most conservative, in some ways it may be the least realistic. The alternatives attempt to reach a better approximation of the true conditions in the market. For instance, calculating market penetration based on 95 percent occupancy rather than 100 percent is a small step toward reflecting the actual conditions under which most facilities operate. Interestingly, if one looks at the financial feasibility components that some of these studies incorporate, full occupancy is frequently depicted as 95 percent rather than 100 percent, whereas penetration is calculated at 100 percent.

Another, more realistic approach to market penetration calculates the ratio in a way that reflects the number of units that are actually expected to fill from within the geographic market area depicted by the demographic statistics. As noted, the market area is typically defined as that geographic area from which most (frequently assumed to be anywhere from 70 to 80 percent) residents will be drawn. Once again, analytical consistency rather than overly conservative assumptions would be more realistic. If a study contends, for instance, that 80 percent of the project's units will be filled from within the market area, then why not calculate market penetration based on 80 percent of the project's units rather than 95 or 100 percent? In fact, the Fitch publication suggests that in calculating penetration rates, a factor of 80 percent should be applied to competitive units in most cases.[17] Alternatively, some analysts come up with a market area draw factor per property. Approximating the number of actual competitive units is complex and rather subjective.

Another approach to market penetration analyses is the application of a range of penetration rates to the qualified pool of households to determine how many units a market can support. This approach has been used primarily in planning studies. The ranges that are applied vary from lows of 3 to 4 percent to highs in the low 20s. This method can be seen as a demonstration of the difference in approaches to calculating penetration in which the lower percentages are typical of those associated with a single facility in contrast to the higher percentage, which might be more typical when all competitors are being included. The low end of this range is thought to reflect the conservative standards that have been established and used by the major accounting firms and underwriters, whereas the high end has been used as an example of what has been achieved in mature markets such as Philadelphia. The latter tends to overlook the fact that Philadelphia's high market penetration has been achieved gradually during a period of nearly 25 years (discussed in detail in the case study of the Philadelphia market in Chapter 8).

Many analysts believe that the most conservative approach is the best approach, which is certainly understandable in an industry that has experienced so many failures. In some ways, however, being overly conservative is the safest way to protect the analyst but not necessarily the best for the client.

Examples of Market Penetration Analyses

To demonstrate the wide variation in determining market penetration rates, the independent living and assisted living demand methodologies of some of the nation's most respected feasibility firms as well as the approach used by Fitch are presented for comparison in Figures 3-7 and 3-8 (only Fitch's methodology is specifically identified). Numerous differences exist in how these firms calculate market depth for both independent living and assisted living. There are many variations in the calculation of qualified households deemed appropriate for assisted living in terms of age and income, and particularly in frailty. Significant differences are also evident in the treatment of existing and planned competitive units. The demand methodologies presented in this section, however, use the same demographic and competitive data in the same market to compare market penetration rates.

The examples in Figures 3-7 and 3-8 clearly demonstrate how market penetration rates can vary significantly despite a constant assumption for the number of age- and income-qualified households. The variation would be even more significant if the analyses were presented using the firm's actual methods for calculating age- and income-qualified households.

Independent Living

The analyses for independent living are presented for the same market using the assumptions shown in Figure 3-7.

Assisted Living

The analyses for assisted living are presented using the assumptions shown in Figure 3-8.

Summary of Market Penetration Rates

Figure 3-9 presents a comparison of market penetration rates as illustrated in Figures 3-7 and 3-8.

A comparison of the results of the various analyses illustrates the dissonance relating to the use and meaning of such terms as *market penetration.* In Analysis B, the term *market penetration* is used to mean the percentage of qualified households

Figure 3-7 **Market Penetration Analyses for Independent Living**

Assumptions Used in Comparative Analysis

Age	75+
Income	$25,000+
Competitive Units	
Total Competitive Units in Market Area	275
Unoccupied Units in Market Area	126
Occupied Units in Market Area	149
Units Planned in Market Area	60
Project Units	100
Total Qualified Households	5,710

Fitch Analysis

		Calculation Guide
Total Age- and Income-Qualified Households	5,710	A
Turnover of Existing Units		
Units Turned Over per Year	28	B = 149 × 20% × 95%
From Market Area	22	C = B × 80%
Turnover Penetration Rate	0.4%	D = C/A
Fill-Up of New Units (Includes Vacant Existing Units)		
Available New Units	160	E
Available (Vacant) Existing Units	126	F
Stabilized Occupancy of 95%	272	G = (E + F) × 95%
Net Residents to Be Captured from Market Area	218	H = G × 80%
New Unit Penetration Rate	3.8%	I = H/A
Saturation Rate		
Total Units in Market Area	435	J = 275 + 100 + 60
Stabilized Occupancy of 95%	413	K = J × 95%
From Market Area	330	L = K × 80%
Saturation Rate	5.8%	M = L/A

Figure 3-7 (continued)

Analysis A

		Calculation Guide
Total Age- and Income-Qualified Households	5,710	A
Less Competition (with Market Area Overlap)		
Existing	122	B
Turnover	21	C = B × 17%
Planned	34	D
Net Qualified Households	5,533	E = A – B – C – D
Adjusted Project Units: 100 Units × 95% Occupancy × 80% Market Area Draw	76	F
Market Penetration Rate	1.4%	G = F/E
Current Market Share	2.1%	H = B/A
Future Market Share	4.1%	I = (B + D + F)/A

Note: The number of existing competitive units includes those located in the market area. It also reflects a market area overlap assumption applied to each individual facility based on information provided by the facility regarding its market area draw. Turnover is assumed to be 17 percent annually.

Analysis B

		Calculation Guide
Total Age- and Income-Qualified Households	5,710	A
Project Units (80% from Market Area)	80	B = 100 × 80%
Competitive Units (100% from Market Area)		
Existing	275	C
Planned	60	D
Number of Units to Be Filled in Market Area	415	E = B + C + D
Market Penetration Rate	7.3%	F = E/A
Project Penetration Rate	1.5%	G = B/(A – C – D)

Analysis C

		Calculation Guide
Total Age- and Income-Qualified Households	5,710	A
Project Units from Market Area (80%)	80	B = 100 × 80%
Occupied Units at Competitive Facilities Resulting from Turnover (20% annually)	30	C = 149 × 20%
Existing Unoccupied Units	126	D
Planned Units	60	E
Total Available Competitive Units	296	F = B + C + D + E
Market Penetration Rate	5.2%	G = F/A

Note: Twenty percent annual turnover is applied to existing occupied competitive units in the market area only.

Figure 3-7 (continued)

Analysis D

		Calculation Guide
Total Planned Independent Living Units in Market Area	60	A
Total Project Units	100	B
Number of Unoccupied Independent Living Units in Market Area	126	C
Annual Turnover of Occupied Independent Living Units in Market Area (20%)	30	D = 149 × 20%
Subtotal of Units to Be Occupied by Market Area Households Age 75+	316	E = A + B + C + D
Subtotal of Units to Be Occupied by Households Originating from Market Area (80%)	253	F = E × 80%
Estimated Units to Be Occupied by Households Age 75+ from Market Area (96.5%)	244	G = F × 96.5%
Estimated Number of Age- and Income-Qualified Households in Market Area	5,710	H
Market Penetration Rate	4.3%	I = G/H

Analysis E

		Calculation Guide
Total Noninstitutionalized Households Age 75+	12,253	A
Existing Occupied Independent Living Units with Estimated Household Income below $25,000	102	B
Vacant/Planned Independent Living Units with Estimated Household Income below $25,000	24	C
Existing Assisted Living Residents (Total Occupied Assisted Living Units)	446	D
Annual Independent Living Turnover of Occupied Units (20%)	20	E = B × 20%
Subtotal: Available Households Age 75+	11,661	F = A – B – C – D – E
Percentage of Age 75+ Households with Incomes of $25,000+	41.8%	G
Total Age- and Income-Qualified Households	4,874	H = F × G
Existing Occupied Independent Living Units with Estimated Household Income of $25,000+	149	I
Vacant/Planned Independent Living Units with Estimated Household Income of $25,000+	186	J
Impact of Annual Independent Living Turnover (20%)	30	K = I × 20%
Subtotal: Available Age- and Income-Qualified Households	4,509	L = H – I – J – K
Project Units to Be Absorbed Assuming 80% Market Area Draw and 95% Occupancy	76	M
Market Penetration Rate	1.7%	N = M/L

Note: The number of units estimated with household income above and below $25,000 would be based on actual data from competitive facilities. For purposes of this analysis, the number of competitive units presented with household incomes below $25,000 does not represent an actual situation. Competitive units presented in the assumptions table are assumed to be filled from those with incomes greater than $25,000 for this analysis.

required to fill all existing and planned units, and the only adjustment made reflecting market area draw is for the property being analyzed. In Analyses C and D, *penetration* refers to the turnover of existing unoccupied and planned units. In Analyses A and E, only the subject property's units are used to calculate market penetration, a calculation that in Analysis B actually is referred to as *project penetration.* Fitch, the bond-rating agency, calculates separate market penetration rates for existing occupied and new (including existing vacant) units and uses the term *saturation rate* to refer to calculations that incorporate all existing and planned (including the subject) units. Only Analyses A and E remove existing units from the pool of qualified households, whereas Analyses C and D do not factor in anything other than turnover for existing occupied units, despite the fact that residents of these communities are very unlikely to move and therefore are not really part of the pool of qualified households.

With the degree of differences in the approaches presented (which represent selected national firms, but not the total universe of major consultants conducting market feasibility studies), it is easy to understand why so many lenders, while anxious to rely on standards such as market penetration rates, have difficulty understanding their true meaning. Clearly, both the terminology and the methodologies vary

Figure 3-8 **Market Penetration Analyses for Assisted Living**

Assumptions Used in Comparative Analysis

Age	75+
Income	$35,000+
Competitive Units	
Existing Units in Market Area	452
Unoccupied Existing Units	6
Units Planned in Market Area	0
Project Units	60

Fitch Analysis

		Calculation Guide
Total Population Age 75+	20,343	A
Income Greater than $35,000	36.8%	B
Total Age- and Income-Qualified Population	7,486	C = A x B
Living Alone	50%	D
Qualified Population	3,743	E = C x D
Requiring Assistance with ADLs	30%	F
Total Qualified Assisted Living Population	1,123	G = E x F
Project Units	60	
Adjustments		
95% Occupancy	57	
40% Annual Turnover	23	
80% Market Area Draw	18	H
Market Penetration Rate	1.6%	I = H/G

Figure 3-8 (continued)

Analysis F

		Calculation Guide
Total Households Needing Assistance with ADLs	892	A
Total Qualified Households		
Baseline Households	459	B
Spenddown Households	107	C
Total Qualified Households	566	D = B + C
Less Competitive Units	250	E
Net Qualified Households	316	F = D – E
Percentage Likely to Move to Assisted Living (30%)	95	G = F x 30%
Project's Unit Potential Assuming 80% Market Area Draw and 95% Occupancy	125	H = G/80%/95%
Project Units	60	I
Adjustment Calculations		
80% Market Area Draw	48	J = I x 80%
95% Occupancy	46	K = J x 95%
Market Penetration Rate	14.6%	L = K/F

Note: Baseline households includes all single-person households and excludes approximately one-half of married-couple households requiring assistance with three or more ADLs. The number of competitive units reflects a market area overlap assumption applied to each individual facility based on information provided by the facility regarding its market area draw.

Analysis G

		Calculation Guide
Age- and Income-Qualified Households	3,445	A
Householders Living Alone	60.7%	B
Total Qualified Households	2,091	C = A x B
Weighted Average Requiring Assistance with ADLs	30.4%	D
Number of Medically Appropriate, Age- and Income-Eligible Individuals Living Alone	636	E = C x D
Unoccupied Competitive Units in Market Area	6	F
Projected and Planned Units	60	G
Total Available Assisted Living Units to Fill in Market Area	66	H = F + G
Estimated Percentage of Units to Fill from Market Area (80%)	53	I = H x 80%
Estimated Net Market Penetration Rate	8.3%	J = I/E
Total Project Units (80% Market Area Draw)	48	K
Project Penetration Rate	7.5%	L = K/E

Note: The percentage requiring assistance with ADLs (30.4%) is based on the weighted average of percentages in U.S. Census Bureau, *The Need for Personal Assistance with Everyday Activities: Recipients and Caregivers,* Current Population Reports, Series P-70, No. 19 (Washington, D.C.: U.S. Government Printing Office, 1990). This firm assumes a turnover rate of 50 percent based on its industry experience.

Figure 3-8 (continued)

Analysis H

Age	Population	Percentage with Four or More Personal Care Activities	Estimated Number	Estimated Demand	Estimated Bed Need	Calculation Guide
65–74	22,464	3.7%	831	20%	166	
75–79	8,859	5.7%	505	30%	152	
80–84	5,934	10.4%	617	45%	278	
85+	5,550	19.2%	1,066	60%	640	
Total	42,807		3,019		1,236	A
Percentage of Households with Incomes of $35,000+					36.8%	B
Estimated Bed Need, All Incomes of $35,000+					455	C = A x B
Number of Beds in Study Area					452	D
Estimated Number Filled by Persons from Market Area (80%)					362	E = D x 80%
Estimated Number Filled by Persons from Study Area with Incomes of $35,000+ (80%)					290	F = E x 80%
Unmet Bed Need in Study Area for Facility with Eligibility Requirement of $35,000+					165	G = C – F

Note: Analysis includes population age 65 to 74.

Analysis I

		Calculation Guide
Project Penetration Rates		
Total Age-Qualified Households	12,253	A
Age- and Income-Qualified Households		
All Households with Incomes of $35,000+	3,445	B
Homeowners with Incomes of $20,000 to $35,000	2,424	C
Total Qualified Households	5,869	D = B + C
Percentage of Households Requiring Assistance with ADLs	27.6%	E
Total Qualified Households	1,620	F = D x E
Percentage Living Alone	60.7%	G
Total Qualified Households	983	H = F x G
Number of Planned Assisted Living Units in Project	60	I
Project Penetration Rate	6.1%	J = I/H
Market Penetration Rates		
Total Qualified Households	983	A
Number of Existing Competitive Beds 100% from Market Area	452	B
Total Qualified Households	1,435	C = A + B
Number of Project Beds	60	D
Total Beds, Including Project	512	E = B + D
Market Penetration Rates		
Preopening	31.5%	F = B/C
Postopening	35.7%	H = E/C

Note: The percentage requiring assistance with ADLs (27.6 percent) is from U.S. Census Bureau, *The Need for Personal Assistance with Everyday Activities: Recipients and Caregivers,* Current Population Reports, Series P-70, No. 19 (Washington, D.C.: U.S. Government Printing Office, 1990). The percentage living alone is estimated by Claritas.

Figure 3-8 (continued)

Analysis J

		Calculation Guide
Total Households Age 75+	12,253	A
Existing Occupied Assisted Living Units with Estimated Household Income below $35,000	51	B
Vacant/Planned Assisted Living Units with Estimated Household Income below $35,000	36	C
Annual Assisted Living Turnover (35%)	18	D = B x 35%
Existing Occupied Independent Living Units	149	E
Subtotal: Available Households Age 75+	11,999	F = A – B – C – D – E
Percentage of Households Age 75+ with Incomes of $35,000+	36.8%	G
Total Age- and Income-Qualified Households	4,416	H = F x G
Existing Occupied Assisted Living Units with Estimated Household Income of $35,000+	446	I
Vacant/Planned Assisted Living Units with Estimated Household Income of $35,000+	6	J
Impact of Annual Assisted Living Turnover (35%)	156	K = I x 35%
Subtotal: Available Age- and Income-Qualified Households	3,808	L = H – I – J – K
Project Units to Be Absorbed Assuming 80% Market Area Draw and 95% Occupancy	46	M = 60 x 80% x 95%
Market Penetration Rate	1.2%	N = M/L

Note: The number of units estimated with household incomes above and below $35,000 would be based on actual data from competitive facilities. The number of competitive units shown with household incomes below $35,000 does not represent an actual situation; it has been created for this analysis. Competitive units shown in the assumptions table are assumed to be filled from those with incomes higher than $35,000 for this analysis.

Figure 3-9 **Summary of Market Penetration Rates in Sample Studies**

Analysis	Independent Living	Analysis	Assisted Living
Fitch	0.4%, 3.8%	Fitch	1.6%
A	1.4%	F	14.6%
B	7.3%	G	8.3%
C	5.2%	H	N/A
D	4.3%	I	31.5–35.7%
E	1.7%	J	1.2%

substantially, in effect rendering it difficult to take penetration standards such as 5 percent (as indicated in the Fitch report) as having a substantiated meaning and value. Discussions with various consultants active in the industry underscore the level of discomfort with benchmarks such as market penetration rates as well as the different approaches in reaching a quantitative basis for conclusions about feasibility. As demonstrated in the examples presented, only some firms calculate what proportion of the qualified market all competitive communities must capture on the aggregate (Fitch's saturation level) to be full. Another variance not reflected in the examples is whether or not competitive communities that are adjacent to the defined market area should be considered quantitatively. Although it is likely that such communities draw some of the residents from the market area, very few firms include them in demand calculations. Of the firms whose studies were used in the comparative analysis, only one includes competitive communities located proximate to the market area, and to simplify the comparison of approaches, it was excluded from the example presented.

Despite reasonable efforts to agree on benchmarks such as 5 percent penetration rates and 15 percent saturation rates for independent living, it is even more complex when assisted living is analyzed. Most agree that various additional screens (household size, requirement for assistance with ADLs) should be applied to the age- and income-qualified households, yet the approach to applying these screens differs from firm to firm. While Fitch suggests that the same standard of a 5 percent penetration rate should be applied for both independent and assisted living, which on the face of it may be reasonable given its methodology, the firm also suggests that 30 percent is a more appropriate saturation level for assisted living, taking into consideration the decrease in the number of qualified households produced by applying household size and ADL screens.

Alternative Approaches to Assessing Risk And Demand for Assisted Living

In response to the growing concern about the lack of standards for evaluating demand and assessing risk for assisted living, several alternative approaches were presented over a period of years during the late 1990s at an annual conference held in Philadelphia (Assisted Living Market Research and Marketing Summit). The conference convener, Anthony J. Mullen, has been honing a methodology for assessing or defining temporary saturation, publishing it and presenting it each year at the conference. The proposed Mullen/CWI Feasibility Guidelines set forth four elements that should be assessed in evaluating whether or not a market is saturated (see Figure 3-10).

Mullen urges that these guidelines be used to complement rather than replace other methodologies for evaluating demand, indicating that methodological sophistication is mandatory in today's market environment, where temporary saturation has been achieved in so many markets. The guidelines are in a state of evolution as the assisted living industry matures, and the third guideline is moving toward being replaced by the establishment of yearly move rates by age cohort.

Figure 3-10 **Feasibility Guidelines**

Mullen/CWI Feasibility Guidelines	**Caution Flags If:**
Comparison of the percentage of the population 65+ and 85+ by the number of nursing and assisted living beds in the primary market area (PMA) and the relationship between these two segments of long-term care	Nursing beds/65+ population > 5.1% Assisted/board and care beds/65+ population > 2.3% Total of both > 7.2% *and/or* Nursing beds/85+ population > 42.0% Assisted/board and care beds/85+ population > 19.0% Total of both > 60.0%
A count of the number of the 85+ population living in group quarters in the PMA. Virtually all of group quarters comprises nursing, assisted living, and board and care beds	Percentage of 85+ population living in nursing and assisted living/board and care exceeds 23% of the 85+ population
A count of the number of new beds coming on line each year in a PMA as a percentage of the number of occupied assisted living beds in the PMA in the previous year	*New* assisted living/board and care beds in the PMA to be absorbed during the current year are 20% or more than the existing and occupied assisted living/board and care beds in the prior year
The average occupancy rate in the PMA for the year in question for those properties open two or more years and an analysis of the move-in rate of new properties	Average occupancy rate in the PMA is 86% or below (non-weighted) for facilities open two years or longer *and* overall absorption is less than previous year *and* if at least one new project of 30 or more beds has move-in rate of two units or fewer after being open at least six months.

Source: Anthony J. Mullen, "An Objective Analysis of the Seniors' Housing and Care Industry from 2001–2005, with a Special Focus on Assisted Living," *An Updated White Paper for a Proposed Definition of Temporary Saturation on a National Basis within the Assisted Living Industry,* 2000.

Evaluation of the Need for Nursing Home Beds

Studies conducted for retirement communities that incorporate nursing home components may include a section on the need for this level of care. For those studies that are prepared for financing, such an analysis is always included in the document. Planning studies sometimes overlook this element of the analysis. Because the number of nursing home beds is controlled in many states by the Certificate of Need (CN) process, the need for beds must be demonstrated and approved during the state's review and approval process. In states where this system is still in place (and the number is declining), the number of nursing home beds needed in each defined region of the state is delineated by the state, so the analysis of need for nursing home beds contained in market studies is typically placed in the context of need that has been established by the state for the area where the project is to be located. At this writing, 14 states have established specific or unique requirements for the development of nursing beds that are to be a part of a CCRC (see Figures 3-11 and 3-12).

Two basic approaches have been taken in studies that include an analysis of bed need for nursing home beds. The first compares bed need projections with the number of beds being proposed for the project. This comparison considers the number of existing licensed beds in the region, the number that have been approved but not yet licensed, and the number that are in the approval process (i.e., have submitted letters of intent or certificate/determination of need application).

The net bed need is compared with the number of beds being proposed by the project to determine whether the state regulating agency will consider there to be sufficient need to warrant approval. In addition, this analysis usually presents the results of a survey of the existing nursing beds in the full market area or a smaller subset. The survey data indicate the number of beds in each facility, the occupancy rate, payer mix, and per diem rates for each. When the data reflect high occupancy rates, they further support the need for the beds to be encompassed by the proposed project.

An alternative approach considers historical use of nursing home beds in the project's service area. Based on information available through the state regulating agency, the number of patient days per year for patients age 65 or older per thousand is divided by the number of licensed beds, yielding an annual historical occupancy rate for the market area. The average annual occupancy rate is applied to the forecast number of elderly (65 or older) in the area for the year during which the project will open to determine the number of beds that will be needed.

Figure 3-11 **States with CN Requirements for Additional Nursing Beds in CCRCs, Including States with CCRC Regulations Only**

States with No CN Requirements for Nursing Beds	Arizona, California, Colorado, Idaho, Kansas, Louisiana,* Minnesota, Nebraska, New Jersey, New Mexico, Pennsylvania, Texas*
States with Standard CN Requirements for Nursing Beds within and outside CCRCs	Arkansas, Iowa, Massachusetts, Michigan, Missouri, Ohio, Rhode Island, Tennessee, Virginia
States with Unique CN Requirements for Nursing Beds within CCRCs (see Figure 3-12)	Connecticut, Delaware, Florida, Georgia, Illinois, Indiana, Maine, Maryland, New Hampshire, New York, North Carolina, Oregon, South Carolina, Vermont
States with Current Moratorium on New Nursing Home Beds**	Colorado, Connecticut, Massachusetts, Minnesota, Missouri, Nebraska, Ohio, Rhode Island, Tennessee, Virginia

*Only Medicaid-certified beds are subject to CN review.

**Moratoriums may be for Medicaid-only beds or under certain conditions may allow CCRCs to add nursing home beds. Oklahoma and South Dakota do not address this issue.

Source: American Association of Homes and Services for the Aging, "Summary of State Continuing Care Retirement Regulations as of 2/12/99."

Figure 3-12 **Unique CN Requirements for Additional Nursing Beds within CCRCs**

Maine, New Hampshire, Vermont	CCRCs are subject to a CN review but traditionally are held to a lesser standard of need. Non-Medicaid nursing beds in CCRCs are not included in need formulas.
Connecticut	A moratorium currently exists, but under certain conditions additional beds may be added to CCRCs to meet demand for independent living life care contract holders.
Delaware	All nursing beds must undergo a CN review; however, nursing beds serving only life care residents are not counted in the general inventory.
Florida	A noncompetitive CN review is held.
Georgia	A special sheltered-bed CN review process for nursing home beds in CCRCs requires that beds can serve only residents of the CCRC.
Illinois	A CCRC variance allows for the construction of one nursing home bed for every five independent living units without a CN review.
Indiana	A CN review exists for all nursing beds, but there are limited exceptions for religious and fraternal organizations.
Maryland	CCRCs are exempt from CN review but are limited to one bed for every five independent living units.
New York	Under Title 46 of the public health code, CCRCs may open up to 1,000 nursing home beds without going through the CN process, but additional beds are subject to CN review. For facilities with more than 90 nursing beds, a geographic CN process exists.
North Carolina	Fifty percent of all nursing home beds in CCRCs are subject to CN review.
Oregon	If the CCRC serves only its own residents, it is exempt from the CN process. Otherwise, it is subject to CN review.
South Carolina	CCRC nursing beds are subject to CN review. The review process differs depending on whether beds will serve CCRC residents or the public at large.

Fill Rate and Absorption

The speed at which a seniors' housing community fills its units is difficult to predict accurately. Like many aspects of this industry, even the definition of the terminology is subject to variation. For some, absorption is defined as the period of time from the beginning of actual project marketing to the point when the facility is open and at full occupancy (typically defined as 93 to 95 percent). Absorption can reflect the number of sales per month during an extended period of time, or it can imply both sales and units filled. The fill period most often reflects the time it takes to reach full occupancy from the point at which the facility opens. Both the rate of sales per month and the rate of fill-up once the facility opens have obvious and significant cost implications for a seniors' housing community.

The market study (or demographic component of the full financial feasibility study) usually addresses the rate at which a facility might be expected to fill once open. This calculation may be based on and affected by several factors, including those that can be somewhat controlled by the team responsible for the community and others that are outside their control. A market study, to the extent that it addresses fill rate, should consider the following factors.

External Environmental Factors

Three major factors that can affect the fill period for a seniors' housing community might be described as external environmental factors, those that are not within the project team's control: 1) the level of education and familiarity of the market's elderly with various seniors' housing options, 2) the extent and nature of the competition, and 3) the condition of the residential real estate market.

On the most basic level, the extent to which a market is educated about and familiar with seniors' housing may affect the rate at which the facility fills. Marketing periods may be lengthier in communities that are unfamiliar with these types of living arrangements and may result in lengthier fill periods.

The competitive environment can have a significant impact on fill rates. More specifically, the fill period may be adversely affected in markets where many new facilities may be trying to market and fill their units at the same time. Slower fill periods can result for any or all of these facilities for several reasons. Elderly consumers and their family members, presented with many choices, may shop around, taking their time to compare facilities. Some who are considering independent living may in fact delay their decisions, believing there is less urgency to make a quick decision because choices are plentiful. On a more fundamental level, some markets are simply trying to absorb more product at a given time than the depth of the market may warrant. Too many competitors opening during a relatively short period of time in a relatively thin market can affect every facility's fill rate. In addition, the comparative quality, both real and perceived, of a seniors' housing community takes on even greater importance in a market environment where numerous facilities are attempting to fill. Quality may be reflected in the program offered by a community, its pricing structure, its location and design, and the facility's sponsorship/ownership and management.

Finally, the condition of the residential real estate market directly affects the rate at which a facility fills. Most people moving to seniors' housing communities move from a home they own and prefer to sell it before moving to a seniors' housing community. Growth in assets that resulted from the activity in the stock market in the 1990s helped many seniors to pay fees without being as dependent on home equity and the sale. This situation differs substantially based on the type of seniors' housing community under consideration. According to ALFA's 2000 annual study, approximately 50 percent of assisted living residents living in the participating facilities in 1999 moved from a private residence, while the ALFA/NIC study reported that 69 percent moved to assisted living directly from home.[18]

The ALFA 2000 study indicates that 79 percent of those in independent living moved from a private residence, while AAHSA reports that 99 percent were estimated to have moved from private residences to the independent living component of a CCRC.[19] The move typically is predicated on the householder's ability to sell the home. In facilities that charge entrance fees, the resident is likely to need the proceeds from the sale of the house to pay the entrance fee. Some residents moving into independent or assisted living rental facilities may need the additional income derived from investing the proceeds from sale of the home to support the monthly rental payment. On a practical and even an emotional level, most people prefer to have completed the disposition of their previous homes before moving to a new one. As has been well documented, moving to a seniors' housing community produces ambivalent and even negative emotions for many people. Waiting until the home is sold, even if not economically necessary, provides a rational excuse for an emotional decision.

Internal Management Factors

The quality and experience of the marketing team and the appropriate allocation of marketing dollars also directly affect the facility's fill rate. One of the most prevalent reasons for seniors' housing communities' getting into trouble, and in some cases failing, is the absence of a well-planned and -executed marketing program designed for this specialized type of housing and service option. Not understanding consumers and the best ways to reach them and close sales can cause an otherwise good project to have trouble filling its units.

The quality, extent, and results of the preopening marketing and sales campaign will affect a facility's fill period. Particularly for retirement communities that have entrance fees or forms of equity ownership, significant presales before opening are typically achieved, or actually required, by third parties such as lenders and state regulatory agencies. The level of presales before opening will affect the pace at which fill-up occurs, typically resulting in a greater fill rate during the early months after opening, with a subsequent plateau effect.

Bases for Fill Assumptions

In studies that present assumptions regarding the project's fill period, the fill rate should reflect many of the considerations just described. For studies being done for planning purposes, if fill assumptions are included, they are typically based on the pace at which competitive facilities in the local market have filled (with particular focus on those that have opened during the last several years). The number of facilities that will be attempting to fill concurrently is also important in developing assumptions about the fill rate. Studies may also consider some of the published general information regarding typical fill rates.

For example, ASHA/PricewaterhouseCoopers reported data from nearly 450 properties that addressed the impact of premarketing on move-in rates (based both on time of premarketing and the budget), absorption by property type, and move-in rates by monthly rent, and presented move-in rates for assisted living facilities by state and market. The study defined absorption as "the length of time from when a property opens until either all portions are sold or stabilized occupancy is achieved."[20] The study excluded premarketing periods from the absorption periods and calculations.

A review of the data in this study also indicates a positive correlation between the length of premarketing and the monthly move-in rate, although premarketing budgets and move-in rates did not appear to be strongly correlated. Further, it observed that, for the most part, lower-priced properties reported higher move-in rates than those with higher prices.

ALFA has also been reporting on absorption in its annual industry studies. Although insufficient data were collected to report on 1999 absorption statistics, Figure 3-13 summarizes net monthly unit absorption for 1997 and 1998.

Given that the makeup of the sample of responding facilities differed from year to year, the slowdown in absorption rates undoubtedly reflects the substantial increase in the number of properties developed in each year and the level of competition this figure represents, an element that would be hard to accurately obtain and factor into either set of statistics.

For studies incorporated into financing documents, particularly tax-exempt bond documents, the data from surveying prospective residents who have paid deposits are taken into consideration. (In these studies, fill rates are usually referred to as *forecast utilization.)* The typical questionnaire sent to depositors requests confirmation of not only their intent to move to the project but also the expected timing of that move.

Figure 3-13 **Net Absorption of Seniors' Housing Units**

	1997	1998
National Average	5.6	3.6
Regional Averages		
Northeast	4.9	3.9
Southeast	5.6	3.3
Midwest	15.1	2.7
West	4.5	5.2

Source: Assisted Living Federation of America, "Overview of the Assisted Living Industry," 1998, 1999.

Finally, the track record or experience of the organization responsible for marketing is a factor. Marketing may be the responsibility of an outside marketing firm or the organization that will own and/or sponsor the community. Some facilities have been built by those with little or no experience, which should be considered in developing the fill rate anticipated for such a project. On the other hand, for seniors' housing communities that are being marketed by professionals experienced in the industry, those professionals' achievements at other facilities can be considered as long as they are tempered by the specific conditions in the local market where the new community is being developed.

Monthly and Annual Fill Rate and Occupancy Level

The pace at which a community fills its units is rarely, if ever, uniform, for many of the reasons delineated earlier in this section. Not all studies provide details on monthly fill rates, however, particularly when a document does not include both a financial analysis and a market analysis. Such studies, typically completed for planning purposes, may provide annualized assumptions regarding the number of residential units that can be expected to be occupied by the end of each year before reaching full or stabilized occupancy, or average net monthly fill rates to the point of stabilized occupancy. This projection may assume that an equal number of units will be filled each month during the overall time required to reach full or stabilized occupancy.

Studies used to support financing may in fact be prepared similarly. To the extent that information on depositors is available, however, approximations reflect the actual anticipated rate of move-ins, at least for those depositors, during the first six to 12 months after the facility opens. Subsequently, the fill rate may be forecast at a relatively consistent monthly pace.

An alternative to forecasting consistent monthly fill rates is to take into account several other factors that affect the velocity of the fill period. The first is a pattern of seasonality that appears to have emerged in the marketing and sales process. Winter and summer months tend to produce slower sales than do fall and spring. In addition, fill rates tend to be accelerated right after opening and frequently fall off once the initial group of depositors is accommodated. It may also be a function of the fact that the most popular units may be reserved and occupied most quickly (similar to other types of real estate) and those that remain may be somewhat more difficult to market.

Finally, fill assumptions (or utilization forecasts) being prepared for studies that include financial projections or forecasts should incorporate assumptions regarding the pace of fill-up as well as turnover. Turnover may involve voluntary withdrawal from the community or may result from death or permanent transfer to a higher level of care inside or outside the community, depending on its programmatic structure. The accommodation of turnover results in a net fill assumption. Turnover begins almost as soon as a facility opens, so it should not be overlooked, even in the earliest months.

ASHA has been reporting turnover statistics in its annual *State of Seniors Housing* report for several years (see Figure 3-14). Recognizing that information for CCRCs may differ, particularly for those that offer independent living units for rent rather than requiring an entrance fee, ASHA has published turnover statistics distinguishing between the two (Figure 3-15). It is interesting to note how much higher the turnover rate in rental CCRCs is compared with nonrental (presumably entrance fee) communities, particularly for independent living units. The statistics on turnover are relatively consistent with those AAHSA reported. With a sample that includes only 19 percent rental CCRCs, AAHSA reported an average annual turnover rate of 17 percent for independent living units in mature communities (those that became operational in 1990 or before).[21] This information supports anecdotal evidence that those moving to the independent

Figure 3-14 **Median Annual Turnover of Residents by Property Type**

Property Type	1996	1997	1998	1999
Congregate	26.0%	19.9%	29.5%	33.0%
Assisted Living (Low Acuity)	49.8%	45.9%	54.4%	60.3%
Assisted Living (High Acuity)	51.1%	57.2%	50.5%	54.2%

Sources: American Seniors Housing Association, *Seniors Housing Statistical Digest, 1999–2000;* American Seniors Housing Association, *The State of Seniors Housing, 2000.*

Figure 3-15 **Median Annual Turnover of Residents in CCRCs**

	1996	1997	1998	1999
Rental CCRCs				
Independent Living Units	23.4%	21.5%	23.0%	24.6%
Assisted Living Units	53.3%	57.6%	64.7%	67.5%
Nonrental CCRCs				
Independent Living Units	13.2%	9.7%	14.9%	12.2%
Assisted Living Units	39.3%	51.8%	55.2%	42.9%

Sources: American Seniors Housing Association, *The State of Seniors Housing, 1997, 1998, 1999, 2000.*

living components of CCRCs charging traditional entrance fees are a somewhat younger, healthier group of individuals.

Estimating turnover for residents of a CCRC who are expected to move to higher levels of care should be based on actuarial assumptions.

Standards and Benchmarks

As evidenced by the discussion of the components of market analysis throughout Chapters 2 and 3, a number of standards or benchmarks for judgments and decisions have evolved in the seniors' housing industry. They are related to the major elements associated with the analysis of market opportunities and speak to the most fundamental assumptions required for such analysis: how the market is defined geographically, how it is defined in terms of the income of households included in the qualified pool, household size, frailty (for assisted living), and acceptable risk as measured by the market penetration analysis.

Geographic Market

The art of properly defining the geographic market area from which a community will draw most of its residents continues to be refined as we learn more about how the elderly respond to options for seniors' housing. If any dominant theme has emerged from the description in Chapter 2 of the various ways in which market areas are defined and the results of more than 20 years of experience, it is that seniors' housing is, for the most part, a neighborhood business. Although some early examples of continuing care retirement and life care communities drew from well outside a local area, the more recent experience of even these facilities corroborates the importance of the local market. Now that most markets throughout the country have some, if not numerous, operating communities, a major rationale for a distant move—that of having no other options—rarely exists. Although there are exceptions to the rule that most facilities are supported by their local market, AAHSA's and ALFA's annual industry studies document the predominance of the local market. According to AAHSA, 25 percent of independent living residents in CCRCs moved from within five miles of the facility, 57 percent from within 15 miles, and 35 percent from more than 25 miles.[22] As frailty increases, so does the propensity to remain close to home. According to ALFA, nearly 70 percent of assisted living residents moved from within 15 miles of the facility.[23]

In addition, the U.S. Census Bureau, in its annual publication about geographic mobility, provides generalized information about the movement patterns of the elderly, which substantiates the localized nature of their movements. For example, nearly 50 percent of those age 65 and older who moved moved to another house in the same MSA. Moreover, 94 percent of the elderly were not movers.[24]

Income Level

The generally accepted practice for determining the minimum income required for households considering a move to independent living units has been based on a ratio of the monthly fee to income, which has settled at a range approximating 60 to 70 percent. Fitch's Public Finance Group references 67 percent as a rule of thumb.[25] The historical percentage of income spent on the monthly fee for independent living has been derived by using national published statistics on how retirees spend their income and deducting certain annual expenses encompassed by the monthly fee required to reside in the retirement community. It has been assumed that the payment of entrance fees, when charged, would be covered by the proceeds from the sale of the home or, combined when necessary with other assets, would eliminate the cost of the entrance fee from the equation of determining necessary income.

While this same approach—establishing a monthly fee-to-income ratio—was adapted for the analysis of assisted living, no clear standard similar to the 60 to 70 percent ratio used for independent living has emerged, and, in fact, some research has eroded the notion of a direct relationship between fees and income. The NIC studies of assisted living customers strongly suggest that residents have significantly less income than expected, given the monthly fees they are paying to reside in these communities.[26] On the other hand, some professionals have argued, publicly and privately, that seniors need much more income than the NIC study suggests. The controversy over the issue of how to determine what income level to use in assisted living market analysis continues. It is obviously a more need-driven product, one where presumably the resident needs less discretionary income than those in independent living. In addition, the comparatively short length of stay argues for the assumption that a resident will spend a higher proportion of his or her income to reside in assisted living than independent living. Various leading consultants in the industry quote rent-to-income ratios ranging from 74 percent to 90 percent (based on a review of numerous feasibility studies included in public offering statements for communities built in the late 1990s). The same Fitch article referenced earlier cites a rule of thumb of 80 percent.

Related to this debate over income is the question of whether or not to factor any measure of wealth into the calculation. As noted earlier, statistics on measures of wealth, other than home values, are nearly impossible to obtain on less than the national level. Information about home values and the proportion of seniors who are homeowners is available locally but with no consistency in terms of the use of home values or other estimates of wealth in analyses done for assisted living communities. Some studies use income derived from investing the proceeds from average home values to offset the level of income required, while others do not recognize this economic variable at all. Few if any studies acknowledge that residents of assisted living are actually spending down the principal of assets to remain in the community.

The relative disconnect between conservative methodology and actual practice became more pronounced as assisted living emerged throughout the 1990s as the fastest-growing form of seniors' housing. The lack of a benchmark for establishing minimum income for assisted living has contributed significantly to the lack of agreement on an acceptable penetration rate for this level of care.

Household Size

While all age- and income-qualified households, regardless of size, are typically included in analyzing the market for independent living units, studies of assisted living have come to further qualify the pool by eliminating most if not all two-person households, particularly married couples. A review of many studies conducted by most of the leading firms indicated that this practice has now become fairly common, with most including only single-person households. The use of single-person households has been further underscored as a commonly accepted practice by HUD in its underwriting standards for the 232 Mortgage Insurance program and by Fitch in its article on measuring demand. This practice reflects the fact that 5 percent or fewer of assisted living units are occupied by married couples. It should be noted, however, that the proportion of single-person households changes rather dramatically when income is applied. The information on household size by income level provided by Claritas, the most commonly used demographic data vendor, is no more refined than above and below the poverty level. The application of income to household size could significantly affect the size of the assisted living market in any given study.

Frailty

It is now commonly accepted that the assisted living market should be further qualified by some measure of the need for assistance with ADLs. These statistics, published by the U.S. Census Bureau and several other sources, are typically based on age and sometimes gender. The degree of variation between different measures of need for assistance with ADLs used by various analysts can produce wide ranges in calculating the number of those who are age- and income-qualified and need assistance. These differences contribute greatly to the lack of consistency in calculating or judging market penetration rates for assisted living.

Market Penetration Rates

The most frequently used quantifiable measure of market potential used in the analysis for retirement communities has traditionally been market penetration. Very low penetration rates, 2 percent or less, were considered in the early years to be acceptable penetration levels to support a project's feasibility.

During the latter part of the 1990s, however, the level of penetration generally considered acceptable increased so that currently many analysts judge projects that involve penetration levels of 5 percent and even higher to be feasible.

Both methodological and interpretive drawbacks are associated with the use of and reliance on market penetration as an arbiter of project feasibility. As noted earlier, how penetration rates are calculated differs widely, ranging from how competition is factored in to how the term *market penetration* itself is used.

More problematic is the use of market penetration standards when they are applied to an improperly qualified pool. In studies done by consulting firms inexperienced in seniors' housing analysis, a problem is created when the market area defined is too large; problems can further arise by such factors as underestimating the minimum income required and by incorrectly identifying and qualifying other competitive facilities.

In studies where the approach is to determine how much product overall the market can absorb, the application of overly aggressive market penetration or saturation standards can misrepresent what that market might be able to bear at a specific time. For instance, as noted earlier, some analysts have assumed that other markets will be able to absorb as much product as Philadelphia, where market saturation or market share levels have reached 15 to 30 percent. This percentage simply is not possible during a short period of time, and duration can easily be overlooked when such an approach is used to size a market's potential absorption.

Two fundamental issues affect *penetration rate* or quantitative analysis of market depth. The first is properly defining the terminology and reaching consensus across the industry on these definitions. The second, which logically follows, is ascribing value and meaning to the results of the analysis.

With regard to terminology, it is important to understand the underlying import of the quantitative exercise. What are the questions we are trying to answer? Two related key questions must be addressed. The first is the percentage of the available market (that is, not already living in a seniors' housing community) the project must capture to fill those units, given certain assumptions about age, income, and the percentage of units expected to be filled by residents of a defined market area. The second, broader question is the percentage of the market that must be captured for the project and all of its competitors to fill the units they expect will be occupied by local market area residents. If agreement can be reached that these are the two most important questions to be answered, agreeing on the specific terminology to describe each should be reasonably easy. Together, these two calculations represent the specific project and place it within the context of the overall market.

It has been our experience that the term *market penetration* has been used to reflect the subject property being analyzed rather than the calculation reflecting what the total competitive universe must capture. This observation is borne out by both AAHSA and Fitch. An AAHSA publication defines penetration rate as "the percentage of the available market that must be captured in order to achieve stabilization. . . . The calculation also reduces the number of eligible households for competitive ILUs available at other communities within the primary target region (market area)."[27] A Fitch report prepared in October 2000 notes the penetration rate shows "a facility's inventory or units relative to market depth,"[28] again supporting the concept that penetration rates relate to a single, specific property.

In some of the examples of market penetration calculations shown earlier in this chapter, it appears that the number of units used in the calculation represented all unoccupied units, which would include those that are being planned, such as the subject, as well as vacant units in existing competitive properties. The results, however, do not take into consideration that those units that *are* occupied are occupied by people no longer available to move to the unoccupied units represented in the calculation. In other words, the divider in the equation, which is total market-area age- and income-eligible households, has not been adjusted to remove those already residing in competitive communities, resulting in an inflated estimate of available households.

In addition, this analysis answered a different question from either of those posed above. Specifically, it addressed the question of what percentage of the market needed to be captured or penetrated to fill all vacant or as yet unbuilt units, which differs from the measures that led to general standards for acceptable levels for market penetration or market saturation, depending on how the term is defined.

For any of these calculations to have meaning and value for providers, lenders, and consultants to the industry, there must be consensus on definitions and the basics of the quantitative analysis. Once consensus if reached, benchmarks can be established for measuring the risk associated with market demand, given the broad base of available data on numerous markets.

On a broader basis, the heavy reliance on market penetration as a key indicator of project feasibility does not take into account the many other critical factors that are necessary for a project's success. Those who are experienced in the use and preparation of market studies recognize that penetration levels are only one of many indicators of a project's potential for success. Market penetration must be considered in the context of the competitive environment: how well are the competitive facilities performing? Are they full, or have several of them been unable to reach full occupancy? What kinds of organizations sponsor or own those facilities, and what impact, if any, has this sponsorship/ownership had on success? What type of program, in terms of pricing and services, appears to be marketable? How many facilities will be in the marketing phase at the same time as the project being analyzed? How experienced is the team that will develop, design, market, and operate the project?

It is more than likely that, as seniors' housing development increases, judgment and experience, in addition to quantitative measures such as market penetration, will be required to evaluate project feasibility. Market analysis will have to be able to assess which new facilities are more likely to succeed in a given market. Beyond that, the experienced analyst will be able to assist a client in developing a strategy designed to position his retirement community for success. It will be too easy, using the benchmarks or rules of thumb from the past, to conclude that a project is infeasible. The job of the experienced market analyst will be to find the *yes* to an otherwise *no* proposition.

Notes

1. PricewaterhouseCoopers, "The Continuing Care Retirement Communities 1998 Profile" (Washington, D.C.: American Association of Homes and Services for the Aging, 1999), p. 24.

2. U.S. Department of Housing and Urban Development, "Guide for Content and Format of a Market Analysis for Residential Care Facilities," Section 232 Programs, Section F.3.

3. R.C. Wetzler and R. Lageman, "Measuring Demand for Seniors Housing," Fitch, Duff & Phelps, October 18, 2000, p. 6.

4. Bureau of Labor Statistics, *Consumer Expenditure Survey,* 1999 [www.bls.gov/CEX].

5. Ibid.

6. Assisted Living Federation of America and National Investment Center, "National Survey of Assisted Living Residents: Who Is the Customer?" 1998.

7. NIC, "Income Confirmation Study of Assisted Living Residents and the Age 75+ Population," 1999.

8. Margaret A. Wylde, Edie R. Smith, and Bernie L. Smith, "Income and Net Worth of Assisted Living Residents and Their Relationship to Monthly Rates of Assisted Living Communities," *Seniors Housing and Care Journal,* Vol. 8, No. 1 (2000), p. 53.

9. American Seniors Housing Association, *Seniors Housing Statistical Digest, 2000–2001*, 2000, p. 24.

10. U.S. Department of HUD, "Guide for Content and Format . . . Section 232 Programs," Section F.3.

11. ALFA, NIC, and PricewaterhouseCoopers, "Overview of the Assisted Living Industry, 2000," p. 16.

12. U.S. Census Bureau, *The Need for Personal Assistance with Everyday Activities by Age: 1991,* Series P-70-33, December 1993.

13. U.S. General Accounting Office, *Alzheimer's Disease: Estimates of Prevalence in the United States,* Report to the Secretary of Health and Human Services (Washington, D.C.: Author, 1998).

14. Herbert J. Sims & Co. and American Association of Homes and Services for the Aging, "From Start-Up to Success: A Statistical Analysis of Emerging Continuing Care Retirement Communities," 1999, p. 25.

15. Wetzler and Lageman, "Measuring Demand for Seniors Housing," p. 6.

16. Ibid.

17. Ibid.

18. ALFA, NIC, and PricewaterhouseCoopers, "Overview of the Assisted Living Industry," pp. 18, 22; and ALFA and NIC, "National Survey of Assisted Living Residents," p. 145.

19. Ibid.; and AAHSA, "The CCRC Industry 1998 Profile," p. 26.

20. ASHA, PricewaterhouseCoopers, and CNC, "Seniors Housing Absorption Trends, 2000," p. 2.

21. AAHSA, "CCRC Industry 1997 Profile," p. 9.

22. AAHSA, "CCRC Industry 1998 Profile."

23. ALFA, NIC, and PricewaterhouseCoopers, "Overview of the Assisted Living Industry, 2000."

24. Kristin A. Hansen, U.S. Census Bureau, *Geographic Mobility: March 1992 to March 1993,* Current Population Reports, Series P-20-481 (Washington, D.C.: U.S. Government Printing Office, 1994), Table 2.

25. Wetzler and Lageman, "Measuring Demand for Seniors Housing," p. 5.

26. NIC, "Income Confirmation Study," 1999.

27. Sims and AAHSA, "From Start-Up to Success," p. 25.

28. Wetzler and Lageman, "Measuring Demand for Seniors Housing," p. 6.

The Sunrise at Bellevue in Bellevue, Washington, includes attractive private and public areas. Architect: Dietrich Mithun Architects

4 Consumer Research

The Use of Consumer Research

Chapters 2 and 3 explore the analytical techniques employed to evaluate many pertinent issues that affect the successful planning and development of a seniors' housing community. Those issues include defining and describing the characteristics of a facility's market area, assessing the size and demographic features of the area's elderly population, and determining the qualities of the competitive facilities that are operating or opening soon in the market area. Chapter 3 addresses the methodologies used to size the demographically qualified market for a project and assess the level of risk associated with its development.

This chapter addresses the use of primary consumer research and its integration into the process of market analysis and planning for seniors' housing. Although secondary environmental research has been the dominant approach to market analysis in this industry, the use of primary consumer research and recognition of its value in product analysis and planning for seniors' housing have increased.

Why does any organization conduct consumer research? On the most fundamental level, it seeks to learn more from those who will use its products and services. Environmental analysis is critical in determining a market's strengths and weaknesses. By ignoring the consumer, planning takes place in a partial vacuum.

Consumer research is conducted to learn more about the target market's awareness, perceptions and attitudes, preferences and desires, behavior and use patterns, opinions, and interests. It is carried out to determine interest in new products and services, to redefine markets and positioning for existing ones, and to refine marketing and advertising strategies, as well as for a variety of other reasons.

Many books have been written on the subject of consumer research, detailing the technical and methodological issues pertinent to the various approaches to designing and conducting the research and interpreting the results. Chapter 2 presents information on several national consumer studies that have been conducted on issues relating to seniors' housing. This chapter discusses the ways in which consumer research has been conducted and used in the planning and marketing of individual seniors' housing facilities. A brief introduction to the techniques typically used—and their advantages and disadvantages from the perspective of general research—is followed by a specific discussion of how consumer research has been used to address key issues in planning a community for seniors. Finally, the chapter includes a discussion of how consumer research and marketing have been intermingled in this industry.

Consumer Research Classifications And Techniques

Consumer research includes two broad classifications —*qualitative* and *quantitative* research. Qualitative research, which usually involves a small sample, is meant to provide descriptive information on respondents' thoughts and feelings.[1] "Qualitative research is characterized by the absence of empirical measurements and the focus on more subjective evaluations."[2] Historically, qualitative research was considered inferior to quantitative research, particularly because of the small samples used. Qualitative research, as a result, was thought to produce results that were deficient in validity and reliability. In addition, some researchers raised concerns over the potential influence of the moderator of qualitative research conducted in small-group settings and the potential for subjective rather than objective interpretation.[3]

Quantitative research, by comparison, usually involves a larger number of respondents, who are meant to represent an even larger universe. It is conducted "for the purpose of obtaining empirical evaluations of attitudes, behavior, or performance."[4] Whereas qualitative research is not meant to be projectable to a larger universe, quantitative research, when conducted properly, can be used for this purpose. A wide variety of techniques is used in conducting consumer research. Data collection methods include in-depth interviews, focus groups, personal interviews, telephone surveys, mail surveys, and other self-administered questionnaires. The most common techniques used in the seniors' housing field have included mail surveys, telephone surveys, and focus groups.

Mail Surveys

Mail surveys often are used to survey those who are thought to have "relatively high interest in the product being studied."[5] Surveying a group of people who have not previously agreed to be surveyed (a "cold" mail survey) is a common technique in studies done during the planning of seniors' housing facilities. It is a relatively inexpensive way to reach a large group of respondents.

In some cases, the target market for a mail survey is defined by geographic boundaries as well as demographic characteristics. For example, a survey might be mailed to all households in Montgomery County, Maryland, headed by an individual age 70 or older having at least $20,000 annual income. A mail survey might also be sent to households that are believed to have a particular affinity with a potential sponsoring organization (e.g., older members of religious denominations or specific churches in a region, alumni of colleges or universities, or members of fraternal organizations).

Both advantages and disadvantages are inherent in the use of mail surveys. On the positive side, when the survey questions are properly framed, this technique eliminates any bias that the interviewer might bring to data collection. In addition, it allows the use of exhibit materials to illustrate the product attributes being studied. Some also contend that older consumers are more likely to return mail surveys than younger ones, a disadvantage for certain products and services but, if true, an advantage for those planning seniors' housing projects.

Many believe that the disadvantages of mail surveys are greater than the advantages. One problem is that there is no control over who in the household completes the questionnaire. In seniors' housing, it would be a problem if someone other than the prospective resident completes the survey. For instance, if a survey is sent to a home in which a younger family member lives, that family member might influence the responses or actually complete the survey. In most cases, however, the absence of control over the respondent may not be as significant a disadvantage in seniors' housing planning, because, in the case of a household occupied by a married couple, both members of the couple actually represent the target market for the community.

A more significant problem with mail surveys is that those who return the surveys are often not truly representative of the total sample. The response rate is frequently tied to the interest of the respondents in the object of the research.[6] Thus, less information than might be desired is obtained from those who are not as interested in the survey subject. In addition, the potential for inaccuracies exists because respondents may be confused by or not understand a question.

Probably the greatest problem with mail surveys is the low response rate. Although various authorities differ somewhat in their estimates of the response rates that can be expected, the range is quite low, typically 5 to 15 percent. Paul L. Erdos, an expert in the subject of mail surveys, suggests that the results are not reliable unless a 50 percent response rate is achieved.[7]

Because of the low response rates achieved by most mail surveys, the data derived are not actually projectable to the total population that the sample frame represents. In some cases, however, the response rate is not considered a major issue, particularly where input is desired that does not necessarily have to represent the total universe being assessed.

Response rates to mail surveys can be increased by certain means. Having a survey sponsored by a known and respected organization may increase the rate of response. The inclusion of a stamped return envelope and a small money incentive have both been shown to be quite effective. Although a deadline for response will not increase the rate of response, it should accelerate it.[8]

Telephone Surveys

A telephone survey is particularly useful when a broad, national sample is desired or when contact is required with respondents from a particular list. In addition, it is an efficient way to call back previous contacts. The telephone survey is a technique used to study attitudes and use and can be used for periodic tracking.[9]

Telephone surveys have been used in several different ways in planning seniors' housing facilities. The most basic use has been to collect information regarding interest in seniors' housing and feedback on project features such as pricing, services and amenities, project sponsorship, and the desirability and acceptability of geographic areas and specific locations. In addition, small sample telephone surveys have been used in conjunction with mail surveys to test whether lack of response to the mail survey could be presumed to indicate no interest in the project.

The use of telephone surveys has numerous advantages, among them the comparative speed of completion (when large, professional centralized interviewing facilities are used) and the high rate of completed responses. Professionals in the field indicate that response rates as high as 80 percent are not unusual.

In addition, it is easier to control many aspects of the telephone survey. Through initial screening questions, the interviewer can control who actually responds to the survey. When telephone surveys are done at centralized facilities, it is easier to supervise and monitor those conducting the interviews. The interviewer is able to clarify questions for respondents who are confused and can also probe for more information when appropriate.

Limitations in the use of telephone surveys are associated primarily with length and the inability to use exhibits or visual aids. What is considered an acceptable length for telephone surveys differs: some authors indicate optimal lengths of ten to 20 minutes, while others say that interviews as long as 30 minutes are acceptable. The amount of material that can be covered is a function of the length of the interview.

Focus Groups

The final technique often used in studies for seniors' housing is the focus group. The focus group is a qualitative technique that may be used when considering the introduction of a new product, when comparing competitive products, and when modifying the features of an existing product.[10] The focus group is used when researchers want to know what people in the target market think about a product and what their needs and attitudes are. It is often the first step in the research process because it helps to define, refine, and identify specific issues that can then be tested through other research means.

The focus group convenes a small group (five to 12 people) in an informal setting for one to two hours. The focus group moderator works from a previously designed discussion guide that governs the topics to be discussed and sometimes the length of time to be devoted to each topic. Focus group moderators should be trained and experienced in this type of group facilitation.

Focus groups are frequently videotaped so that the tapes can be reviewed before interpreting the results. Taping can be a particularly helpful tool for gauging participants' nonverbal responses.

The advantages of focus groups are that they allow the researcher to develop hypotheses for further testing, can be helpful in structuring questionnaires to be used in later phases of research, or can be used for interpreting the results of research. Some advocates of focus group research suggest that the focus group, compared with personal or in-depth interviews (two other forms of qualitative research), may result in more candid responses because participants may feel more "protected" by the group environment than in a one-on-one setting such as a telephone survey or face-to-face interview.[11]

On the other hand, some suggest that the group setting results in less candid responses or even unwillingness to participate and the potential for some individual participants to dominate the discussion.[12] In addition, the success of the group depends largely on the moderator's skills. As mentioned, the result of the focus group cannot be projected to a larger group.

Psychographic or Lifestyle Research

Psychographic is a word pioneered by consumer research expert Emanuel Demby in the 1960s. He defined psychographic research, an approach to market segmentation, as follows:

1. Generally, psychographics may be viewed as the practical application of the behavioral and social sciences to consumer research.
2. More specifically, psychographics is a quantitative research procedure that is indicated when demographic, socioeconomic, and user/nonuser analyses are not sufficient to explain and predict consumer behavior.
3. Most specifically, psychographics [seeks] to describe the human characteristics of consumers that may have bearing on their response to products, packaging, advertising, and public relations efforts. Such variables may span a spectrum from self-concept and lifestyle to attitudes, interests, and options, as well as perceptions of product attributes.[13]

A term sometimes used interchangeably with psychographic research is *lifestyle research*. The distinction between the two appears to be that psychographic research refers to people's personality traits, whereas lifestyle research refers to activities, opinions, and interests (AOIs, as described by William D. Wells and Douglas J. Tigert).[14]

Psychographic research is used for several key reasons. It is a valuable tool for identifying and explaining target markets. It leads to a better understanding of consumers' behavior. It also provides information that can be used for strategic marketing and, if conducted and used properly, should minimize the risk associated with introducing new products.[15]

Psychographic research has not frequently been a component of consumer research done for seniors' communities. Several large national companies involved in seniors' housing also have attempted psychographic research to understand and segment their buyer profiles. This research was applied to elderly households in markets targeted for development (see Chapter 6 for more detail).

Issues Addressed through Consumer Research on Seniors' Housing

Direct consumer research in the seniors' housing field has been implemented to address a broad variety of questions and issues that arise in the development of a single facility. Quantitative consumer research has been conducted to actually estimate demand for a specific project. Both qualitative and quantitative research methods have been used to learn more about the general level of familiarity with and interest in seniors' housing, specifically what older consumers may or may not want in the design, program, and pricing for a facility, and perceptions of such issues as site location and sponsorship.

Knowledge of and Familiarity with Seniors' Housing

Consumer research can be used to begin to gauge the level of familiarity with today's senior living options, such as continuing care, life care, congregate housing, and assisted living. In a focus group, participants may be asked, before being presented any information on a specific community, to describe what they perceive seniors' housing to be like. This question can be asked about services and programs, as well as about architectural and design features. It also can be addressed more indirectly, by inquiring about participants' perceptions of what type of person moves to a senior community or asking participants to name seniors' housing facilities they know of or have visited.

Asking these types of questions at the beginning of a focus group provides the research team with an opportunity to determine the preconceived notions that participants may have of retirement living. In cases where there is little familiarity, the responses may suggest that seniors' housing is closely associated with participants' perceptions of an old age or nursing home. In markets where elderly consumers have had more exposure to newer concepts, this knowledge may be reflected in their responses.

In survey research, questions that address familiarity are likely to be somewhat more direct. The questionnaire may require that respondents indicate directly how familiar they are with various seniors' housing concepts described verbally or in writing (depending on the research approach) or may list a number of local seniors' housing communities and ask whether respondents are familiar with them or have visited them.

Developing a sense, through consumer research, of how knowledgeable the target market is about the concept of seniors' housing helps the team plan the strategy for marketing the facility. Less familiar markets require a marketing campaign that has a substantial educational component and focus. Highly competitive markets, where the elderly are more familiar with seniors' housing, require the marketing strategy to differentiate the facility from other competitors.

Familiarity with and Acceptance of Site

Given the critical importance of site acceptability, consumer research can be a useful tool for evaluating how the elderly perceive the site or location where a senior facility is to be developed. Clearly, the validity of responses to questions regarding location depends on participants' familiarity with the subject area. In focus groups, the use of locational maps can be supplemented by a verbal description of the location and of landmarks that may help participants to recall it. In telephone survey research, a verbal description of both the specific location and identifying landmarks can be used. Self-administered questionnaires can provide a description of the project that includes both a narrative description of the site and a locational map, if desired, which respondents may be asked to refer to in evaluating a site. Participants may be asked to answer questions that determine both their familiarity with the site and their willingness to consider moving to a seniors' housing community on that site.

Questions regarding willingness to move may be asked, even of those who have already indicated that they do not plan to move to any seniors' housing community. For studies in which site acceptability rather than willingness to move is the key issue, information from all participants can be valuable.

In some cases, consumer research is used to compare the acceptability of alternative locations. This choice may be site specific or even broader when an organization is attempting to determine where (a town or geographic area) to develop a seniors' housing community. Religious and fraternal organizations with memberships that represent a broad geographic area have used this approach. When such organizations begin to plan the development of a seniors' housing community, they may seek to determine the geographic preferences of the membership.

For certain specific types of locations and projects, site acceptability may be even more critical. Colleges and universities that are planning to develop seniors' housing communities on their campuses may seek to determine the extent to which they will be able to draw from alumni who have moved away from the area. Although the market made up of nonlocal alumni may not be the only or the largest target segment for a facility, it is still quite useful, when project marketing begins, to have determined whether a specific marketing program should focus on this group. Hospitals and nursing homes that are considering the development of seniors' housing communities may wish to test locational acceptability, whether the institution plans to build on its existing campus or off site. The issue of on-site development should be tested to determine whether the market may resist moving to what could be perceived as too institutional a setting. The issue of off-site development may be tested to be certain that the alternative location still allows the organization to have the benefits associated with operating a facility within its sphere of influence.

Interest in and Willingness to Move to a Seniors' Housing Community

The issue of interest in or willingness to move to a seniors' housing community may be one of the least satisfying issues addressed by consumer research. Inquiries about whether participants would consider moving to the community being planned are typically incorporated into both telephone surveys and self-administered questionnaires. The question may address respondents' interest in the concept, their willingness to consider moving to any seniors' housing community, and their willingness to consider moving to the facility being researched. In addition, an accompanying question regarding the potential timing of such a move, if one is contemplated, may be asked.

Problems associated with questions of this type are related, in part, to the fact that a move to a seniors' housing community is still perceived by most of the market as somewhat negative. It is frequently motivated by declining health, the death of a spouse, or some other event that reminds an individual that living on his or her own may not be the most manageable option.

For years, consumer research reflected the demographic flaw that characterized other forms of market research for seniors' housing: it was addressed to age segments—those age 65 to 74—that were very unlikely to be ready to consider such a move. Based on the experience in the industry to date, it is now known that few people below the age of 75 move to seniors' housing communities. Including a younger group in the sample is unlikely to yield very meaningful results, because the question is being posed to people who are not ready to make the decision. Their ability to anticipate whether they would consider such a move under the right circumstances is questionable—particularly for those who equate a seniors' housing community with a nursing home. Even for those who do not, being asked to respond to the likelihood of doing something that is comparatively unfamiliar at some future date is not likely to produce a reliable response.

For consumer research firms with depth of experience in the seniors' housing industry that have asked the same questions for numerous projects, the responses to these questions may take on additional meaning. By comparing the response rates across several projects and/or markets, the analyst is able to assess whether research respondents for a specific project are expressing greater or lesser degrees of interest and willingness to move. It can be even more powerful if the firm takes the time to go back to researched facilities to determine how accurate the research has been.

Market Area Draw

As discussed earlier, well-planned and correctly designed interviews with key informants during the fieldwork stage of market analysis can provide substantial information useful in determining boundaries of the market area. During that level of research, however, issues regarding draw areas may emerge that cannot be fully evaluated without going directly to the elderly target market for feedback.

Testing the ability to draw from different geographic areas enables the analyst to confirm or refine the initial assumptions about market area definition developed during the fieldwork. Consumer research can help to prioritize geographic areas, refining the definitions of primary and secondary market areas, which can then be tested and evaluated by comparing the market's level of interest in or willingness to consider moving to a specific location in each of two or more defined geographic areas. When such research allows a market of secondary importance to be confirmed, market penetration analyses can be modified to distinguish between primary and secondary market areas. It also can be particularly useful in evaluating the opportunity for a seniors' housing community development for an organization that is inexperienced in this area and that may be expecting a wider geographic draw than is likely to occur.

Results may provide powerful evidence that residents of certain geographic areas are more or less oriented toward a move to a specific site or location. When consumer research is being used to develop or refine market area boundaries, the sample that is surveyed should be selected to have significant enough representation in each area to be tested to draw conclusions from the results.

As indicated, consumer research can be a valuable tool in determining whether prospective residents of a senior community might be drawn from nonlocal areas. This research may be used to test an affinity group, with the sample representing nonlocal members of a religious denomination or fraternal organization, or alumni of a college or university. It may also be designed to determine whether individuals from nonlocal geographic areas with no formal ties or affinity to an area would be willing to move there. Such an approach, for example, may be used in research to test locations in seasonal or resort trade areas to determine whether the major markets or a specific market from which visitors typically come would also result in potential moves by retirees.

Preferred Features

One frequent use of consumer research is to learn more about what project features the target market prefers for a specific community. Questions about a project's features address approaches to and levels of payment, programmatic issues, and design features and amenities. They may be addressed through any of the major methodologies, although questions about certain types of project features, particularly design and perhaps even payment alternatives, are easier to research using focus groups and self-administered questionnaires.

Payment Approaches and Pricing

Direct consumer research may be used to help determine whether the payment approach being considered is acceptable to the target market.

Emery Photo; courtesy AIA

At Friendship Village at Dublin in Dublin, Ohio, renovation updated the 1970s era retirement community, giving it an inviting residential appeal. Architect: James Michael Milligan

Decisions about payment approaches may be facilitated by testing a specific concept or by structuring questions that require the respondent to indicate a preference among several options. In the event that the organization planning the project has a specific preference for the structuring of payments, testing that preference will provide guidance on the acceptability of the preferred approach. Testing payment structures can also be particularly useful for assessing the reaction to a payment approach different from that currently dominating a market. For instance, consumer research in the form of a brief but widely circulated questionnaire was conducted for a proposed rental project, the Bellingham, in the Philadelphia area, a market that was dominated by the CCRC endowment or entrance fee. Survey respondents demonstrated a strong interest in, in fact a preference for, a rental alternative.

Testing actual pricing levels is done in several ways. If a questionnaire is being used, specific prices to be charged can be indicated in questions about whether the respondent would be able to afford and willing to pay those rates. An alternative to this approach is to present price ranges and request participants to select the price range they would be able to afford and willing to pay. One shortcoming of this approach is that people tend to select prices on the low side, hoping that doing so might influence pricing decisions.

When prices are tested in focus groups, the results can be rather interesting, depending on the approach to the question. In some cases, negative responses may indicate that prices are too high. If, on the other hand, participants are asked to indicate what they think it would cost to live in a seniors' housing community (once the design, amenities, and services are discussed and understood), they may actually come fairly close to estimating the correct price. This outcome is related, in part, to the increased perception of value that may occur when people understand what goes into making up the price charged for a seniors' housing community.

Learning more about how a targeted market segment responds to pricing can be critical to continued planning and development. In the worst case, if the research uncovers substantial price resistance or determines that the greatest interest in moving to the facility is displayed by those who cannot afford it or who select the lowest possible price ranges, it may be necessary to significantly modify the project's features or to abandon the project altogether.

Program Features

Program features in a seniors' housing community refer to the specific type and frequency of services provided. Services may include meals, housekeeping and maintenance, transportation, linens and laundry, health care and wellness services, and social, recreational, and cultural activities. Consumer research may be structured to refine existing program assumptions or to develop the basic framework of services to be offered. Questions may address preferences, including frequency of service where appropriate (e.g., how many meals per day or per month, how often housekeeping should take place) and whether to include services in the fee structure or to offer them on an as-used basis.

One of the most important program issues tested through consumer research concerns the area of health care services. In particular, consumer research frequently is carried out for communities that are considering offering a continuum of care to determine whether residents prefer to have nursing care available as part of a community's program. Applicable questions include whether nursing care must be offered, whether it should be included as part of the physical development plan for the site, whether residents prefer to pay as they use it or insured life care is more desirable, and whether the presence and availability of nursing care enhances the proposed community's attractiveness.

Responses to questions on program features are affected by the participant's stage of life or readiness to move to the facility. To obtain the most useful profile of what the target market is looking for, it is best to focus on the responses of those who are actually interested in the specific facility or are contemplating a move to a similar facility. The less ready one is to make such a move, the more likely he or she is to desire fewer services and to prefer the pay-for-service approach. Frequently, the apparent desire for the pay-for-service approach belies the extent to which residents may actually use these services. What might appear before moving in to be a fair philosophy can become perceived as an annoying nickel-and-dime philosophy once residents have lived with it for a period of time.

Design and Amenities

Surveys and focus groups are frequently used to evaluate design features of seniors' housing communities. Issues tested range from the broad to the narrow. For instance, the research may attempt to test respondents' reactions to the general building type, asking about preferences and acceptability of high-rise, mid-rise, and low-rise apartments, detached cottages, and townhouses. Given that many sites do not afford a range of options, this type of question is more likely to be found in a survey that is not site specific but may also be designed to determine locational preferences. Respondents may also be asked to indicate preferences for unit types (detached units versus apartments) and unit sizes (number of bedrooms). The latter types of questions help define or refine the unit mix before architectural plans are completed.

Some questionnaires also request respondents to provide feedback on other design considerations, including the functional use of common space. Some design amenities that may be included in a survey are a convenience store, banking facilities, guest accommodations, a meeting and recreation room, an arts and crafts room, a woodworking shop, a card and game room, an indoor pool, an exercise room, a library, a chapel, a beauty salon/barber shop, a coffee/snack shop, community garden plots or a greenhouse, and personal storage space.

Influence of Sponsorship

Many communities are sponsored by nonprofit organizations. Frequently, consumer research carried out for such facilities includes questions about the influence of the sponsorship on the respondent's interest in moving to the planned facility. The study may attempt to determine whether members of the sponsoring organization have a different level of interest in moving to the facility than the general population or whether the influence of the sponsor is a positive, negative, or neutral factor among the overall elderly target market.

These issues can be tested in several ways. One approach is to directly inquire whether the sponsor will influence the decision to select or move to a seniors' housing community. A less direct alternative is to design the research to compare the interest in moving to the facility expressed by the two different groups, the general elderly population in the market area and members of the particular sponsoring organization. This strategy is clearly facilitated when lists of elderly members of sponsoring organizations can be obtained for the geographic area being targeted. Before implementing this approach, the two lists should be screened to avoid duplication.

Timing of Move

The point at which respondents would consider moving is a critical consideration in project planning. This issue is addressed in consumer research studies conducted for seniors' housing to determine several things. Although the most basic question is whether there appears to be a short-term market or pent-up demand for the project among those responding to the research, the issue also can be crucial in the design of data analysis.

All the responses may be interesting, but it is most useful to consider those derived from people who are actually ready (or close to being ready) to move. These individuals represent the true target market. Cross tabulating the responses of those indicating interest by when they would consider moving may yield important differences in preferred design and programmatic features.

In some cases, mail and telephone surveys are conducted before carrying out focus group research. Survey respondents may be requested to participate in this next level of research. Targeting those who indicated interest in moving to the planned facility in the relative near future is a good idea, as these individuals are likely to indicate a much truer picture of what they will consider in making the decision than those who are farther from being ready to move.

Factors Influencing the Decision to Move

Consumer research can provide some insights on why respondents would consider a move to a seniors' housing community. This information can be pursued with a mail or phone survey or a focus group. Responses derived from questions of this type allow those creating and marketing the facility's program to design strategies that respond to the motivations of potential residents. Factors that may be tested in a survey include such things as the desire for companionship, security, freedom from housekeeping and maintenance chores, a more independent lifestyle, and a desire to have access to and assurances about future health care services.

In addition, it can be quite instructive to learn why respondents would not consider moving to a seniors' housing community. Those who indicate no interest or uncertainty about their interest may provide extremely valuable feedback, particularly with regard to future project marketing and positioning. For instance, if a substantial number of respondents indicate they would not consider moving to such a facility because they are too healthy and independent, an effort can be made to alter their perceptions of the seniors' housing community as a facility for the frail, inactive elderly, and they might become prospects rather than rejects as a result. Success in doing so might require a change in marketing strategies and collateral materials used in marketing the facility. It may also require retraining personnel involved in marketing and sales. It is just as helpful, if not more so, to understand the barriers that must be overcome in marketing the community as it is to know what factors are positive influences.

Profile of Respondents

Both telephone and mail questionnaires almost always seek information that will allow a profile of respondents' characteristics to be developed. This information may include basic demographic data as well as information on health status. The types of demographic data sought may include gender, marital status, age/spouse's age, household composition, housing tenure, current housing type, estimated annual income, estimated equity value of personal residence, length of time at present residence, monthly mortgage/rental payment, and education.

Questions on health status may range from a very general question asking respondents to rate their overall health status (excellent to poor) or may involve more complex queries regarding functional capacity. The latter might include questions about the respondent's (and when appropriate the spouse's) ability to handle certain basic ADLs, such as using the stairs, getting in and out of a bathtub, bending/stooping, walking a few blocks, carrying heavy packages, lifting large items, getting dressed, and eating; use of a cane, walker, or wheelchair; visual limitations; and hearing impairment.

Like the question regarding readiness to move, questions about health status facilitate an analysis of the degree of dependency that characterizes those interested in moving to the seniors' housing community, thereby providing a better understanding of the actual target market. This information will influence many program and design factors as well as the overall orientation of the marketing program.

Consumer Research for Assisted Living Communities

Although consumer research that directly targets the consumers or end users of seniors' housing has become fairly common, it is much more difficult to successfully structure and carry out consumer research intended to plan an assisted living community. Two issues make consumer research for this product type difficult.

The first issue relates to the need-driven nature of the assisted living product and the frailty level (frequently cognitive as well as physical) of the end user. Seniors who need assisted living may have difficulty responding to any form of consumer research, exhibiting difficulties in hearing and understanding questions. For those seniors who are not yet ready to make a move to assisted living, projecting their feelings and desires to a time when their capabilities are likely to have diminished is difficult and fundamentally unreliable. Responses from seniors who are not ready for assisted living are likely to produce research results that are not the same as those that would truly describe the needs and preferences of someone ready to make such a move.

The second issue that creates a challenge in conducting consumer research intended to help plan a specific assisted living community is the importance of adult children in making the decision for an older family member to move to assisted living. Once again, unless that adult child is actually facing the near-term decision to help a family member move to assisted living, he or she may not have thought about the various issues associated with the decision and the type of community he or she would consider and select. Further, screening and finding potential appropriate adult child respondents can be time-consuming and therefore costly.

Despite the shortcomings in using consumer research directed toward a specific assisted living development, several national studies of great significance have shed light on the characteristics of both the assisted living resident and the adult child decision maker.

"National Survey of Assisted Living Residents: Who Is the Customer?" published in 1998 by ALFA and NIC, presents the results of a comprehensive analysis of contemporary assisted living communities.[16] Managers of 178 communities and their 1,023 residents were surveyed, resulting in a comprehensive profile of communities and residents. While the array of information resulting from this study is extensive, several critical points were made with regard to assisted living residents:

1. The reported incomes and net worth of residents in assisted living communities are substantially lower than currently presumed by feasibility standards and industry benchmarks. This finding has dramatic implications for the future of the industry and may indicate that the industry could be two to three times larger than presumed.
2. Assisted living residents are similar in most demographic characteristics to nursing home residents, but nursing home residents have far greater limitations.
3. Residents' length of stay differs significantly by type of payer, suggesting that residents could stay longer in assisted living if funds were available to pay for it.
4. The satisfaction with the quality of life in the assisted living community, as measured by a single key question, is high for residents of these communities.
5. About half the residents of assisted living communities believe that it was mostly their idea to move to the property. Only 8 percent of residents had no one else involved in the decision-making process. Even though the family may initiate and drive decision making, marketing messages—especially brochures—must be tailored to both groups, and must appeal to the resident.
6. This research confirms previous industry research regarding the profile of typical assisted living residents and contributes new information in many areas, particularly related to the health, physical, and cognitive status of residents.

"NIC National Survey of Adult Children: How They Influence Their Parents' Housing and Care Decisions" reports the results of more than 1,500 telephone survey interviews with adult children age 45 to 64 who are or have been or expect to be responsible for the well-being of a parent, relative, or other older adult.[17] Its purpose was to learn about their roles, knowledge about, and influences on their decisions regarding their relative's housing and care. Some of the study's major conclusions include:

1. Adult children in this category are relatively uninformed about options for independent and assisted living.
2. Terminology about seniors' housing and care was confusing and varied, with 11 different categories used to label congregate living and 22 to label assisted living.
3. More than one-fifth of the adult children whose parent lived at home without services and nearly one-third whose parent received home care felt their parent should move, primarily because of needed health care.
4. Only a small proportion considered either assisted living or independent living as an option for care.
5. More than three-fourths said they had not discussed the cost of care with their older relative, and a like amount said they would provide financial assistance, although nearly two-thirds did not know how much they would contribute.
6. Less than half indicated that their older relative would have sufficient income to pay for seniors' housing or care.
7. More than three-fourths of those whose family members lived in independent or assisted living housing were involved in the decision to move.

The results of these studies, particularly "Who Is the Customer?" have undoubtedly influenced the assumptions used in conducting market feasibility studies for assisted living communities. Of particular significance and certainly the most controversial finding is the one relating to the income levels of assisted living residents that emerged from the first study. Sixty-four percent of residents reported an annual income of $25,000 or less, despite the fact that the mean annual cost of living in the communities surveyed was $24,433.[18] This finding was confirmed in NIC's follow-up study, "Income Confirmation Study of Assisted Living Residents and the Age 75+ Population." Most experienced seniors' housing feasibility consultants have used actual monthly fees proposed for the subject assisted living community to estimate minimum income (as described in Chapter 3). An article published in *Seniors Housing and Care Journal,* however, cautions against using income and assets as a major indicator of demand.[19] To date, most feasibility consultants have not abandoned the approaches to calculating the minimum income that were used in the past, but it will not be surprising to see some changes occurring in what may be considered an overly conservative approach to sizing the market.

Interpreting Consumer Research

A number of issues need to be raised with regard to the analysis and interpretation of consumer research for seniors' housing. They relate to the newness of this industry and to the continuing lack of understanding of the actual target market for most seniors' communities.

Lack of Familiarity with Seniors' Housing

Although seniors' housing has been introduced in most communities, the elderly target market continues to have a very substantial lack of familiarity with and understanding of this concept. Seniors' housing is confused most often with nursing or old age homes and perceived as being a place for the very old, very frail, and often ill segment of the market because they have no other choice. It may also be confused with assisted living, a term that gained enormous market recognition during the 1990s. Alternatively, seniors' housing may be confused with adult communities (i.e., those that target consumers above age 50 but offer few if any services) or with subsidized apartments for the elderly that exist in most markets. Given this confusion and lack of understanding, research conducted among respondents with limited knowledge of the product being tested can yield spurious results. How can one truthfully indicate preferences for something that is fundamentally not understood?

In some cases, the research design incorporates questions that are meant to yield information on respondents' familiarity with the concept being tested. In many cases, this type of question is left unasked. Even when research attempts to determine whether respondents understand various concepts of seniors' housing, rarely are the responses of those who indicate that they are familiar with the type of housing compared with the responses of those who are not.

When respondents are questioned about their knowledge of the product, the results, even when not analyzed as suggested above, can be helpful in determining the type of marketing campaign that needs to be conducted. In markets where respondents seem to have a low level of familiarity and awareness, marketing campaigns clearly need to address the issues of educating the market. In other areas, where awareness is higher, marketing strategies may emphasize differentiating the planned community from others in the market.

Reaching the Target Market

Consumer research for seniors' housing has frequently used data from respondents who do not fit the profile of the target market, particularly in terms of age and income. Many surveys and focus groups reach out to a population older than age 65, rather than older than 70 or 75. As a result, the data often reflect the responses of a substantial number of individuals who are not yet likely to be in the market for seniors' housing. The inclusion of the younger group in this research also can result in an oversampling of couples. When data obtained from such surveys are analyzed on an aggregate basis, the results may be skewed. Younger respondents' answers to many questions are likely to be different from those of their older counterparts. Although we know that age alone is not necessarily directly correlated with interest in seniors' community living, the evidence is clear that such communities draw only occasionally from among the young elderly. At the very least, survey results should be analyzed comparing responses by age group, even if they are broadly defined as those above and below age 75.

In addition, there can be a problem in terms of obtaining data from respondents who are potentially income qualified. When the sample frame uses a list of people who have been income qualified, this point is less of an issue, although there is still evidence that a percentage of those supposedly income qualified will not be (or will not describe themselves as being) qualified.

When the sampling frame incorporates a list representing an affinity group, such as members of religious denominations and fraternal groups or hospital mailing lists, the ability to prequalify the list in terms of income is minimized. Surveys that incorporate both types of sampling frames may find that the pool they have reached is largely nonqualified, particularly with regard to income. As a result, although the responses may be interesting, unless they are screened and analyzed by using the demographic data requested on the survey form, the potential for misinterpretation can be substantially increased.

The Analyst's Bias

One historical complaint from users of feasibility studies is that they have never seen a negative one, implying that all feasibility studies reinforce or support the outcome desired by the client. Moreover, consumer research might be manipulated or misinterpreted to reinforce the analyst's bias. Although this outcome is not necessarily common, some firms that conduct research appear to be oriented toward a particular seniors' housing format, such as continuing care communities that charge an upfront entrance fee. On some occasions, despite survey data suggesting that some other payment mechanism such as monthly rental is favored, recommendations have been made to the contrary because the firm conducting the analysis is primarily experienced in continuing care projects that charge entrance fees. This approach is particularly troublesome when these studies are conducted by research firms that also offer the client marketing and management services. When consumer research studies are commissioned, users should carefully evaluate the results to be comfortable that recommendations actually coincide with and are supported by the data.

On a more basic philosophical level, some take issue with the overall way in which older members of our society are viewed and evaluated.

> We no longer know what such terms as *senior, retiree, maturity market,* and *elderly* mean in qualitative or quantitative terms. We are attempting to find our directions in older markets amid statistical and semantic babble that is largely centered on age as the main determinant in market research, planning, and program execution.[20]

"Lifestyles and attitudes, not age, drive older consumer behavior."[21] Author David Wolfe has criticized the design and interpretation of consumer research aimed at seniors and points out the shortcomings inherent in using a single method of studying older consumers. "How good a survey instrument can someone who is not older create for older respondents? And once such an instrument has been created, how well can such a person interpret the results?"[22]

Relationship of Consumer Research to Marketing

Although a distinction clearly does or should exist between consumer research and project marketing, the two can be and are intermingled. In particular, mail surveys have been used not only to determine preferences of the target market but also to initiate marketing on several levels. First, a survey may be considered an initial step in the marketing program in terms of building awareness. Survey questionnaires accompanied by a description of a proposed project begin the process of letting the target market know that a seniors' housing community is planned. Second, surveys can be used to generate a list of initial leads

Jaime Ardiles-Arce; courtesy AIA

Sun City Kanagawa in Japan includes a clinic, lifestyle service center, assisted living facility, and therapy rooms. Architect: Nihon Sekkei

in several ways. The survey form may include a space for respondents to provide name, address, and phone number. This information might be optional and requested of those who wish to remain informed of the progress of the project planned. An alternative is to include in the mailing a separate reply card that gives recipients an opportunity to indicate their interest without obligating them to respond to the questionnaire. The questionnaire or reply card can also be used to obtain names and addresses of others whom respondents believe may be interested in the project.

Finally, consumer research can be used to identify an initial group of interested individuals who may be invited to continue their involvement in project planning and marketing through membership in an advisory committee. This technique allows prospective residents to develop a sense of ownership in the community, which can result in valuable ongoing feedback in project planning and in reaching their peers through involvement in marketing activities.

Many might argue strongly against confusing consumer research with project marketing. Unfortunately, it has been difficult to persuade many organizations of the value of consumer research (as well as the value of non-consumer-based market analysis). The lack of interest in and understanding of consumer research—and inadequate budgets—can result in the desire to blend marketing research with marketing when an organization is at all inclined toward research.

Notes

1. William R. Dillon, Thomas J. Madden, and Neil H. Firtle, *Marketing Research in a Marketing Environment* (St. Louis: Times Mirror/Mosby College Publishers, 1987), p. 131.

2. Thomas L. Greenbaum, *The Practical Handbook and Guide to Focus Group Research* (Lanham, Md.: Lexington Books, 1988), p. 6.

3. Wendy Gorman and Roy Langmaid, *Qualitative Market Research: A Practitioner's and Buyer's Guide* (Brookfield, Vt.: Gower Publishing Co., 1988), p. 1.

4. Greenbaum, *Practical Handbook and Guide to Focus Group Research,* p. 6.

5. Jeffrey L. Pope, *Practical Marketing Research* (New York: Amacom, 1981), p. 39.

6. Dillon, Madden, and Firtle, *Marketing Research in a Marketing Environment,* p. 139.

7. Paul L. Erdos, *Professional Mail Surveys* (New York: McGraw-Hill, 1970), p. 144.

8. L. Kanuk and C. Berenson, "Mail Surveys and Response Rates: A Literature Review," *Journal of Marketing Research,* November 1975, p. 452.

9. Pope, *Practical Marketing Research,* p. 35.

10. Eric J. Soares, *Cost Effective Marketing Research* (Westport, Conn.: Greenwood Press, 1988), p. 51.

11. Ibid.

12. Ibid., p. 63.

13. A. Weinstein, *Market Segmentation* (Chicago: Probus Publishing Co., 1987), p. 109.

14. Ibid.

15. Ibid., pp. 109–111.

16. Assisted Living Federation of America and National Investment Center, "National Survey of Assisted Living Residents: Who Is the Customer?" 1998, pp. vii–xiv.

17. NIC, "NIC National Survey of Adult Children: How They Influence Their Parents' Housing and Care Decisions," 2000.

18. ALFA and NIC, "National Survey of Assisted Living Residents: Who Is the Customer?" pp. xviii & xxii.

19. Margaret Wylde, "Income and Net Worth of Assisted Living Residents and Their Relationship to Monthly Rates of Assisted Living Communities," *Seniors Housing and Care Journal,* Vol. 8, No. 1 (2000): 59.

20. David A. Wolfe, *Serving the Ageless Market* (New York: McGraw-Hill, 1990), p. 12.

21. Ibid., p. 13.

22. Ibid., p. 24.

James Parker, courtesy AIA

The Gilchrist Center for Hospice Care, Towson, Maryland. Architect: Faith Nevins and Marks, Thomas and Associates, Inc.

5 Financial Analysis and Feasibility Studies

Is the project financially feasible? What will the project have to charge, given the costs associated with development and operation? Is the land cost appropriate for the size of the project being considered and its target market? Should the facility charge entrance fees or rent? What will it cost to build the community, and can the debt be serviced? These and many other questions are addressed in the financial analyses conducted for seniors' communities. Like market analysis, financial analysis can be used for planning purposes and ultimately is required by most financing sources as part of the documentation for the transaction.

Financial analysis and financial feasibility are directly related to the results of and decisions made based on market analysis. On the most fundamental level, the pricing structure and fees that form the basis for revenues must be considered appropriate in the context of the local market and economic segment being targeted. Many decisions regarding the community's features—both architectural and programmatic—are related to what has been learned about the market. And to varying degrees, the absorption and fill rates that drive the projection of revenues and expenses are a function of market conditions and the experience of competitive facilities in reaching full occupancy.

Financial Planning and Preliminary Financial Analysis

In planning the development of a seniors' housing community, financial analysis can and should be a critical element. If a market analysis has been conducted and supports proceeding with the project, financial analysis and testing what-if scenarios should follow. Financial analysis should take into consideration the guidance and recommendations that result from the market analysis. In some ways, the ultimate test of market feasibility relies on financial analysis. For until some level of financial analysis is conducted, the analyst and client cannot be certain that the recommended size, price, and programmatic features will result in a financially viable project, given the attendant financial considerations. A key in continuing to plan and implement the development of a seniors' housing community is that the major features that affect the community's financial performance must be weighed and evaluated. The financial analysis is an iterative process because of the interrelationship of the project's key elements. For instance, project sizing, the level of services, and the economic target market affect unit pricing. Preliminary financial analyses can be used to test the impact of each key variable that affects the financial performance of the community and to answer questions about potential project viability and performance.

Contractual Structure

Preliminary decisions may be reached early in project planning regarding the type of contractual structure to be employed in the project. An organization may have determined, for instance, whether it prefers to charge an entrance fee, offer its units for sale as a condominium or cooperative, or charge a straight monthly rental fee. How residents will pay for the right to reside in the community and receive services must be further refined, however. For example, for projects with entrance fees, it must be decided whether those fees will be fully or partially refundable. Nonrefundable fees are typically as much as 50 percent lower than refundable fees. This differential is tied to the magnitude of cash infusion from turnover of the units. All else being equal, a nonrefundable entrance fee structure yields more cash to the community when a unit turns over than does a refundable entrance fee structure. This additional cash, along with monthly service fees, can be used to support the operations of the community. The community charging a refundable entrance fee receives less upfront usable cash and therefore must substantially support operations from the monthly service fees because so much is used to pay the refund of the prior occupant.

In some cases, entrance fees become nonrefundable immediately upon the resident's move into the seniors' community. In other cases, a grace period is written into the residency agreement allowing for some portion if not all of the fee to be refunded if the resident chooses to leave the community during a short, specified period after moving in.

Refundable entrance fees can be structured in a variety of configurations. For instance, the fee can be fully refundable, or a percentage of the entrance fee may be refunded to the resident or his or her estate. Partially refundable fees, which return 75 to 90 percent of the initial fee, are not unusual. Sometimes, entrance fees are in effect amortized at a specified rate, such as 2 percent per month. In some cases, facilities that amortize entrance fees do so over 50 months, so that after this period, the fee is totally nonrefundable. In other cases, the entrance fee amortization may stop at a certain point, providing a partial refund (e.g., 60 or 70 percent).

The impact of refundability is not felt until a project matures and begins to experience turnover in its units. Financial projections are often done for five-year periods, thereby minimizing the effect of turnover and the financial obligations that are implicit in the way projects have been structured. For planning purposes, financial analysis for projects with refundable entrance fees are more useful when constructed on a ten-year basis, providing the organization with a better understanding of how turnover will affect the facility's cash flow, balance sheet, and financial position.

In the case of rental facilities, decisions must be made about whether, given the debt service and operation costs, the monthly rental will be affordable to the market being targeted. Because no front-end fees are available to pay down some of the construction or permanent financing, charges for a rental project are less flexible. Although some modifications can be made by treating certain services on a fee-for-service basis, few ways exist other than increasing the equity contribution to lower the monthly fees charged to residents.

Project Sizing

Decisions regarding size of the seniors' housing community are instrumental in analyzing its financial viability. The factor having the most direct influence on a community's maximum development potential is the parcel of land on which it will be developed and the zoning regulations that govern the site. The market analysis, however, provides feedback and guidance to the developer on project size in the context of potential market size and competitive activity. These factors help the architect and developer consider alternatives regarding overall size of a planned seniors' community. They also influence decisions about the potential for building the development in single or multiple phases.

The components that will be encompassed by the seniors' housing community are all factored into the financial analysis. Options regarding types of units, levels of care, unit mix and size, and amount and use of common space all play important roles in financial planning and analysis. Once again, feedback from the market influences these issues.

During preliminary financial analysis, issues regarding project size and configuration can be evaluated. For instance, development phasing can be assessed to determine the components that would be required in each phase and costs associated with their development, which in turn directly influence operating expenses. Scenarios can be evaluated to determine how large the first phase of a project must be to be self-supporting without placing an undue financial burden on the residents who occupy the units at this stage of the project.

Pricing

The price required for residents to live in the community is clearly key to the community's financial viability. In many cases, market analysis provides the initial guidelines on what price ranges are best suited to the economic target market sought and how those prices compare with prices charged by other facilities in the market area. The market analysis may result in specific recommendations on price ranges by unit type. Market-driven and market-acceptable pricing must, however, be tested to determine whether it is achievable given the cost of developing and operating the proposed community. What may make great sense in the context of the market may be difficult to achieve, given the realities of costs associated with building and running the community.

Certain issues should be kept in mind when testing a proposed pricing scheme. For projects that plan to charge entrance fees, those fees should reflect the same economic target market as the monthly fees. For example, a community that offers its units for entrance fees starting at $200,000 should be charging commensurate monthly fees. Low monthly fees combined with high entrance fees send a mixed message to the market. In addition, it is unlikely that a community that targets the affluent could realistically offer low monthly service fees. Affluent consumers' expectations for service dictate higher costs associated with the number and quality of staff and the type of food service program. These two items alone make up the largest share of the operating expenses that typically drive monthly fees.

Financial analysis is also critical for projects such as most assisted living communities that plan to charge only monthly rent. Once again, the analysis must test the fees that appear to be marketable to determine whether, given the cost of debt service and operations, these rates are achievable. Early financial analyses can be used to determine whether additional equity, for instance, needs to be raised for the project to lower the costs associated with servicing the debt. They are also useful in determining whether certain services need to be modified or perhaps offered on a fee-for-service basis.

A frequently underestimated pricing element, particularly in CCRCs, is the *second-person fee* charged for an additional resident in a unit. Some CCRCs add a second-person fee to both the entrance and monthly fees. Many others have limited the second-person fee to the monthly charges. The critical factor with regard to second-person fees is whether the community offers nursing care on a self-insured basis, as traditional CCRCs or life care communities have done. In the event that the community is self-insuring, the second-person fee must accommodate the additional costs of providing this care to two residents in a single unit. Although the additional costs associated with other services are relatively incremental, the costs of providing long-term nursing care are the same for the first resident of a unit as for the second and must be treated as such when determining project pricing.

Services

A critical element in evaluating the potential financial performance of a proposed seniors' housing community is the level of services. Operating expenses for a community directly reflect the services being provided and offered to residents. The operating budget must be constructed to reflect the staffing, food, and other costs necessary to operate the community. This point is also where the developer can and should evaluate using contract service providers or handling all services in house.

To a large extent, the service program is dictated by the relative level of independence and/or functional capacity of the market being targeted and the economic segment to which the community is planned to appeal. The frailer the population, the heavier the service program. The more independent the target market, the fewer the services that must be used and paid for in the standard fee structure. In addition, projects that target a more affluent market reflect it in their service packages.

Assisted living facilities often have a tiered pricing structure to reflect the differing levels of care provided to residents. Typically, a facility may offer three levels of care based on the amount of personal assistance an individual resident may require in the course of a day. Personal assistance services are usually priced based on half-hour or hourly increments, with as much as $300 to $400 per month

Michael Pyatok; courtesy AIA

Puyallup Silvercrest Senior Housing includes 41 one-bedroom apartments for low-income senior citizens of Puyallup, Washington. Developed for the Salvation Army, it is built on a two-acre parcel located adjacent to an existing Army Corps building that will provide support services. The plan preserved a small stream and wetland area, and the entire site is accessible to disabled persons. The project was built with HUD 202 funding. Architect: Ronald F. Murphy

differential between levels of service. Estimating the mix of care residents require (and the associated revenue and expenses of providing the additional services) is difficult for new facilities. One needs to estimate not only the care level of the resident upon entering the facility but also whether or not the resident will require a different care level as he or she ages. Factors such as the target market, programs offered, design of the facility, and mix of residents at other similar facilities in the market area need to be evaluated and considered when estimating the mix of care level for residents in a new facility.

For communities that incorporate nursing care, costs associated with providing the care must be evaluated. Will the community offer a limited amount of free care to residents or a fully insured package of long-term care services? If the free care is to be limited, how many days should be provided, and should they be cumulative or available only on a yearly basis? What are the operating expenses associated with the provision of long-term health care? How much will be recovered directly from fees, and how much will have to be subsidized by creating reserves from entrance and monthly fees? A most important consideration, particularly for facilities that are to be self-insured, is the anticipated turnover and use of the health care unit. As mentioned, the typical five-year period reflected in financial projections will not provide enough time to evaluate these issues and should be extended to at least a ten-year period for purposes of analyzing the financial implications of health care coverage.

Development Costs

The four major categories that contribute to the cost of developing a seniors' housing community include land, site improvements, construction costs, and marketing costs. In addition, the architect's fees, legal and accounting fees, the developer's fees (if applicable), and financing costs are all part of the total project cost.

Several issues must be considered and factored into the financial analysis when planning the development of a community. Land costs must be kept in line with total development costs and must reflect the economic market segment being targeted. Other than for projects targeting an extremely upscale market or in markets where average housing values are very high, land costs, including site development, can be expected to fall into a range of $10,000 to $15,000 per unit. One must consider the costs associated with site preparation and improvement. Sites that require excessive costs to develop a project will add substantially to the unit cost, which must be considered in evaluating whether the project will be affordable to the market being targeted. Construction costs can cover a very wide range based on such factors as type of facility, materials and finishes, and the presence of union labor requirements. Controls over these development costs must be maintained to keep project pricing in line with the target market.

Early studies tended to underestimate marketing costs, which are affected by numerous factors, including the type of marketing program and marketing media being used as well as conditions in the market. For example, for projects targeting a broad geographic area, marketing costs will be higher than for those targeting the immediate local area. The longer the fill period, the higher the costs of marketing a community, and a slow residential resale market, such as that characterizing the late 1980s and early 1990s, can contribute. Marketing costs may also have an indirect relationship to the depth of the market, with lower costs in deeper markets and vice versa. Per-unit costs for marketing seniors' housing communities may range from $10,000 to $13,000 for CCRCs, with exceptions at both ends of the range, and $3,000 to $5,000 for assisted living facilities.

Debt Structure

Once the basic assumptions associated with revenues and expenses are formulated, financial analysis can be used to evaluate the debt structure for the seniors' community. For rental facilities, alternative scenarios balancing equity and debt can be evaluated, particularly with regard to their impact on pricing. When the framework for the financial projections and assumptions has been established, the amount of equity required to bring the pricing of the project in line with the target market can be tested, enabling the developer to assess whether sufficient equity can be found to both meet the requirements of a lender and bring project pricing in at a level acceptable to the market.

For projects that involve the payment of an entrance fee, how much long-term debt will be required can be analyzed, given the equity being put into the project and the use of resident entrance fees if allowable. A balance may be achieved that will permit some entrance fee funds to be used to pay down the construction loan, thereby reducing debt. For those entrance fee projects that are financed through tax-exempt bonds, restrictions regarding the use of resident funds must be factored into this analysis. As described earlier, many states have legislation and regulations that restrict the use of resident funds. In addition, as detailed earlier, rating agencies have very specific restrictions on the use of entrance fee funds for bonds that are to be rated. Start-up facilities cannot be rated, however, because they have no history.

Another component of the debt structure that emerges during the financial analysis is the potential need for a working capital loan during the project's start-up years. An operating cash shortfall is likely to occur during the early years as the community moves toward full, stabilized occupancy. In addition, the difficulty of accurately projecting fill-up and the experience of most facilities suggest that operating reserves should be planned to accommodate variations in performance from those projected or forecast. The way in which the project is capitalized governs the extent to which working capital loans may be necessary. When factoring in debt service, however, it is critical that this issue be dealt with appropriately.

Risk

All organizations, whether for-profit or nonprofit, must evaluate the risk associated with proceeding with the development of a seniors' housing community. The financial analysis is a tool for measuring and determining the level of risk involved and the level that is acceptable to the organization. Some key variables considered in this assessment are the project's reserve funds, cash balances, and capital replacement reserves. In cases where the financing involves tax-exempt bonds or in some states that regulate CCRCs, reserves are stipulated by the investor, underwriter, rating agency, or state regulations.

Once all the assumptions have been made and financial projections prepared, the organization that will own the community can determine whether, given cash flow, debt service, and reserves, the return warrants the level of perceived risk associated with the undertaking. For some nonprofit organizations, depending on their reasons for developing the project, reaching a break-even point and adequately funding replacement reserves may be sufficient to warrant proceeding with the project. For those that seek to generate excess revenue to achieve other organizational goals, a surplus cash position may be necessary before the decision to proceed can be reached. The issue of risk and reward for proprietary organizations is more difficult. For publicly held corporations, the overriding objective of satisfying stockholders has made seniors' housing a difficult area for diversification because of the lengthy development and start-up period during which investment far outweighs returns. Even for private, for-profit organizations, the perceived level of risk has not always matched the quality of the financial returns, particularly during the generally lengthy start-up period.

Financial Screening Criteria

A market analysis for a seniors' housing community involves establishing a minimum income for elderly households to estimate the size of the pool that may qualify for residency. Once the financial analysis has been conducted during planning for the community, it is important, given the refinements made to pricing, to look back and determine whether the income criteria originally established are still appropriate. Most people involved in the seniors' housing industry assume that monthly fees should not be more than 50 to 65 percent of household pretax income for independent living and 75 to 80 percent for assisted living. Using these numbers as a test, the developer should reexamine the assumptions made in the market analysis and make any necessary adjustments to determine whether, given the realities of project pricing, a sufficient potential resident base still exists.

Financial Forecasts for Use in Financing Documents

Financial feasibility studies for a project are of interest to a broad spectrum of parties, including management, lending institutions, and government agencies. Financial feasibility studies for projects financed by tax-exempt bonds generally include a financial forecast. The American Institute of Certified Public Accountants defines financial forecasts as:

> ...prospective financial statements that present, to the best of the responsible party's knowledge and belief, an entity's expected financial position, results of operations, and changes in financial position. A financial forecast is based on the responsible party's assumptions reflecting conditions it expects to exist and the course of action it expects to take.[1]

The financial forecast is appropriate for general use documents, such as public offering statements. *General use* refers to the use of the financial forecast by lenders or investors with whom the responsible party (i.e., the sponsor or owner of the project) is not negotiating directly.

Financial Guidelines

The investing public, made up primarily of banks, pension funds, institutional investors, and individuals through direct purchase or mutual funds, has historically applied investing criteria from other industries (i.e., real estate and health care) in evaluating the credit of a seniors' housing community. In recent years, however, as more and more seniors' housing communities have been developed and financed and their actual financial results gathered and analyzed, certain guidelines and investing criteria have emerged specific to the industry. In addition, some accounting and auditing standards for CCRCs have evolved.

Some of the more sophisticated financial guidelines for investment in CCRCs have been developed by the major credit-rating agencies, specifically Standard & Poors and Fitch, Duff & Phelps. None of the rating agencies as a matter of company policy issue an investment-grade rating to a start-up CCRC unless there is some investment-grade form of third-party credit enhancement supporting the underlying financing. The rating agencies believe that a start-up project credit profile is too risky to warrant an investment-grade rating. The single most important element of risk in a start-up project is the initial fill-up period, which consumes both time and large amounts of capital. Start-up CCRCs are still financed by both conventional lenders and through the issuance of nonrated tax-exempt bonds, although at generally higher rates of interest than investment-grade-rated debt.

Another useful source of financial information on CCRCs is issued by the Continuing Care Accreditation Commission (CCAC), an independent accrediting organization sponsored by AAHSA. In conjunction with Ziegler Capital Markets Group and KPMG, CCAC publishes financial ratios computed from the audited financial statements of accredited CCRCs.

Although the rating agencies do not issue investment-grade ratings to start-up CCRCs and, conversely, start-up projects are usually not submitted to the rating agencies, the rating criteria issued by the agencies and the financial information contained in the CCAC ratios publication can serve as valuable guidelines. The developer of a project is advised to be familiar with the rating guidelines because they can be useful during the financial structuring of a start-up facility and are often incorporated into the underwriting requirements of both lenders and investment bankers. The next five subsections reflect some of the financial guidelines incorporated into the rating criteria and information contained in the CCAC survey.

Fitch has issued guidelines for rating freestanding assisted living facilities. Start-up assisted living facilities generally do not have the financial characteristics necessary to achieve an investment-grade rating. Unlike for CCRCs, rating guidelines for assisted living do not address such areas as presales, but financial characteristics such as liquidity and debt service coverage are evaluated.

Presale Requirements

Rating agency guidelines encompass both the market and financial areas of a project. The most significant market guideline is that a minimum number of residential units must be presold. Some guidelines also address refundability of the deposit. Various presale levels are set forth, depending on the period an organization has been in operation (more or fewer than five years) and whether the organization operates multiple facilities. The minimum presale requirements range from 50 to 75 percent of the total project's independent living units being financed. A presale is defined as a minimum deposit of at least 10 percent of the entrance fee or $1,000, whichever is higher.

Entrance Fees and Escrow Funds

The guidelines concerning the relationship between entrance fees and project costs are flexible, depending on the scope of services being offered. Entrance fees or up-front fees and any equity contributions should equal at least 60 percent of total project costs. Total project costs include the debt service reserve fund, if applicable, and funded interest. For communities charging entrance fees upon completion of a project and beginning of operations, a percentage of the initial entrance fees received should be escrowed and restricted for refunds, debt service, working capital (to be considered a loan and repaid within 24 months), and replacement of plant, property, and equipment.

Debt Service Reserve Fund

A project financed with bonds usually includes a debt service reserve fund. Generally, a minimum of one year's annual debt service (principal and interest) is to be funded at the time of bond closing. In certain circumstances, an acceptable letter of credit for the full amount or for any deficit in the debt service reserve fund may be substituted.

Operating Reserve Fund and Overall Cash Reserves

Both state regulations (if applicable) and lenders usually require operating cash reserves. Typically, a single reserve fund can satisfy the requirements of several entities. For instance, in many states, the debt service reserve fund required by the lender or investor is sufficient to meet the reserve requirements of state regulations applicable to CCRCs. Many lenders and bond covenants, however, require an operating reserve fund to be funded in addition to those cash reserves required by state regulatory agencies. Typical operating reserve fund requirements range from 30 to 60 days' worth of cash operating expenses.

Many lenders also require a reserve for capital improvements and replacements. This cash reserve fund is usually funded over time and can be borrowed from periodically for necessary capital expenditures.

Overall cash reserve requirements vary, depending on the program of services offered. Facilities that offer health care guarantees of service that are not covered by resident charges are required to maintain a ratio of total cash reserves available (including the operating reserve fund, the reserve for capital improvement fund, and letters of credit) to total debt (reserve ratio) equal to the higher of 30 to 35 percent of total outstanding debt or at least three times annual debt service. Facilities that cover health care services through a fee-for-service arrangement or do not offer such services generally are required to have a lower overall reserve ratio.

Funded Interest

Funded interest during construction should be equal to the anticipated interest expense on the loan during the construction fill-up periods. It is recommended that an additional three to six months of interest expense be funded as a contingency for construction delays.

Debt Service Coverage

All bond financings include covenants by the borrower that it will maintain rates charged to residents at a level high enough to produce a minimum debt service coverage. Debt service coverage measures the ability of a project to service debt from ongoing operations by measuring the ratio of funds available for debt service to debt service. Both annual operating and nonoperating income and annual cash flow from entrance fees resulting from unit turnover (net of refunds) are used as funds to cover annual debt service. Typical rate covenants require annual debt service coverage for entrance fee projects (the ratio of available funds to annual debt service) of at least 110 to 120 percent. This ratio should not include reserve funds (i.e., debt service reserve fund or escrowed entrance fees) but cash flow generated from annual operations. The debt coverage ratio of 110 percent should apply by the third full year of operation. The minimum debt service coverage ratio for rental projects, especially those financed by banks, tends to be closer to 120 percent. Meeting these minimum coverage requirements does not alone indicate that the project is financially feasible and will be able to satisfy underwriting criteria.

Financial Feasibility

The financial structure of a seniors' housing community influences the approach to the financial analysis of a project. The financial analysis of projects structured as rental facilities is relatively straightforward and should concentrate on revenues, expenses, and cash flow ratios, such as operating margin and debt service coverage.

Financial analysis of entrance fee projects, especially those that subsidize future health care costs, is more sophisticated. The financial analysis of these projects should, in addition to revenue and expense ratios, focus on liquidity ratios (i.e., days of cash on hand), profitability ratios (i.e., operating ratio), and capital structure ratios (i.e., debt service coverage).

Amortizing entrance fees for financial reporting evenly over the expected life of residents may understate the financial viability of certain well-managed facilities.

The factors that must be considered in developing assumptions for revenues, operating expenses, and cash flow are described in the remainder of this chapter.

Revenues

The seniors' housing community's revenues and cash flow can be generated through the payment of entrance fees, condominium or cooperative purchase prices, membership fees, and/or monthly fees, which may cover the costs of operations and some or all of the debt service for the facility. The revenue assumptions must reflect the anticipated absorption or fill pace and should also take into consideration that some turnover will begin even in the first year of operation. In addition, they should reflect any predetermined policies regarding price changes that may be planned during the initial fill period as well as planned annual increases in monthly and upfront fees based on the stipulations expressed in the residency agreement. Some nonoperating revenue in the form of interest earnings or dividends can also be generated, particularly for communities charging upfront fees. Whether interest income is classified as operating or nonoperating revenue depends on whether management considers the income to be essential for ongoing operations. If the nonoperating revenue is essential to supporting ongoing operations, it should be classified as operating income.

Entrance Fees and Condominium and Cooperative Purchase Fees

Depending on the financial structure of the community, revenues and cash flow can be generated through the payment of upfront fees (entrance fees, condominium or cooperative fees, and membership fees) and/or monthly fees. The generation of revenue can begin once a unit is reserved, although particularly with entrance fees, the reservation deposit is often protected against use by the developer and placed in an escrow fund (which may be governed by state regulations in states with CCRC legislation). Once the community is operational and residents begin moving into the units, the revenue volume generated by payment of the full upfront fees accelerates at the pace at which units are absorbed. Depending on the way the community is operated, the full fee may be paid at the point at which the unit is occupied or at an earlier stage subsequent to the final and firm reservation. In some cases, communities require that an upfront fee be paid in phases before and at the point of occupancy. These arrangements should be described specifically in the residency agreement. Some facilities have special introductory pricing during a specified time period; however, upfront fees may be increased for units occupied after the specified time.

If all or a portion of the entrance fee is nonrefundable, that portion of the fee is earned equally over the average life expectancy of a resident, typically considered approximately 12 years after moving into the community. If the entrance fee is refundable, the refundable portion of the entrance fee is amortized over the remaining asset life of the unit, and the nonrefundable portion is amortized over the average life expectancy of the resident. Increases in entrance fees and condominium or cooperative fees can be factored into the projection as units turn over and are reoccupied.

Many CCRCs have contractual arrangements with their residents to provide future services. The future cost of these services is compared with the unamortized portion of the entrance fees or deferred revenue. If the projected cost of the services exceeds the unamortized deferred revenue, then an unfunded liability exists and is recorded on the facility's balance sheet as a liability. If deferred revenue is greater than projected costs, nothing is recorded on the balance sheet. Sound actuarial assumptions regarding mortality and morbidity rates of residents are important to the calculation of the costs of future services. Most investors expect a CCRC to have an up-to-date actuarial study.

Monthly Service Fees

In seniors' housing communities, monthly fees are typically designed to cover the costs of operating the community and a portion of annual debt service. The proportion of debt service covered depends on the type of resident contract. For those communities that employ a fee-for-service contract, monthly service fees should be set to cover debt service as well as operating costs. Although most seniors' communities rely to some degree on entrance fees received from unit turnover to help cover debt service, the greater the reliance on entrance fees, the greater the risk. For rental facilities, monthly fees must also be sufficient to cover the debt service and to set aside some funds for replacement reserves. In life care communities, a portion of the monthly fee is also intended to cover the resident's future health care costs. The generation of revenue through monthly fees accelerates at the rate at which the community expects to occupy its units and is therefore based on the use or absorption schedule developed. As indicated, it is best to be conservative in forecasting a community's fill rate, particularly given the experience of existing facilities. Revenue based on monthly fees should take into account the payment of second-person occupancy fees. The percentage of units forecast to have second occupants is based on a number of factors. The first is the type of community. Seniors' communities offering independent living units have a much larger proportion of second occupants (usually married couples) than assisted living units. In assisted living communities, a second occupant is more likely to live in a unit designed for shared (or semiprivate) occupancy where each occupant is charged a separate fee. In independent living, the unit mix must be considered. A community with a large number of two-bedroom units might expect a larger percentage of double occupancy than one with small one-bedroom and studio units. In addition, some consideration should be given to the fact that in independent living, double occupancy is likely to decline as the community matures and residents lose spouses to death or transfer to the health care unit (whether or not it is part of the community). Forecasts as high as 40 percent double occupancy may be appropriate in the early years of the community, but a decline to 25 percent might be anticipated after seven to ten years. Monthly fee revenue should be increased annually based on the consumer price index or some other index. The basis for the increase is usually delineated in the residency agreement.

Additional revenue might be generated by allowing residents to purchase more meals than the contract specifically includes in the monthly fee. Additional sources of revenue are fees for guest services (meals, overnight accommodations) and for additional use of other services, such as housekeeping and specially arranged transportation.

Monthly fees in assisted living facilities should reflect the mix of care service provided to residents. If no empirical evidence exists in the market area with respect to the mix of care levels, a reasonable assumption is that 25 to 30 percent of the residents of a new facility probably require additional services.

Health Care Unit

Use of the health care unit is influenced by the general demographics of the area population where the seniors' community is located as well as the residents of the community, the ratio of residential units to nursing beds in the community, demographic characteristics of residents residing in the community, state regulations regarding nursing units in CCRCs, medical screening criteria and philosophy employed by management, and provisions of the resident care agreement regarding use of the nursing unit.

For communities with a health care (nursing) unit, routine revenue is a function of the number of patient days times the daily room rate. As with other types of living units, these rates should be increased annually. Ancillary revenues reflect the additional fees paid for therapies and drugs (as well as use of the beauty or barber shop) and are sometimes forecast as a percentage of routine revenues (4 to 5 percent is typical).

In life care communities that insure the resident against the cost of long-term health care in the health care center, residents who are transferred usually pay the monthly service fee as their base rate. Additional items, such as extra meals (not covered by the monthly service fee), drugs, and therapies, are paid on a fee-for-service basis. Arrangements in other seniors' housing communities may differ, depending on how the resident contract is structured. This structure affects both temporary and permanent transfers. For instance, in some newer communities, a certain number of "free days" in the health center are provided to the resident annually or cumulatively. Contractual allowances must be factored into the health care revenue forecasts based on regulations of third-party payers (Medicare or Medicaid).

Nonoperating Revenue

Several sources of nonoperating revenue are possible for a seniors' housing community, particularly one that charges entrance fees. Interest earnings represent the major source of nonoperating revenue (in some instances interest earnings may be classified as operating revenue). Interest earnings may be generated on escrowed entrance fees or, for bond-financed projects, on trustee-held funds, including the debt service reserve fund, bond funds, and other reserve funds. When developing assumptions on interest-generated nonoperating revenue, it is important to match the appropriate interest rate to the liquidity requirements of the funds being invested. For example, operating reserve funds should be kept in highly liquid investment vehicles, such as money market funds. Reserves that are less likely to be called on can be invested in longer-term instruments.

Other sources of nonoperating revenue include bequests and contributions (which may be more pertinent for nonprofit than for for-profit facilities). In cases where estates and other sources provide contributions and bequests to facilities, the specific conditions under which the bequest has been made must be taken into consideration in the forecast. Bequests and contributions can be unrestricted and used to fund operations as designated, used to fund a specific capital project, or placed in a capital replacement fund.

Operating Expenses

It is critical that the pattern of operating expenses reflect the characteristics of the program that the seniors' housing community will offer. A wide range of expenses exists, based on such items as the number of employees, number of meals and type of food being served, and nature of the services offered. Staffing and other expense patterns are not necessarily interchangeable from one community to another unless those communities have similar programs, operating philosophies, overall sizes (in terms of building and campus), and economic target markets. For example, a facility that intends to target and serve an upscale market should reflect residents' expectations. Larger living units and more staff to provide more services should be anticipated, as should increases in salaries and food costs. Assisted living facilities that will offer residents multiple levels of care must match staffing levels and other costs to residents' estimated use of higher care levels.

Forecasting expenses should also reflect the fact that certain types of expenses are overhead and fixed (that is, incurred even before the facility opens), while others are variable or incremental. Fixed expenses include administrative costs, real estate taxes, utilities, and a certain staff level in each department. Other expenses such as certain service staff (housekeeping, food service) and food costs tend to vary based on the level of occupancy.

Salaries/Wages and Employee Benefits

The number and type of employees at a seniors' housing community should reflect both the service program and, to a certain extent, the community's economic target market. Facilities designed to serve an affluent target market, for instance, might have higher staff-to-resident ratios than those designed to serve a moderate-income group. Staffing for seniors' housing communities, for purposes of developing operating forecasts, is always expressed as ***full-time equivalent*** workers.

Labor costs, including employee benefits, represent the single largest expense in the operating budget. These costs may range from 50 to 60 percent of all operating expenses. Salaries and wages must be comparable with those available in the geographic area. Underestimating salaries and wages is not unusual in forecasting operating expenses. In some cases, underestimating is caused by using starting salaries as comparables rather than salaries being earned by people with more experience in particular positions. Forecasts for certain positions, particularly in health care facilities, must take into consideration whether union contracts apply and must reflect not only appropriate salaries for union employees but also contractual obligations regarding wage increases. Those increases may exceed the rate of inflation, which is typically used in forecasting wage increases for nonunion staff. Forecasts for expansion of facilities should also take into consideration typical salary and wage rates for similar positions.

Employee benefits reflect the policies of the organization that owns and/or manages the community and may be based on historical experience at similar facilities or, in cases of expansion, at the facility itself. Expenses for benefits are generally increased during the forecast period because of the likelihood of increases in health benefits and periodic increases that occur in Social Security, unemployment, and other taxes.

Food

The cost of food reflects the type of food service program offered and the economic target market of the community. In some seniors' housing communities, particularly those oriented toward less affluent markets, choices on the menu may be more limited than in facilities targeting an affluent market. This factor must be taken into account when estimating food costs. Food costs are calculated per meal and are variable. The number of meals estimated should reflect the occupancy level of the community as it fills as well as the rate of double occupancy. In communities that include only one meal per day in the fee, the number of individuals who will take additional meals if they are available must be estimated. In addition, some allowance must be made for guest meals.

In some newer communities that offer a pay-as-used meal program, forecasting food costs is somewhat more difficult. To maintain a greater level of control over this rather significant budgetary item, communities might consider offering a certain number of meals per month as part of the service program covered by the monthly fee. This approach allows for greater planning in budgeting and food purchases. Even in communities that offer only a pay-for-service meal program, patterns of consumption emerge rather soon after the facility has a critical mass of residents, thereby allowing better planning for future food service budgeting.

The statistical basis for estimating food costs historically was influenced by the more institutional counterparts of seniors' housing communities: nursing homes and hospitals. In recent years, however, estimates for food costs have improved as the information base has improved. Annual studies by the American Association of Homes for the Aging and ASHA include information on meal costs from facilities that participate in those studies. In addition, food service management companies that specialize in seniors' housing communities can provide valuable input about estimating food costs.

Utilities

The most reliable way of calculating utility costs is per square foot, rather than using estimates from supposedly comparable facilities. Utility costs are influenced substantially by several factors, making comparisons with other facilities difficult. Utility costs vary based on, in addition to overall size of the facility, age of the facility, type of construction, presence (or lack of) energy conservation systems, and region of the country.

Assumptions for utility costs should be based on all these factors. Accuracy depends on consultation with the architect for the community and with local utility companies. The utility company should provide not only current rates but also information on potential rate increases. Rather than increasing rates annually, utility companies tend to raise rates periodically, and increases frequently are higher than inflation rates for the area.

Real Estate Taxes, Insurance, and Other Operating Expenses

Real estate taxes have become part of the budget at both for-profit and nonprofit facilities. In the latter case, payments for the actual tax rate or a payment in lieu of taxes may be required as municipalities seek to protect their tax base. Estimates of real estate taxes can be based on the appraised value of the new facility, if available, or on construction costs if no appraisal is available. Local taxing authorities should be consulted to find the area's tax rates. Assumptions about real estate taxes should also take into consideration the availability, if pertinent, of any tax abatement provisions that may apply to the facility.

Estimates for property and liability insurance can be developed by consulting with representatives of insurance companies.

Other operating expenses that should be included are administrative costs of the community and repair and maintenance. Administrative costs are typically fixed and cover those items required to operate the facility's office and management functions. Repair and maintenance expenses are frequently underestimated for new facilities when management assumes incorrectly that few repairs and little maintenance will be required. Underestimating is also a problem for seniors' housing communities built on large campuses, which require substantially more staff and materials than more compact facilities. The size, layout, and design of a seniors' housing community directly affect costs associated with maintaining it and must be taken into consideration in making assumptions.

Depreciation and Interest

Depreciation is a noncash fixed expense. A fixed cost for a project is a cost whose total amount is unaffected by changes in the number of residents living in the facility. For financial reporting purposes and typical feasibility studies, annual depreciation is calculated on a straight-line basis over the expected useful life of the asset. Depreciation expense is adjusted to correspond to increases in plant and equipment (capital additions) during the period covered by the feasibility study. Depreciation, because it is a noncash expense, is generally not significant in determining a project's financial viability.

Interest expense is directly related to the terms and size of the loan. Interest expense on tax-exempt bond issues is generally paid semiannually to the bondholders. The facility usually makes monthly payments to a trustee bank, however, which in turn pays bondholders every six months. Important analytical tools in determining a project's financial viability include the amount of annual debt service payments (interest and principal) in relation to annual cash flow generated by the project (debt service coverage ratio) and to cash balances (cash to debt ratio).

Note

1. Financial Forecasts and Projections Task Force, *Guide to Prospective Financial Statements* (New York: American Institute of Certified Public Accountants, 1986), Section 200.04.

Rick Alexander; courtesy AIA

The "wandering garden" at the Forest at Duke in Durham, North Carolina, was designed specifically for the cognitively impaired residents of the community. The garden includes a variety of paths, benches, an arbor with a gate that residents can open and pass through, a pond with a waterfall, and swings beneath a trellis. Architect: Alan Moore

6 Market Segmentation

What is market segmentation? How does it affect the seniors' housing industry? What are the various segments that constitute the aging market? What distinguishes one segment from another? How does one evaluate which segments a seniors' community will serve? How does one plan, design, and market seniors' communities for differing market segments?

Market segmentation is an established and important part of marketing. Wendell R. Smith first described the concept in 1956 in *Journal of Marketing*. Smith compared two alternative marketing strategies, market segmentation and product differentiation. He described segmentation as the viewing of "a heterogeneous market (one characterized by divergent demand) as a number of smaller homogeneous markets in response to differing product preferences among important market segments."[1] Segmentation is a way to identify, understand, and better meet customers' needs and desires. A survey conducted in 1986 of 303 marketing executives ranked segmentation third among 18 "pressure points" most important to the marketing function.[2]

Although segmentation originally was applied primarily to the consumer products industries, it has found application in other industries. In the 1980s, segmentation began to emerge as a component of both analysis and marketing strategies in real estate and health care. Increasing competition and complexity led to a greater focus on marketing. In these industries, where marketing had not been particularly sophisticated, segmentation strategies became part of the marketing equation.

As segmentation has developed over the past several decades as an intrinsic part of marketing, a substantial body of related literature has appeared. Many writings have resulted from academic explorations of segmentation, although numerous examples of real-world applications and examples also have been described. Like many other aspects of market research and marketing, however, definitions and dimensions of market segmentation have been subject to widely varying descriptions and interpretations. In an article that appeared roughly 20 years after Smith's seminal article defining market segmentation and market differentiation, the same *Journal of Marketing* published a piece on the persistent confusion between the two terms. The authors point out that their "review of 16 contemporary marketing textbooks reveals considerable confusion"[3] and indicates that segmentation has been viewed both as a form of research and as a marketing strategy.[4]

This chapter explores market segmentation and its application to seniors' housing. The background information on segmentation is not intended as a thorough review of the literature in the field but as a basis for the discussion of the application of segmentation to the seniors' housing industry.

Components of Market Segmentation

Market Segmentation describes the many approaches to segmenting markets and discusses some of the most common dimensions of segmentation. The author groups the bases for segmentation into two broad categories: "physical and behavioral attributes."[5]

Physical Attributes

Physical attributes common to segmentation include such things as geographic area and demographic and socioeconomic characteristics. For example, a market may be geographically segmented according to a national, statewide, or local scope, or might be defined by population density, climate-related factors, or standardized classifications such as those created by the U.S. Census Bureau.[6]

Demographic segmentation is related to population characteristics, such as individuals, households, family size, age distribution, gender, marital status, and ethnic and religious background. Socioeconomic measures of market segments include income, educational levels, occupational information, housing tenure, housing values or rents, types of dwelling units, and so forth. Demographic and socioeconomic characteristics are frequently considered together as *demographics.*[7] Although demographics is one of the most common approaches to market segmentation, it has limitations. The sole use of demographic segmentation may lead to the incorrect stereotyping of consumers as similar when "in reality they may have different interests, attitudes, and perspectives on life."[8]

Behavioral Attributes

Behavioral attributes include psychographics, product use, benefits, perceptions, and preferences.[9] (Psychographics or lifestyle research was discussed in Chapter 4.) Simply expressed, psychographics attempts to create classifications delineated by attitudes, perceptions, and personalities, grouping people with greater similarities into various market segments. Psychographics represents the marketer's attempt to better understand consumer behavior and to develop marketing strategies that appeal to those market segments identified as important. Unfortunately, market analysis based on psychographics is much more complex and expensive than that based on geography and demographics. Several psychographic and/or lifestyle studies have been conducted on a syndicated basis, however, and have become part of the common segmentation knowledge base. Some of the best known are the Value and Lifestyles (VALS™) Program created by SRI, PRIZM Neighborhood LifeStyle Clusters, owned by Claritas, and ACORN, owned by CACI Marketing Systems.

VALS™ sorts people into an eight-part typology. The main dimensions of the typology are self-orientation and resources. Under the VALS™ system, people are assumed to be motivated by one of three self-orientations: principle, status, and action. Resources refer to the full range of psychological, physical, demographic, and material means and capacities people have to draw on. The eight segments of adult consumers who have different attitudes and exhibit distinctive behavioral and decision-making patterns include actualizers, fulfillers, achievers, experiencers, believers, strivers, makers, and strugglers.[10]

PRIZM is predicated on the assumption that one's choice of where to live, being among the most basic of consumer decisions, reflects other aspects of one's lifestyle. Thus, PRIZM assigns individuals to market segments based on where they live. PRIZM establishes LifeStyle Clusters, which are neighborhoods with statistically similar demographics or lifestyle profiles. Using a complex statistical analysis that encompasses both demographic characteristics and consumer behavior, neighborhoods in the United States have been assigned to one of the 62 PRIZM clusters across 15 social groups. Neighborhoods are defined primarily by ZIP codes but are available by census block groups and postal ZIP codes plus the four-digit extension.

CACI's ACORN® (A Classification of Residential Neighborhoods) divides neighborhoods into 43 clusters and nine summary groups. Neighborhoods are analyzed and sorted by 61 lifestyle characteristics such as income, age, household type, home value, occupation, education, and other key determinants of consumer behavior. Market segments were created using a combination of cluster analysis techniques.

Benefit segmentation is related to the identification of consumers' motives and buying behavior. Weinstein describes benefit segmentation as one of the most useful but most difficult to measure bases of segmentation. In benefit segmentation, "the marketer must try to determine precisely what the prospect wants or needs."[11] Product differentiation and promotional strategies are then designed to appeal to targeted market segments based on benefits offered by the product or service. Benefits go beyond product features and may satisfy physical, emotional, or psychological needs.

Generational Differences

In recent years, a significant amount of attention has shifted to the influence of "generational markers" on how members of different generations vary in their responses to many life experiences. In *Generations: The History of America's Future, 1584 to 2069,* William Strauss and Neil Howe identify 18 generations. Strauss and Howe contend that "among these generations, we find important recurring personality patterns—specifically four types of 'peer personalities' that have (in all but one case) followed each other in a fixed order. We call this repeating pattern the 'generational cycle.'"[12] In the book, among other things, the authors discuss the current generations: the G.I. (born 1901-1924), the Silents (born 1925-1942), the Boomers (born 1943-1960), and the 13ers (America's 13th generation, born 1961-1981). It is the G.I.s who were served by the seniors' housing industry for most of the latter part of the 20th century, but that market is now transitioning to the Silents. The impact of each generation's peer personality has been explored by many others since *Generations* was published in 1991. For example, *American Generations* includes chapters on how various generations are reflected in terms of such things as attitudes and behavior, education, health, households, housing, income labor force, population, spending, and wealth. The book is primarily statistical in nature, using data collected by the federal government.[13] By contrast, *Rocking the Ages* is a book on generational marketing that the authors describe as "a strategic business perspective that studies these cohort effects and highlights what's relevant for better business decision making."[14]

In recent years, more attention has been focused on the differences between the G.I.s and the Silents. Research on the Silents, conducted in the late 1990s by Brooks Adams Research surveyed members of this cohort nationally and provided insights into their views on retirement and retirement housing. The study highlighted changes in preferences with regard to payment, unit types and sizes, services, and amenities. It also illustrated differences between the G.I.s and the Silents with regard to seniors' housing.

Segmentation and Marketing Strategies

Physical and behavioral attributes provide a way of viewing or describing the market. They are useful in segmentation research encompassing both primary and secondary data. Market segmentation is also considered a management strategy, however. Marketing managers may design ways to reach and influence the market to make buying decisions based on identification and analysis of their key market segments. As a marketing strategy, segmentation can be used to increase both market penetration in the major existing target market segment and use among smaller segments that may not typically be targeted. Although some degree of penetration of any *one* of these secondary targets may not substantially impact sales, aggregate penetration of several secondary segments can be very effective. Because the use of a segmentation strategy presumes that the market for a product consists of segments with different needs and wants, a marketing strategy that employs segmentation techniques involves developing marketing approaches that appeal to these different segments.

As mentioned, the health care industry, specifically hospitals, has focused on market segmentation as a means to increase market penetration and to compete effectively. This general interest in marketing among health care professionals has emerged only in the last decade or so as the industry has been beset by the more difficult reimbursement environment created by the prospective payment system, the need to carefully allocate resources, and the increasing amount of competition, especially for private pay patients. A guest editorial in the *Journal of Health Care Management* describes market segmentation as a "critical factor for survival and growth" in the changing environment for hospitals.[15] Hospitals have added new services and products in their efforts to increase market share and add new market segments to their base. In an example of vertical integration, some institutions have embarked on developing a specialized niche in servicing the elderly segment of the market. Through the addition of such things as a home health care program, specialized elderly social services, and skilled nursing and assisted living facilities, hospitals are able to meet many of the health care needs of their elderly market. The addition of a seniors' housing facility also illustrates a market segmentation strategy, one that a number of hospitals employed during the last two decades. The use of benefit segmentation in the health care industry was described in a 1986 article that concluded that "distinguishable benefit segments can be found in a hospital's market. Segmenting patients in terms of benefit importance provides hospital managers an opportunity to develop unique services sought by specific segments of the population and to develop positioning strategies."[16]

Segmentation versus Differentiation

In contrast to market segmentation, which focuses on attempting to identify and then meet consumers' needs, market differentiation is "concerned with the bending of demand to the will of supply. It is an attempt to shift or change the slope of the demand curve for the market offering of an individual supplier."[17] Some describe differentiation as an alternative to segmentation, while others consider it as complementary to segmentation or as a way to implement segmentation. Differentiation involves strategies designed to distinguish a specific product or service from those that are similar or even identical. Product differentiation can be based on real or perceived differences and may involve both physical and nonphysical characteristics. A 1956 article classifies differentiation as a promotional strategy or approach to marketing, characterized by the heavy use of advertising and promotion. In contrast to segmentation, differentiation results in a "horizontal share of a broad and generalized market," whereas segmentation tends to "produce depth of market position in segments effectively defined and penetrated."[18]

Market Segmentation and Seniors' Housing Research

The analysis conducted in planning a seniors' housing community employs some of the more fundamental aspects of segmentation research. In the early planning stages, the project team, including the market analyst, must ask and adequately answer certain basic questions that frame the subsequent analysis of the market and are, under the best circumstances, oriented toward a basic segmentation analysis. Those questions might include:

- Whom are we trying to serve? What are the attributes of the market segment that will be most responsive to the facility we are planning?
- Where do our future residents now reside, and how far can we expect them to move to relocate to our facility?
- What are the features of a seniors' housing community that our target market will seek in making this choice?
- What will motivate our prospective residents to consider moving to a seniors' housing community, and what will motivate them to choose ours over others?

In many cases, the greatest focus has been placed on the first question regarding the socioeconomic and demographic characteristics of the potential target market. In other cases, efforts have been made to understand the behavioral attributes of the target market.

Physical Attributes

On the most basic level, all market studies for seniors' housing communities have employed some degree of segmentation analysis. As discussed in detail in Chapters 2 and 3, market studies in effect represent an effort to apply a series of qualifying screens designed to reveal the demographic profile of the pool of qualified prospects for a project. The first screen, which frames all the rest, is designation of a specific geographic area determined to be the facility's market or service area. Analysts seek to answer several questions regarding the geographic trading area. The first is likely to be what constitutes the boundaries of the local market for the facility. The second, depending on circumstances, may be whether the seniors' housing community can expect to draw more than a small portion of its residents from a larger regional market. More than a few seniors' housing communities have been successful in drawing significant numbers from nonlocal, noncontiguous markets. Those that have done so often have other characteristics that in effect create an opportunity for a segmentation strategy. For instance, facilities associated with retired military officers, in targeting that specialized market segment, have drawn residents from throughout the country. Seniors' housing communities associated with certain religious or fraternal organizations have drawn residents from the regions where their membership is strong. Thus, geographic and affinity group segmentation can and do interact, and they must be considered in market analysis.

Market studies that do not include a consumer research component focus much of their effort on devising and applying a series of qualifications designed to quantify the pool of eligible households in the defined geographic market area. The first qualifier has been age. In the early years as seniors' housing products began to proliferate, the elderly were defined as those age 65 or older, and all persons in this rather large age category were considered eligible in the market analysis. As the industry matured and data from a broad base of experience became available, studies acknowledged that the group that seemed most likely to enter such communities was at least a decade older. Age segmentation therefore began to more accurately reflect the realities of the market, once those realities had been studied and documented.

Market analysis further qualified or segmented demographics by recognizing that the unit of analysis had to be households rather than individuals. Further demographic breakdowns therefore reflected the number of households headed by an individual who was qualified in terms of age. Further segmentation on this level occurs in distinguishing between assisted living, which generally focuses on one-person households, and independent living, which incorporates both one- and two-person households.

The third level of demographic segmentation involved economics, specifically household income. The analysis took into consideration pricing structure and levels proposed for the project being analyzed, determining the necessary economic profile of the household that would qualify. In other cases, analysis of the economic characteristics of the elderly in the geographic target market resulted in a decision to target those at a certain economic level. The most frequently used measure of economic status in market analysis has been annual household income. In some cases, however, the analysis also took into consideration such things as housing tenure, for example, whether one owned or rented a home. The latter was considered particularly important for projects charging entrance fees because of concern about the source of capital needed to pay those fees. Homeownership was considered the most reliable (or easily identifiable or measurable) indicator that a household would have the necessary capital to pay the entrance fee for seniors' housing communities that require an upfront payment.

As discussed in Chapter 2, one difficulty encountered in demographic segmentation of the elderly housing market had been the absence of readily available data that break down and cross tabulate demographic characteristics on more distinct levels than age by income. Sources such as the American Housing Survey, which provide more detail by housing tenure, do so for larger regions than are typically designated as the geographic target market for specific facilities. The development of the Senior Market Report (SMR) by Project Market Decisions represents a significant advance in the ability to conduct demographic segmentation studies. The

SMR breaks down the demographic profile of elderly households into a highly defined and useful series of cross-tabulations, and it does so for any specifically defined geographic area. Data in the report begin by dividing elderly households into two large pools, homeowners and renters. For each group, the report provids cross tabulations of age by five-year cohorts and income. The distinctive feature of SMR data is a breakdown by age and income for four specific household types: single males, single females, married couples, and others. Thus, it becomes possible to quantify much more discretely defined demographic market segments. Recognizing that seniors' communities, for instance, have typically filled a majority of their units with single women, one could quantify the number of single female householders in a defined market area.

More important, the SMR and its related software, the Senior Market Area Report Tabulation (SrMART®) system, permit and encourage the use of a sensitivity analysis or what-if approach to evaluating a potential development. What if the average age of residents is 80 rather than 78? What if fees have to be raised by $200 per month? What if couples cannot be attracted to at least 30 percent of the units? SrMART® allows the analyst to answer these questions and more. It facilitates a much clearer understanding of the demographic strengths and weaknesses of a given market. The SMR also provides information on median housing values of elderly owners by age and income, thereby extending the analyst's ability to consider the impact of the home's value on the project's affordability. Project Market Decisions's products enabled substantial advances to be made in demographic segmentation research.

Behavioral Attributes

Although demographic analysis allows for partitioning markets into those with certain basic similar characteristics, segmentation analysis must be extended to the more critical aspect of identifying those with similar purchasing behavior. As discussed in detail later, age and income are not necessarily the best or even most accurate determinants of consumer behavior. Certain studies, particularly those for assisted living/personal care facilities oriented toward the frail elderly, attempt to segment the market according to level of frailty. As discussed in Chapter 4, attempts to quantify data relate to the need for assistance with ADLs and/or IADLs. The assumption that drives this form of segmentation is that those individuals who need certain types of assistance represent the target market for the personal care or assisted living facility.

Behavioral segmentation continues to be rather elusive to market analysts and those who develop, market, and manage seniors' communities. Most project-specific consumer research studies attempt to gain information on interest in moving to a community, timing of such a move, and features desired. Surveys also typically include a series of questions on demographic characteristics.

But few studies have included questions designed to learn more about respondents' lifestyle and what motivates them. Unfortunately, any behavioral information obtained is rarely subjected to a rigorous or sophisticated analysis to determine the relative value of independent variables. Using a technique referred to as *conjoint analysis* to simulate real-life decision making, however, ProMatura Group evaluates which features, services, amenities, and unit styles and sizes influence the decision about the subject development, and which features respondents would be willing to pay more for. Results can be matched to the characteristics or various market segments that are or are not interested, and interests can be differentiated by segment.

Problems

Although great emphasis has been placed on demographic segmentation analysis in seniors' housing, some experts argue that age-based segmentation actually has significant shortcomings. *Serving the Ageless Market,* for example, argues against the effectiveness of segmenting seniors by age. Its second principle for what the author calls *maturity markets* is the age-correlate principle: "Age is a correlate, not a determinant, of consumer behavior in maturity markets and hence should not be used in defining and predicting specific consumer behavior of older people."[19]

The reliance on age and the lack of understanding of the diversity and complexity of senior markets have led to many of the industry's problems. During the 1980s and 1990s, the amount of press about the graying of America helped to fuel increased activity in seniors' housing. This activity was a response to what many perceived as an already large and rapidly growing market segment known as *the elderly.* Countless articles informed us that it would be the fastest-growing segment of the population for decades to come and that, contrary to popular opinion, the elderly had plenty of money to spend. The resultant "silver rush" in seniors' housing demonstrated, in many cases, a lack of understanding that this perceived monolithic market segment actually comprised myriad segments with different demographic and socioeconomic characteristics and different life experiences that shaped their behavior as consumers.

Several issues create difficulties in conducting more sophisticated forms of segmentation analysis for seniors' housing, particularly those that extend beyond demographic segmentation. As mentioned, segmentation research can be expensive, particularly when added to the requisite supply and demand–oriented market studies typically conducted for development of seniors' communities. Despite the emergence of large national public companies in the 1990s, the majority of organizations involved in development of such communities were still local or regional nonprofit sponsors or local or regional development firms, which were not likely to allocate the resources necessary for lifestyle- or behavior-oriented segmentation research. In many cases, these organizations planned to undertake only one such development, and those planning several developments did not perceive sophisticated segmentation research to be a necessary tool in planning.

Product Segmentation in Seniors' Housing

As seniors' housing has matured and developed, an increasing degree of product segmentation has occurred. Given that a continuum exists from the most independent to the most dependent and frail elderly, facilities that emphasize different points along this scale have been created. An article in *Contemporary Long Term Care* discusses product segmentation for retirement housing and describes five products: the leisure model, the quasi-leisure model, the services model, the medical model, and the personal care model.[20]

The leisure model is oriented toward the most active retirees (not the subject of this book) and has frequently been referred to as the *active adult community.* Consisting typically of individual homes (freestanding or attached), this community is geared toward empty nesters who no longer need or desire to live in a larger single-family home. Frequently, these facilities incorporate substantial recreational features and amenities. Without a medical infrastructure or the typical support services found in CCRCs or congregate facilities, the leisure model targets the discretionary consumer—the youngest, most independent, and potentially largest market segment.

In contrast to the leisure model, congregate housing (the services model), CCRCs (the medical model), and assisted living facilities (the personal care model) are need-driven. The article warns about the limitations of combining a need-driven product with the economic realities of the market most likely to be attracted to such products, that is, single women over the age of 75, the poorest of the elderly demographic segments. It raises concerns about whether the market for such products is actually as large as those in the industry originally believed.

In the quasi-leisure model, an effort is made to combine some features of the leisure model with some from the medical model. Combining both lifestyle and health-oriented elements, the quasi-leisure model represents an effort to create a bridge between products oriented to the very independent elderly and products serving those who are more frail. While characterizing it as an effort on the part of the industry to "broaden the base from need driven to discretionary," the authors warn about potential confusion that could result from trying to market such a community.[21]

Whether one agrees or disagrees with this depiction of CCRCs as need-driven, data corroborate the demographic profile of the average resident as female, single, and close to age 80. The missing element in this profile continues to be related to behavioral characteristics. One can speculate, based primarily on anecdotal data, that the behavioral similarities that bind this segment have to do with a need for security and a concern about the ability to carry on as health fails or to afford the increasing costs of health care that accompany deteriorating health. Although those characteristics seem evident, experience talking with people who have moved to seniors' communities demonstrates other, more affirmative traits: interest in making new friends, having the freedom to enjoy new experiences, a sense of independence and not wanting to rely on or burden children, and perhaps a penchant for planning ahead. These somewhat conflicting characteristics belie the need-driven profile described in this study.

Nevertheless, the types of available facilities represent products that segment the elderly market according to the ability to function independently. The active adult community or retirement village attracts those with the greatest ability to live independent lifestyles. CCRCs and congregate housing facilities seem to draw older and somewhat less active retirees. Assisted living facilities draw from the frail segment of the market, from among those requiring more regular assistance with ADLs. Nursing homes are designed for those who are incapable of living independently and who may be burdened with a chronic health problem.

Segmentation has also occurred in assisted living communities based on physical and cognitive frailty. Many assisted living communities create a specially designed wing dedicated to those with some form of memory impairment resulting from conditions such as Alzheimer's disease or related disorders. Moreover, some assisted living models have been created to serve only this segment of the market.

Economics has also been a form of segmentation in seniors' housing, although with limits. Most facilities that include substantial service packages, including health care, have been oriented toward the middle- or upper-middle-income population. Even congregate housing facilities that may not include a health care package have targeted the same economic market segment as traditional CCRCs, which in many ways has been dictated by the economics of developing and operating such communities. Although developers have spoken about creating similar facilities oriented toward the moderate-income segment, it has been an elusive goal. The lower-income market has been served, albeit insufficiently, by government-subsidized housing for the elderly. The elderly who fall between government-subsidized housing and typical market-rate facilities, however, have been the unserved market. During the 1980s and 1990s, a number of facilities were developed to target the wealthy elderly. The three suburban Philadelphia facilities described in Chapter 8—Waverly Heights, the Quadrangle, and Beaumont at Bryn Mawr—are examples of communities that target the affluent. In some ways, these facilities have taken segmentation a step beyond pure economics. Although their pricing structures are similar, each facility has evolved a special niche within the well-to-do elderly living on Philadelphia's Main Line. Originated for Quaker Haverford College alumni, the Quadrangle developed a reputation as the retirement community for the intellectual or academic set. In contrast, Beaumont at Bryn Mawr and perhaps to a lesser degree Waverly Heights drew residents from the more social set, the country club set, the old moneyed families of the area.

Variations in pricing structures have also attempted to segment the market. As the traditional nonrefundable life care entrance fee gave way to rental and equity pricing, operators attempted to appeal to different motivations for buying a unit. Rental fees appealed to those who did not wish to make a long-term commitment, who wanted to know that they could move if and when they wanted to without a financial penalty. The equity models, which include cooperatives and condominiums, were designed to appeal to those who desired to make an investment and to continue to realize the benefits associated with owning real estate.

Several efforts have been made to appeal to more independent elderly, perhaps younger individuals (still in their 70s) and more couples. Unbundled or fee-for-service programs have emerged to attract a more independent segment of the market, one that is turned off by too much assistance. The design of a facility has also been used to reinforce the image of independence. Communities that include villas, townhouses, cluster homes, and cottages send a message that they want a younger, more active market.

Although these variations in the features of the product appear to be approaches to segmentation, they have not actually been studied in a way that verifies that these variations do in fact attract distinctly different market segments.

The Marketing Message: Benefit Segmentation

As described earlier, benefit segmentation is one of the most valuable but most difficult to evaluate forms of segmentation. Understanding the motivations behind buying behavior and designing marketing strategies to appeal to these motivations have been as elusive in the seniors' housing field as in consumer products, health care, and real estate. It may be that difficulties arising from proper benefit segmentation have been largely responsible for the limitations thus far in motivating seniors to move to less need-driven forms of seniors' housing.

It can be argued that seniors' communities and their emphasis on independent living represent a contradiction in terms, a mixed message that defies effective translation from a marketing perspective. A contradiction is inherent in associating the concept of independent living with an array of services that carry the message that one may no longer be as capable of caring for oneself as in the past. The message "we'll take care of you," whether blatantly carried in marketing brochures and through marketing personnel or hidden behind the promise of an independent lifestyle, still rings through to prospective consumers. And to those consumers, the fear of losing independence is very strong.

Marketing professionals often confess that seniors' housing is a negative sell, that they are selling a product to a market that does not want it or does not want to admit that it needs it. Where does this persistently negative perception of the seniors' community come from? In part, it is an image formed in the past among a target market that grew up with only negative connotations of old age homes informing their perception of group living quarters for the elderly. These early images associated with seniors' living were negative, invoking fear of dependency and concerns that such institutionalization would be an end to life as they knew it.

Mature individuals need to continue to enjoy life-affirming experiences or *life satisfaction.* Marketing approaches for seniors' housing, however, have traditionally focused on the real estate and the services rather than on the opportunity to enhance life experiences. Few people moving to a seniors' community are trading up in terms of their physical surroundings. Services can connote a negative, rather than a positive, factor that marketing professionals may believe them to be. Many seniors interpret the service package as a form of regimentation and of limitations on their freedom and independence.[22]

What few facilities have succeeded in doing is positioning themselves using the *gateway-to-experience principle.*[23] Often, when people who have chosen to move to seniors' communities are asked to describe what life is like for them, it is the *experiences* that they describe. They do not talk about how beautiful their apartment is or how much they like the services. When services are mentioned, they are presented in the context of life-enhancing experiences. Residents enjoy meals, not because they relieve residents of cooking but because they have opportunities in the dining room to meet and talk with interesting people. People who are happy with the choice they have made to live in a seniors' community often talk of their ability to pursue life-long interests with greater freedom and more time. Few have stopped doing what has always been important to them, unless deteriorating health has prevented them from pursuing their interests. An important question is why such a difference exists between the actual experiences of many living in seniors' communities and the messages that are used to promote and position them.

The concept of differentiation has begun to emerge in markets with numerous seniors' communities, which are therefore characterized as highly competitive. Interviews with marketing professionals indicate that most attempt to employ marketing techniques that differentiate their facility from similar facilities. Unfortunately, differentiation is difficult in an industry that does not thoroughly understand what motivates its consumers to choose to move. Emphasizing physical characteristics or differences in pricing may have some limited success but probably does little to broaden the base of interested consumers. Based on the description of differentiation discussed earlier,[24] strategies such as those employed in seniors' housing are more likely to be used to insulate the business against price competition than to increase the depth of the market for the product.

Unity Health Systems: An Example Of Segmentation Strategy

As noted, hospitals have begun to employ market segmentation in the face of the increasing complexity of their environment and the impact of competition. In particular, the knowledge that inpatient services were declining in favor of outpatient procedures has prompted many hospitals to diversify to reach new market segments. Some conditions that gave rise to these strategies in the health care field have led hospitals to expand into the seniors' housing field. For example, Unity Health Systems in Greece, New York (adjacent to Rochester in Monroe County), has employed segmentation strategies effectively to protect and enhance its position in the market. Unity Health Systems, however, did not merely develop a single facility or program for the elderly in its effort to diversify from its traditional acute care model. The institution developed a full range of facilities, programs, and services, in effect employing a strategy for increasing its reach to multiple elderly market segments. Critical to this strategy, particularly throughout the 1990s, was forming partnerships with various local community groups to provide housing and services for seniors. Unity Health Systems's wide variety of housing and programs enables it to reach seniors of all income levels.In the early 1970s, a citizens advisory group that had raised funds from major industries in the Rochester area donated a 154-acre campus in Greece, New York, to Park Ridge Hospital. Park Ridge opened a 120-bed nursing home in July 1972 and by 1975 had added the 194-bed community hospital that was to become its anchoring identity in the market. Because of its experience in the nursing care field, the New York Department of Health asked Park Ridge in 1982 to take over the operations of a bankrupt facility located in Rochester. When this facility was later sold at auction, Park Ridge acquired the 120-bed facility, naming it Park Hope. As shown in the accompanying chronology, Park Ridge continued throughout the 1980s to pursue its strategy of becoming a major provider of housing, care, and services for the elderly in Monroe County. In 1998, Park Ridge Hospital merged with another local hospital, St. Mary's Hospital, and the two became Unity Health Systems. This merger fostered further development of both facilities and services for seniors, particularly through community partnerships with various organizations. In 2000, for example, Unity Health joined with a local organization to provide services—delivery of meals, home maintenance, housekeeping, grocery shopping and delivery, and companion services—to seniors in their homes.

1972	Park Ridge Nursing Home
1982	Acquisition of Park Hope Nursing Home
1985	Approval for HUD 202, Section 8, elderly housing project
1985	Lifeline Emergency Response System
1990	Day at the Park (adult daycare program)
1990	Village at Park Ridge (congregate/assisted living facility)
1990	Park Ridge at Home (home care program)
1992	Unity Living Center (nursing home)
1992	Resch Commons (HUD 202 elderly housing project)
1998	Unity Health Systems (merger with St. Mary's Hospital)
1999	R.L. Edward Manor (HUD 202 elderly housing project, community partnership)
1999	St. Bernard's Park (independent living and social adult day program, community partnership)
2000	Woodland Village (independent living apartments)
2000	Senior Services Program (community partnership)

Rather than pursuing a direction that would have allowed Park Ridge to serve only a single segment of the elderly market, Park Ridge extended its influence and service to those seeking care both inside and outside the home, targeting several economic levels, from those requiring Medicaid to middle income. During the late 1980s, Park Ridge laid the groundwork for developing a comprehensive program of adult daycare and home care services and expanded into the middle-income congregate housing market. Through its combination of housing, long-term and acute health care, and support services, Park Ridge Hospital has successfully targeted the elderly as a specialized market. Recognizing that the older market comprises many segments that respond differently to the various options for housing and health care services, Park Ridge has employed segmentation strategies that enabled it to increase its penetration of the market in the Rochester area. The feedback that Park Ridge has obtained as it has expanded and diversified points to the influence of the hospital and its excellent reputation for care as the single most influential force in consumers' decisions to seek housing or long-term care services from Park Ridge.

Interestingly, although many experts in the seniors' housing field believe that housing should not be located on a hospital's campus, it has been a positive feature of the attraction of the Village at Park Ridge congregate and assisted living facility. Residents involve themselves in many of the programs and hospital activities available to them on the large campus. From volunteer services in the hospital to involvement in the children's daycare program operated on the campus, residents have found a way to continue to contribute to the community of which they are still a vital part.

Notes

1. Wendell R. Smith, "Product Differentiation and Market Segmentation as Alternative Marketing Strategies," *Journal of Marketing,* July 1956. Reprinted in Donald W. Scotton and Ronald L. Zallocco, *Readings in Market Segmentation* (Chicago: American Marketing Association, 1980), p. 5.
2. A. Weinstein, *Market Segmentation* (Chicago: Probus Publishing Co., 1987), p. xi.
3. Peter R. Dickson and James L. Ginter, "Market Segmentation, Product Differentiation, and Marketing Strategy," *Journal of Marketing,* April 1987, p. 1.
4. Ibid., p. 3.
5. Weinstein, *Market Segmentation,* pp. 44–45.
6. Ibid.
7. Ibid.
8. Ibid., p. 12.
9. Ibid., p. 44.
10. Copyright 1997, SRI Consulting, http://future.sri.com/VALS.
11. Weinstein, *Market Segmentation,* p. 46.
12. William Strauss and Neil Howe, *Generations: The History of America's Future, 1584 to 2069* (New York, William Morrow & Co., 1991), p. 8.
13. Susan Mitchell, *American Generations* (Ithaca, N.Y.: New Strategist Publications, 2000).
14. J. Walker Smith & Ann Clurman, *Rocking the Ages,* The Yankelovich Report on Generational Marketing (New York: HarperBusiness, 1997), p. 4.
15. N.K. Malhotra, "Market Segmentation and Strategic Growth Opportunities for Hospitals," *Journal of Health Care Management,* June 1986, p. 2.
16. D.W. Finn and C.W. Lamb, Jr., "Hospital Benefit Segmentation," *Journal of Health Care Management,* December 1986, p. 32.
17. Smith, "Product Differentiation and Market Segmentation," p. 4.
18. Ibid., p. 4.
19. David B. Wolfe, *Serving the Ageless Market: Strategies for Selling to the Fifty-Plus Market* (New York: McGraw-Hill, 1990), p. 86.
20. R.L. Rohrer and R. Bibb, "Product Segmentation and Marketing Challenges in the Seniors' Housing Industry," NASLI Technical Bulletin M-1, n.d. Reprinted in *Contemporary Long Term Care,* May 1986.
21. Ibid., pp. 18–19.
22. Wolfe, *Serving the Ageless Market,* p. 74.
23. Ibid.
24. Smith, "Product Differentiation and Market Segmentation."

Jaime Ardiles-Arce; courtesy AIA

Sun City Kanagawa, an assisted-living facility in Kanagawa, Japan, displays a dignified, tranquil, and, most important, non-institutional character. Architect: Nihon Sekkei

7 Relationship of Feasibility Analysis To Performance

How does the actual experience of a seniors' housing community differ from the assumptions developed or presented in a feasibility study? Should studies be expected to predict actual outcomes? Which assumptions are more or less likely to correspond to performance and why? What issues related to feasibility and performance are beyond the scope of the feasibility study, and should they be? What allows a seniors' community to defy performance norms? This chapter addresses these questions, focusing on how and why study assumptions and actual performance vary. The information presented is framed as a guide for those who use such studies, enabling them to critically evaluate the work that is done and to refine their expectations for the feasibility process.

How and Why Performance Can Differ from Feasibility Analyses

The actual characteristics and performance of a seniors' community often differ from those assumed or recommended in market and financial feasibility studies. Some reasons for this discrepancy are justifiable; others result from poor work. A market study conducted to help plan a community may demonstrate a significant degree of variability from the actual project as a result of such factors as the time that elapses between the study and implementation of the final stages of the development process, the perceived value of the study's recommendations by the organization receiving them, and the involvement of parties other than the study's commissioner. Financial feasibility studies prepared for inclusion in financing documents may not vary as significantly from actuality, because most, if not all, key decisions affecting the design, price, and to some extent marketing of the facility have already been set.

Market Analysis

Thorough market analysis conducted by experienced professionals can yield valuable results that can be used in planning the development of a seniors' community. Several events can intercede, however, that cause the community, once opened, to differ from some recommendations of the market study. External factors that can cause this differentiation are the regulatory process and the elderly consumers themselves. Although changes enforced through the approval process may or may not be desirable, those resulting from direct input of prospective residents can be of great value. Even extremely high-quality market research and direct consumer research cannot replace the input gained from people who are actually ready to move. They represent the ultimate test of what will and will not be acceptable in the market. The following subsections discuss several areas in which the recommendations of a market study may differ from actual performance or outcomes.

Market Area Definition

Studies that use a radius or county approach to define market area are probably most prone to differ from the origin of actual residents. This type of analysis rarely takes into consideration any other features or characteristics of the market that are likely to differentiate responses from one area to another. As noted in Chapter 2, geographic and psychological boundaries and socioeconomic distinctions between neighborhoods are not accounted for when analysts automatically resort to a radius or county location to define market area.

The more care taken in conducting market analysis and consumer research, the more likely the study will accurately depict the area from which most residents will be drawn. Chapter 2 discussed the issues that should be considered when defining market areas for seniors' communities. For example, specific comparison of the qualities of the neighborhood where the site is located with those in the surrounding area yields a market area definition that takes into consideration the similarities and differences. Attention to the site's accessibility and distances to other parts of the region also help to form a more realistic appraisal of market area definition. Considering the experience of other competitive facilities located in the same or similar local areas is also helpful.

One benefit of using direct consumer research is to refine the market area definition. Market analysis that combines fieldwork with telephone or mail surveys can provide extremely valuable insights about the acceptability of the site and the areas from which prospective residents will be drawn. Properly structured, consumer research can be used to compare geographic areas in terms of the level of interest they produce, thereby facilitating market area refinement. This approach has value in determining the overall boundaries of the market and in establishing the hierarchical relationship among primary and secondary markets.

In studies conducted for planning rather than financing, the definition of a market area is more speculative and therefore likely to differ more significantly from actual performance. Planning studies are frequently conducted during the early stages of the development process, prepared to assist an organization in reaching critical decisions about whether to proceed with development and what the project's features should be. Feasibility studies conducted for CCRCs in states that regulate them or for financing frequently have the benefit of geographic origin data about prospective residents from presales or deposits. In states that regulate the industry, it is not unusual to find that high levels of presales are required before approval. Sources of financing—both underwriters for tax-exempt bonds and a growing number of direct lenders—also impose substantial presales requirements, thus leading to the ability to draw market area boundaries that conform to actual data generated by presales. Rental retirement communities, on the other hand, rarely begin significant premarketing before construction and therefore do not have the benefit of an advance look at who will be moving in and where they are coming from. This statement is true as well for assisted living facilities, where preopening marketing usually does not begin until six months before opening the building.

The definition of a market area, particularly as it appears in a planning study, provides a guide for future project development. Well beyond the control of the analyst is the actual implementation of the marketing program. Decisions about the use of techniques to generate leads, such as direct mail, printed matter, and electronic media, affect the origination of prospective residents. For instance, using neighborhood sections of large metropolitan newspapers produces leads based on distribution of the newspaper. In comparison, using electronic media such as television and radio may produce very different results.

Identifying the Target Market

As discussed in Chapter 2, most market analyses address demographic, and to some extent socioeconomic, characteristics of the market targeted for a project. In sizing the pool of potentially qualified households, studies tend to delineate the target market according to age, income, and, in some cases, housing tenure and household type. Even when dealing with such fundamental characteristics of the market as demographics, however, studies often do not employ refinements appropriate to the specific character of the market being targeted by a project. For instance, studies conducted for facilities being developed for middle-income households rarely eliminate households in the upper income ranges from the qualified pool.

With the advent of systems such as SMRs (Senior Market Reports) created by Project Market Decisions, analysts have increased the ease with which they can delineate and evaluate a facility's potential target market. A more refined data system lends itself to the creation of sensitivity analyses, which encourage the analyst to identify highly specified demographic strengths and weaknesses in a specified geographic market area. Thus, for example, one can evaluate what is necessary to reach the largest possible base or how to adjust unit mix and sizes to reflect the nature of the targeted household composition.

Many experienced professionals in the seniors' housing industry assert that qualitative factors override demographic characteristics in the market for seniors' housing. Issues such as the importance of the constituency represented by an affinity group may not be adequately addressed. Cultural, religious, and ethnic differences among the elderly living in a geographic area are rarely considered in market studies because of (at least partly) the quantitative orientation of such studies. Those who are least impressed by market analysis have concluded that one cannot expect much more from market analysts than a judgment about whether a reasonably sized population base is available from which to draw.

Facility Size, Phasing, and Characteristics

The likelihood that the size, phasing, and characteristics of a seniors' housing community will differ from recommendations included in a market study is increased if the study is conducted during early planning stages of the project. In the early stages, it is likely that several factors that control ultimate decisions about such features have not yet been finalized. The regulatory approval process can have the most significant effect on the characteristics of a community. Market studies done before receiving necessary zoning approvals may recommend total project size based on what appears to be supportable in the market area. Although such a study is likely to take into consideration the size of the subject parcel and the size of a project that could be accommodated on the site, actual size may vary once it has gone through the zoning process. Zoning may result in the ability to build more or fewer units than recommended in a market study. Pursuing full buildout may be irresistible, given the potential for increased revenue and/or profits, but it may be inadvisable, given market conditions. In such cases, phasing a project should be considered, if possible, to avoid flooding the market with too many units at once.

Because early planning studies are often completed before the actual design phase, architects are likely to render some changes to the number of units recommended by the study. Many architects interviewed for this book who specialize in seniors' housing indicated that they prefer not to proceed very far with a client before a market study is completed. They believe that the study, if conducted properly, will provide valuable information for both the overall design and the architectural program.

Projects that propose to include health care services subject to review by a state's department of health also may change between the analysis and the approval process. Most analysts consider projected bed need for a specific area and the economics of operation when recommending nursing home beds, in particular. The approval process under a state's Certificate of Need (CN) regulations can be highly political, however. Depending on numerous factors, including how many organizations are competing for beds, who those organizations are, and other issues that are difficult to generalize, an application for 120 beds may not necessarily result in either approval or outright rejection for the full complement. Often, fewer beds are approved than requested, particularly when several applications in a geographic area are being reviewed simultaneously. This kind of outcome cannot be anticipated in a market study conducted before submission of a CN application.

Perhaps the most extreme instance of differentiation occurs when the study recommends the inclusion of health care beds and services but necessary approval cannot be gained. For example, the analyst may conclude that in the specific market under consideration, health care needs to be part of the community's service program for the project to compete successfully. In such a case, the market feasibility judgment might have been negative had the health care component of the project been eliminated.

In some seniors' housing communities, flexible design permits changes in the unit mix. Under such an ideal scenario, unit mix may be adjusted as marketing takes place to respond to prospective residents' actual preferences. Studios and one-bedroom units, for example, may be designed so that they can be combined in the event of greater demand for two-bedroom units. Such adjustments result in a change not only in unit mix but also in overall size (i.e., number of residential units) of the community.

Recommendations for project pricing included in a market study done for planning purposes must be tested to evaluate whether they will result in a financially viable project. Often, the pricing levels recommended by a study are based on a consideration of the target market that the client's organization wishes to serve as well as prices already charged for similar communities in the market area. Suggestions offered for pricing levels, however, should be viewed only as a guide or range for consideration until they have been further tested through a financial analysis for the project. In some markets, where few or no seniors' communities are in operation, it is difficult for the market analyst to accurately anticipate acceptable prices. In such markets, elderly consumers may experience sticker shock because they are comparing fees with real estate prices without considering the value of the services. Pricing levels in these markets may go through several refinements during early marketing or premarketing, which can occur long after the market study has been completed.

Absorption

The rate at which a community can market and occupy its units is a nettlesome component of market analysis. When various industry professionals were asked about ways in which feasibility studies varied from actual performance, absorption was the area most frequently pointed to. Perhaps the greatest gulf lies among the absorption rate that is forecast, the rate desired by the client, and the reality of the fill period. Studies that have the most reliable basis on which to project absorption are those conducted for the financing of seniors' communities charging entrance fees, because it is the only type of community that is typically required to achieve a high (60 percent or more) level of presales with a substantial deposit before financing the development. With presales of this magnitude, even though some prospective residents will change their minds, it is easier to develop a closer approximation of the actual fill rate than for any other type of community.

One of the most egregious errors plaguing development of congregate housing during the early to mid-1980s was extremely aggressive absorption forecasts that were nearly impossible to achieve. One result of this error was a lack of sufficient working capital to sustain the longer fill period actually experienced by most of these independent living communities. During the 1980s and 1990s, far more conservative absorption or fill projections for independent living units were used as a result of the sobering evidence presented by most facilities built during that time.

During the 1990s, many types of organizations involved in this segment of the industry made similarly aggressive projections for absorption of assisted living units. Public companies projected rapid absorption, pressed by the necessity of indicating when stabilized occupancy would occur and begin yielding positive cash flow and returns to investors. Many companies, confident of their own capabilities and the power of their "branding," assumed that they could outperform other entrants in the same markets where they were building. More than any other segment of the industry, assisted living could be characterized by building too much, too fast, and in too many markets throughout the country. ALFA's annual overview of the industry reflected declining average absorption rates during the period from 1997, when it reported a net monthly absorption rate averaging 5.6, to 1998, when the same statistic was 3.6.[1] In a survey of national providers conducted in 2000 (representatives of approximately 15 companies participated), 44 percent of respondents indicated that their actual absorption rates had fallen short of their own projections in 50 percent or more of the communities that had opened since January 1999, and another 22 percent indicated that it had been the case in 25 to 49 percent of their communities opening during this period. Even with study, "average" absorption may vary greatly in either direction, making it extremely difficult to predict.

Several identifiable factors, however, can create a variance between absorption and fill forecasts and actual performance. As noted, studies have tended to contain overly aggressive estimates of the absorption pace. Currently, the National Investment Center provides national move-in rate statistics on its Web site *(www.nic.org)* in the section on key financial indicators. Statistics are shown by product type on a quarterly basis. Accurate or useful information from local competitors reflecting local market conditions is frequently lacking, however. Problems with obtaining local comparable data can stem from several sources. For instance, for newer facilities that provide the best insights on fill periods, changes in marketing and management personnel may make it difficult to obtain an accurate picture of the facility's fill rate. In addition, competitors may be unwilling to share the information with analysts. Alternatively, studies done for projects in markets where no recent facilities have been built have no local comparable facilities on which to base estimates of absorption. How rapidly a facility filled five to ten years ago bears little relation to the conditions of the market today. And studies conducted by firms inexperienced in seniors' housing may lead to overly aggressive projections of absorption.

Unfortunately, it is difficult to translate either a study's penetration (demand) analysis or consumer research into accurate projections of absorption. The penetration analysis is enlightening only to the extent that it reflects the number of facilities that may be attempting to fill simultaneously. The greater that number, in general, the greater the likelihood that the fill period may be longer for each than expected. Consumer surveys that inquire about both interest in moving and timing of the prospective move to a seniors' housing community can provide only broad indicators useful in annual absorption estimates. Usually, even respondents indicating interest in moving to the proposed facility cannot accurately pinpoint when they will be ready to make the move, unless they are ready at the point when the survey is conducted.

Analysts today frequently err on the conservative side, especially if the project team is working with lenders or underwriters experienced in the seniors' housing industry. Although projects may achieve stabilized occupancy more rapidly than forecast, many entities in the financial community require that studies be based on extremely conservative assumptions.

One factor that significantly affects a facility's fill period is particularly difficult to evaluate: the condition of the housing market in the facility's market area. Most residents moving into a seniors' housing community, particularly into independent living, sell a home before the move. For communities that are not strictly rental, this sale historically was usually necessary for the resident to pay upfront endowment or condominium/cooperative fees. This situation changed somewhat for those entering the market in the mid- to late 1990s. Analysts are seeing a new generation needing to liquidate portfolios rather than sell homes. Particularly during volatile markets, such as those experienced in 2000 and 2001, however, they may be unwilling to do so. A declining market for housing resales can slow absorption considerably. For example, the near-depression conditions of the real estate market in the Northeast and parts of the Southwest in the late 1980s and early 1990s had a trickle-down effect on the seniors' housing industry, making it more difficult to market and fill units.

Perhaps the most critical factor that may not be accounted for in market studies is the input of experienced marketing staff and consultants in designing and implementing the marketing program for a seniors' housing community. The chances of achieving a healthy absorption rate are increased significantly by the presence of experienced marketing personnel. Unfortunately, many organizations have not pursued this critical component—and have suffered as a result. Marketing conducted, for instance, by individuals who treat the seniors' community as if it were another real estate sale may be headed for trouble when they find that prospects are making a lifestyle, rather than a real estate, decision. As mentioned, most residents of seniors' housing communities make a tradeoff in terms of real estate quality when they make this move. Overemphasizing the real estate features of a seniors' housing community may be a nonproductive marketing strategy. Although the quality of the marketing program is clearly a key to the successful absorption of any type of seniors' housing community, the field still contains comparatively few experts. While the number has grown significantly, the ratio of marketing talent to projects undertaken means that many projects will not reap the benefits of highly qualified marketing personnel.

Absorption projected by the study done for planning purposes and that prepared for financing may differ. During planning stages, absorption projections included in the study may be forecast before knowing who will be responsible for marketing the project. When a feasibility study is conducted for financing purposes, the likelihood increases significantly that this personnel decision has been made and therefore can be taken into consideration by the feasibility firm, and that a certain level of presales has been achieved as well.

Financial Analysis

Feasibility studies done for use in financing transactions also are likely to show less variance in the financial performance than are financial analyses done during the planning process. This section focuses on factors that may cause changes following the feasibility study done for planning and the feasibility study conducted at the point of project financing.

Construction Costs

Although it is preferable that feasibility studies for financing purposes be conducted when most, if not all, project components have been finalized, it is not always possible. One critical cost that may not be set at the point of financing is the construction contractor's guaranteed maximum price. Without this figure, overall project costs may change as a result of last-minute alterations in design, delays in the construction period, or increases in construction costs. A number of factors can contribute to design changes. For instance, changes in management may result in the requirement to modify elements of the design to suit the experience and approach of the new team. On a more mundane level, problems may be found during construction that necessitate change orders because they were overlooked previously. Some developers anticipate the variability by building a 5 percent contingency into the overall construction budget. Others, however, are not prepared with this type of cushion. The best way to minimize or avoid changes in construction costs is to get input from team members, including management and interior designers, as early as possible in the design phase.

Operating Expenses

The largest component of a seniors' housing community's operating expenses is staff salaries and benefits. A number of factors pertinent to staffing can result in changes in operating expenses. For instance, subsequent to the feasibility study and financing, staffing patterns that were assumed during planning stages may be changed. It is difficult to generalize about why these types of changes are made. One major reason is perhaps a change in key management personnel. One community had trouble because managers did not understand staffing levels described in the feasibility study and did not understand the importance of sticking to the plan outlined by the feasibility study—and that failure to do so may lead to a different style and philosophy of operating the community. In some facilities, an outside management firm may be brought in if dissatisfaction arises with the original firm. In others, internal management personnel may change. And sale of the property during the period of a feasibility study's forecast (usually five years from opening) is likely to result in different operating expense patterns from those forecast.

Problems in the labor market can result in the unanticipated need for higher pay or bonuses to attract and retain qualified personnel. The nursing shortage that continues to plague the health care industry overall is a good example of difficulties that can occur in meeting forecast operating expenses. As many leave the nursing professions, both hospitals and nursing homes (including those that are part of seniors' communities) find themselves resorting to unexpected financial measures to properly staff their units. The same kinds of problems have occurred among unskilled staff as seniors' housing and health care facilities find themselves competing with national franchises in the fast-food business, for instance, which are able to offer better hourly wages and benefits.

Another component of operating expenses subject to variability is the cost associated with taxes, utilities, and insurance. Although tax increases have a greater impact on seniors' housing communities owned by for-profit organizations than by nonprofit organizations, both types of facilities have been subjected to the unexpected. The surprise for nonprofit organizations may come in the form of payment in lieu of taxes. As local governments feel increased pressures to generate revenue, even those seniors' housing communities that are tax exempt may find themselves negotiating some form of payment in lieu of real estate taxes, when previously none was required. Unanticipated increases in costs of local utilities can also be troublesome and difficult to predict. Utility costs may also be hard to forecast for facilities that have heating and air-conditioning controls in each independent living unit but do not require residents to pay their own utility bills.

Finally, operating expenses may increase if a facility experiences a significantly slower fill period than forecast and needs additional working capital. If those responsible for the facility have not set aside reserves to cover unplanned start-up losses, the only solution may be a working capital loan. And interest payments on such a loan, which may not have been anticipated, add to the burden of a community's operating expenses.

Revenues

The most significant differences in actual and forecast revenue occur when a project does not fill as expected. Although the fill rate may be more rapid than anticipated, it is much more likely to be slower than forecast. Overly competitive market conditions during a project's fill period may yield a decision to offer incentives to prospective residents. Although an organization may account for this contingency in its budgeting process, it is difficult for a prefinancing feasibility study to anticipate that this policy will become necessary. It is difficult to raise rates before residents have moved in, but many feasibility studies project this situation, leading to problems.

Some seniors' housing communities have adopted a pricing strategy that allows residents to choose from several options. Although this strategy may be planned before financing the project, it is difficult to predict the ultimate distribution of alternative pricing schemes. Some facilities offer different options for entrance fees, with higher refundable fees and lower nonrefundable fees. Others have mixed entrance fees with rental options. Facilities that achieve substantial sales before financing have better databases from which to forecast than do those with scant or no premarketing results. Because of the level of attrition normally experienced from presales, however, it is still difficult to predict the ultimate breakdown of preferences for pricing schemes. Another effort to provide residents with greater choices—the trend toward offering pay-for-use services, particularly for meal service—makes forecasting revenues very difficult.

A similar problem can occur for assisted living communities that offer tiered pricing schemes. Such pricing strategies are now more common than an all-inclusive single monthly fee. Tiered pricing or increases in pricing are based on the resident assessment done at admission and reflect the specific needs of each resident, something that is difficult to forecast before opening. This approach may be somewhat easier for the national chains, based on their experience across a large number of communities, but for smaller providers it is likely to be much more difficult. Very little published data are available relating to the acuity level at entry for those moving to assisted living.

Finally, revenue forecasts are affected if an unexpected amount of turnover occurs in the early years of a facility's operation. It may have been a problem as congregate housing communities offering no health care services discovered that they were attracting an older and frailer group of residents than anticipated. As residents' frailty and needs increased, many of these facilities were unable to continue to serve them. The resultant moves to assisted living facilities or nursing homes yielded higher turnover and longer periods of vacancy than planned. High turnover has also been a problem in facilities that may have relaxed their standards in screening and admitting residents to independent living units. This decision often occurs in facilities that are experiencing difficulty attracting residents, especially when the fill period is stretching beyond what was forecast. Exacerbating the problem of an extended fill period is the necessity to admit higher numbers of frail or ill residents so that facilities experience higher than anticipated rates of turnover, thus necessitating the remarketing of the independent living unit. In other cases, facilities experiencing marketing problems may admit residents who do not have the necessary finances to sustain fee payments. Although this problem may not manifest itself during the facility's early years of operation, it eventually can become a significant problem.

Clearly, a feasibility study cannot anticipate all the potential problems in marketing, filling, and operating a community. Even when assumptions are conservative, they may not accurately reflect the events that take place once a seniors' community is open or the measures necessary to counter them.

When Studies Forecast Outcomes Most Accurately

Experience of Analysts

As noted, market analyses conducted for seniors' housing communities can vary tremendously. Studies conducted by organizations that have specific and significant experience in the seniors' housing industry are most likely to accurately anticipate performance. As many markets have become more competitive and the industry becomes more complex, this case has become increasingly apparent. Analysts have to be able to combine the best analytical methodologies with the most informed judgment based on their experience in the industry. Those judgments have to take into consideration both quantitative and qualitative factors, such as the nature of the competition and its timing, the character of the market, the niche opportunities to meet underserved market segments, and the experience of the project team.

Differences in the experience and objectives of those conducting the market study can and do affect methodologies as well as results. Minimal or superficial experience can, for instance, result in reliance on benchmarks as absolutes. Limited experience can lead to the use of overly simplified methodologies to define market area (such as use of a radius) to less than thorough competitor analyses and unrealistic dependence on market penetration rather than less quantitative but more valid measures of market feasibility.

In some cases, market analysis is conducted by an organization with a vested interest in its outcome. In-house analysis by inexperienced personnel often leads to self-serving prophecies of market potential—which can be a particular problem for organizations feeling pressure to do something with a piece of land they already own or for whom survival depends on successful diversification.

Significant differences are apparent in market analysis in the real estate, health care, and seniors' housing industries. Yet many studies of seniors' housing have been done by organizations that previously had focused on more traditional residential real estate projects or acute or long-term health care facilities. Reliance on the fundamentals of the supply and demand/need analysis may result in missing the qualitative and subtle differences required to accurately assess the market for a seniors' community.

Time Spent in Local Market

It is the market feasibility consultant's job to quickly become knowledgeable about local market characteristics and conditions that can affect the success of a seniors' housing development. Although numerous small consulting practices are located in and focus on their own local markets, many firms with specialized expertise in seniors' housing are called on to conduct studies in markets throughout the country. The expectation of a client choosing the latter type of firm is that this firm will be able to bring the depth of its expertise and knowledge of national trends and various markets to the specific market where the client's project is to be located. The client can expect such a consulting firm to spend enough time in the local market to develop an understanding of its particular dynamics and characteristics. When a market study is conducted without benefit of sufficient local knowledge, the results suffer. Each market has its own idiosyncratic history and character that affect the development and acceptance of seniors' housing.

For example, the study conducted for Fiddler's Woods (now successfully operating as the Lafayette Redeemer) in Philadelphia appears to have overlooked a critical feature of the marketplace. Fiddler's Woods was to be built in the northeast section of Philadelphia, a highly urbanized neighborhood characterized by middle- to lower-middle-income residents. The market portion of the feasibility study assumed that Jewish residents from throughout the five-county Philadelphia metropolitan area (the Pennsylvania portion) would make up the market for this project. Local knowledge would have prevented that assumption from being made. For families whose improved economic conditions allowed them to move to suburban neighborhoods, returning to the northeast part of town at the end of their lives was not a form of nostalgia in which they were likely to indulge. Usually, local fieldwork is limited because those who commission market studies wish to limit the budget for the work as much as possible. The unwillingness to spend what is necessary to conduct a thorough, professional analysis is a shortsighted decision in a process that ultimately requires significant funds. Properly conducted market studies that allow for sufficient time in the local market can help not only prevent projects from being built for which little market support exists but also shape decisions that prevent spending funds for redesigning or retargeting marketing efforts.

Relationship between the Study and Development Timing

A market or feasibility study represents a picture of conditions at a specific time. Although it represents the best effort to look into the near future on items such as competition, it cannot be prescient. Conditions are fluid in nearly every market and can change in ways that alter analyses and recommendations. Thus, most financing sources, particularly underwriters handling tax-exempt bond financing, require that the study date not exceed 90 to 120 days before the financing date so it represents the most likely conditions, characteristics, and assumptions to be employed in the project being financed. Studies conducted well before that point must be updated to reflect the most current market conditions.

Frequently, however, when market studies in particular are conducted well before project financing and no update is required, the study's findings and recommendations and project performance vary greatly. Sources of capital willing to accept outdated studies encourage this risk, a decision that may be made in an effort to control costs. Thorough market studies provide strong information bases on competitive facilities, which can readily be updated periodically by the feasibility analyst or by the development organization's staff.

Team Function

The ability to conduct a thorough and meaningful study is enhanced immeasurably if key members of the project team—developer, sponsor, architect, managers, and marketing professionals—have already been assembled. The feasibility analyst benefits if the architect has been selected and can provide valuable insights about the site's development potential. The sponsor, managers, and marketing team will have an indelible effect on the seniors' housing community, and it is important that the feasibility analysts have their input. The development process is an interactive team effort that should be initiated as early as possible in the planning process. For feasibility consultants, having the benefit of the team's input allows better translation of what appears to be possible for the market to what can be accomplished, given the team responsible for the project.

Issues That Studies May Not Address

The success of a seniors' housing community is a function of many factors that traditionally have been beyond the scope of feasibility studies. Those factors—design, development, marketing, and management—must come together and be implemented properly to increase the chance for success. As the industry has grown, players have recognized to a greater extent the critical influence each component has on performance. Although feasibility studies completed for financing purposes may cite the experience of the key team members, analysts often are not in a position to render in-depth judgments about team members' capabilities to carry out the project.

Design

The architectural design of a seniors' community must not only be in keeping with the surrounding environment but also include specific design features that meet the needs of the target market. A significant body of knowledge about specialized design features in housing for the elderly increases the potential for inclusion of necessary design features. Issues such as walking distances between living units and a community's service core and special features in the living units must be considered. The acceptability of overall design features (such as whether a facility includes independent cottages or villas, garden homes, or low-, mid-, or high-rise structures) is critical to architectural feasibility. Many architectural firms routinely conduct their own feasibility tests to determine the acceptability of overall design and features. Architects can refine project features by listening to reactions of and feedback from prospective residents in formal or informal focus groups.

Most market and financial feasibility studies, however, do not incorporate a review of a facility's architectural plans. Market studies conducted during the planning process rarely have the benefit of completed or even preliminary architectural plans. Even at the point of financing, architectural issues are not a focal point for most feasibility consultants. The extent to which design is considered is cursory in most cases, and rarely if ever have poor designs resulted in negative feasibility studies.

Marketing and Management

Marketing is critical to the success of a seniors' housing community, particularly in the increasingly competitive environments where most new projects find themselves. Many feasibility consultants now recommend in their planning studies that the development team include an experienced marketing firm or individuals who have marketed other seniors' housing communities. Feasibility studies completed for financing also include a description of the experience those responsible for marketing the community should have. As recently as a decade ago, feasibility studies usually did not seriously consider the presence of experienced marketing personnel a component of a project's feasibility. Project feasibility was assumed to be contingent on successful marketing, as reflected in the language frequently found in financial feasibility studies. As more and more projects experienced difficulties during their fill periods, however, the importance of good marketing was recognized. Although the evidence is primarily anecdotal, it appears that feasibility consultants are now much more reluctant to issue final studies for financing purposes without the assurance that experienced marketing personnel will be part of the project team.

Essentially, much of what has been said about marketing is echoed in the area of management. Although feasibility consultants do not actually review the résumés of key management personnel, they are likely to consider their qualifications. Today, feasibility consultants as well as lenders consider qualified management a requirement. Some experts in the industry believe that management is the single most critical element that contributes to a project's success. Consumers, having seen many newspaper accounts of failed projects, make management a high priority when considering the move to a seniors' community.

Projects That Do Not Play by the Rules

It is highly likely that numerous successful seniors' housing communities are operating in every part of this country that do not conform to what appear to be industry norms. Many of these communities have existed for more than a decade; others have opened more recently. In most instances, a traditional market feasibility study might not have concluded that the projects were feasible, particularly if they had relied on certain benchmarks or standards. Probably the most common trait among seniors' housing communities that have defied the standards is their ability to draw from broad, nonlocalized markets. Although the majority of seniors' housing communities draw most residents from the local geographic area, a number of communities have been able to extend their reach beyond a typical local market and to sustain such a pattern successfully.

It can be extremely difficult for a typical market analysis to evaluate the potential for a project that must defy the norms to become successful. Clearly, many elements that are difficult to measure contribute to the success of such communities. For instance, it is unknown whether the appeal of a vacation destination can be translated into a year-round residential attraction and whether the team involved in a project has the skills and resources necessary to craft a marketing campaign to reach and draw residents.

To the extent that analysts rely entirely on benchmarks that reflect the typical rather than the unusual, the potential for development opportunities that will yield unpredictable results may be missed. In the future, market analysis must become more sophisticated and responsibly creative as unusual projects are assessed. The use of consumer research will become a much more important and necessary tool in conducting such studies. Survey research is a critical component in the initial approach to evaluating new development opportunities. The use of early premarketing campaigns will also become part of the market feasibility process in certain cases, using the results to support and demonstrate a potential project's ability to defy the norms.

Note

1. Assisted Living Federation of America, National Investment Council, and PricewaterhouseCoopers, "Overview of the Assisted Living Industry, 2000," Table 1, p. 11.

Barry Rustin Photography; courtesy AIA

At Chai Point in Milwaukee, Wisconsin, a 208-bed, skilled nursing facility provides a skilled care dementia center, assisted and independent living apartments, an adult daycare center, and a daily lunch program for 100 nonresidents. Architect: David Kahler

8 Market Maturation and Saturation

What is the effect of being one of the first seniors' housing communities to open in an area? When is the market for seniors' housing saturated? How does market maturation differ from market saturation? What impact do various market conditions have on the marketing and fill-up of seniors' housing communities? How do older communities adjust to changing market conditions? How do the characteristics of seniors' housing developments differ from one market to another? These critical questions must be addressed by those involved in the seniors' housing industry, as they represent the most fundamental issues affecting a project's success.

This chapter addresses these issues directly and through examples. Three regional case studies are presented; they are distinctly different in terms of the history, development, acceptance, and success of market-rate seniors' housing, and the study areas were selected to illustrate these differences. All three case studies are updated from material that appeared in the first edition of this book, *Retirement Housing Markets,* published in 1991. The Philadelphia area, known throughout the country for its exceptional concentration of nonprofit life care CCRCs, is a market that, according to many who do not understand its dynamics, is saturated. But Philadelphia may be one of the best examples of how the market for seniors' housing matures over time, belying the theory that it is saturated. In contrast, during the 1980s Cincinnati represented how market saturation can occur, how it affects the overall market, and how it can stabilize over time. The south Florida market was chosen to illustrate how relatively rapid expansion can succeed in a market.

The distinctive nature of seniors' housing contributes to the difficulty in answering the most fundamental question: when is a market saturated? Although seniors' housing is in some ways a hybrid shaped by the real estate, health care, and hospitality industries, it does not enjoy the benefit of well-formulated theories and methodologies that allow one to comfortably judge when too much product has been developed in a market. The effective demand calculation models that can be applied in assessing residential real estate developments cannot be directly translated to seniors' housing. Unlike much of the health care industry, the determination of need for seniors' housing is not regulated (other than for nursing care and, in some states, assisted living). (Some states regulate aspects other than the quantity of supply.) Therefore, the industry is not subject to the franchising of supply represented by the Certificate of Need process that still controls the nursing home business in many states. Finally, because the seniors' housing industry is still evolving, no reliable historical pattern can be examined to predict the limitations of future demand that will shape supply requirements. Only as recently as the late 1990s were any efforts made to develop national standards for judging saturation, and they were directed primarily at assisted living in response to the development boom that occurred during the mid- to late 1990s.

Market Maturation and Saturation In Seniors' Housing

Defining Market Maturation and Saturation

Defining market saturation and what actually constitutes a "saturated" market is very difficult in seniors' housing. Virtually none of the experts interviewed for this book had a ready definition or description of market saturation. A factor that contributes to the difficulty in pinpointing, quantifying, or defining saturation is the relative newness of the seniors' housing concept as we know it today. Probably few if any markets have achieved their ultimate development potential, and the saturation issue may well be an iterative one as a result of the combined effects of demographic growth in the target market and the increased acceptability of the product that comes with the successful absorption of new projects.

In reality, market maturation and market saturation must be separated and not confused. Is the Philadelphia area, with its 63 seniors' and 66 assisted living communities, saturated, as some believe it to be, or is it representative of the *maturation* process, which allows increasingly high penetration levels to be achieved? Given the difference in the development time line for seniors' versus assisted living communities in this market, can it be a mature seniors' community market and a saturated assisted living market? Saturation should not be measured by the number of projects and units in a given market; it is more likely a function of the relationship between timing and quantity than quantity alone, an effect of the rapid pace of development over a short period of time. Two of the case studies—Philadelphia and Cincinnati—illustrate the impact of time on a market's ability to continue to absorb new communities.

One should be wary of assuming that a market is saturated because projects are performing poorly. Without doubt, many seniors' communities that have opened were poorly conceived, marketed, and managed, factors that have contributed to their poor performance. Many developers in the 1990s assumed there were no limits to the number of assisted living communities a single market could absorb in a short period of time. Bad projects can cause a market to be judged as saturated when saturation is not the actual problem. They can also create image problems for the entire industry in the area, which may affect the performance of good projects being introduced in the same market.

Existing quantitative methodologies (whether referred to as market penetration or market saturation analyses) should not be relied on as the sole or even most critical arbiter of market saturation or as a sign that a project can achieve success. In many instances, the numbers may indicate *no,* but the real answer should be *yes.* This outcome is a function of several factors. To begin with, efforts to size the market and measure saturation are driven by decisions that are reached regarding market area definition and the qualifications of the market segment to be considered. To the extent that such determinations accurately reflect the real conditions of a specific market, quantitative analysis may be useful. But incorrect judgments about any of the criteria that drive the quantitative analyses can lead to faulty judgments based on faulty measures.

On a more fundamental level, one still has to ask whether there is an agreed-upon quantitative measure or benchmark for market saturation. As the industry expanded and more facilities were successfully developed and filled, early "acceptable" penetration levels for independent living of 2 percent or less began to increase to 3, 4, 5, and higher percent. A study of statistical information on 34 nonprofit CCRCs financed from June 1994 through August 1999 revealed that the average penetration rate for eligible age- and income-qualified households age 75 and older was 7.7 percent (the median was 6.4 percent).[1] Penetration rates reported in this study ranged from a low of 3.5 percent to 10.4 percent. The ability of a market to absorb a new project is predicated on much more complex variables than those that can be quantified and measured demographically.

"Measuring Demand for Senior Housing" characterizes market saturation levels of 15 percent and 30 percent as the maximum levels for independent and assisted living, respectively, beyond which a significant credit risk is perceived.[2] A series of guidelines dealing with assisted living temporary saturation is being developed and refined by Anthony J. Mullen; it has been described in successive papers presented by Mullen at his annual Research Summit in Philadelphia. Mullen ties temporary saturation to a series of factors, the most important of which reflect the proportion of new beds being opened in the current year as they relate to existing and occupied beds in the previous year, and below-average occupancy rates and the move-in rate for new facilities opened for at least six months.

Segmentation, for instance, is a factor. Seniors' housing communities that offer an alternative to entrance fees, such as rent or equity, or facilities that target an underserved economic or social market segment may succeed in otherwise highly developed areas. Some communities in the Philadelphia area support this notion. Bellingham, an affordable rental community, achieved steady lease-up in a market that offered few rental opportunities, particularly in the suburbs. Some developments that originally charged entrance fees and faltered converted to rental communities and succeeded. The Quadrangle, Beaumont at Bryn Mawr, and Waverly Heights, which all opened within a three-year period on Philadelphia's prestigious Main Line, were the first to specifically target a very affluent clientele. Taking advantage of sites that were well-known estates, all three communities successfully filled up and have waiting lists. Although these communities and others developed in the 1990s helped to increase the Philadelphia area's overall penetration to levels that would turn many developers away from this market, the projects have been successful. Good projects, well planned and targeted, with high-quality teams implementing them, belie the numbers.

Factors Contributing to Saturation

The most significant factor contributing to a sluggish or saturated market is the introduction of too many facilities over too short a time period. Although the level of penetration achievable in any given market can be expected to expand over time, reaching higher levels of market penetration should not be expected to occur easily in a relatively brief period. The case study for Cincinnati presents a good example of overdevelopment of seniors' housing communities during a three- to four-year period in the 1980s, leading to difficult market conditions for many facilities and a quantity of product that took many years to absorb. The scant number of seniors' communities that opened between 1990 and 2000 is a testament to the earlier overbuilding. The pattern of overbuilding repeated itself in the assisted living segment in this market during the late 1990s.

The quality of projects being introduced also figures in issues related to maturation and saturation. Some projects have been successful despite a saturated market. In Cincinnati, the Seasons is a highly successful project that opened toward the end of the very heavy development period. Like the three upscale Philadelphia projects mentioned, the Seasons targets an affluent clientele and is located on a site that attracts that market segment. The high quality of the facility, its premier location, the caliber of staff, and persistent marketing efforts contributed to its success. Although during the initial fill-up of the community, the Seasons had the highest fees in the market, it successfully attracted residents who were seeking a top-quality product regardless of price. Throughout the 1990s, the Seasons maintained full occupancy and today has a waiting list of up to three years. The Seasons is, at least in part, a story of how success can be a function of market segmentation. Identifying the right market niche and employing the right tactics to reach the target market segment, particularly in highly competitive markets, is a strategy that should increase the chances of success.

Warning Signs of Market Saturation

While little agreement exists about what constitutes a saturated market, many professionals who have been involved in projects in markets that appeared to be overbuilt indicate that there are warning signs. Most analysts look at how the competition is performing for an indication of whether a market is saturated. Facilities that have never reached full occupancy and that are languishing well below 90 percent occupancy may be a sign that there is too much product in the market, particularly if they are otherwise sound projects on their own merits. Facilities that have not yet filled that are having difficulty substantially improving occupancy levels may also be a red flag. Yet another warning sign could be a market where numerous communities are developed in a short period of time, thereby causing fierce competition and resulting in slower absorption.

A common condition with seniors' housing communities during the 1980s and again in the 1990s with assisted living has been the inability of some development groups to overcome the tendency to think that, regardless of market conditions, their project will be so special that they will have no competition or that their national name recognition means they will not be affected by local market conditions. This ego-driven philosophy has caused many organizations to proceed with development plans despite the advice of their consultants and others in the market.

Effect of Maturation and Saturation On Seniors' Housing Communities

Marketing New Communities

In areas that have experienced a significant amount of seniors' housing development, marketing new facilities frequently employs a strategy of differentiation. The need to continue educating the market does not necessarily disappear in markets where a number of facilities are already in operation. In these markets, consumers may have become much more informed and sophisticated in evaluating their options, as they have shopped the various communities in the market. Their questions typically reflect this knowledge, and marketing professionals must be in a position not only to explain the basic concept embodied by their specific community but also to differentiate it from the rest, if possible. Attention to distinctive programmatic, financial, or architectural characteristics must be translated into a strategy that allows potential residents to focus on the special benefits of moving to the community they are visiting. In Philadelphia, for instance, Beaumont at Bryn Mawr distinguished itself from its direct competitor, Waverly Heights, by emphasizing that it was the only life care facility in Philadelphia that offered residents the chance to own the facility. With its structure as a cooperative, Beaumont legitimately distinguished itself in what became a very important way. Residents at Beaumont are affluent and accustomed to making investments in real estate, and they were attracted to the ownership structure.

Although the physical setting and architectural design of a community are important, they should not be the focal points in selling a community or distinguishing it from competitors. Many who have become involved in the seniors' housing industry have learned, some the hard way, that residents are not attracted to the real estate, per se, but to the tangible and intangible aspects of the lifestyle. Those moving into any type of seniors' housing community are not trading up in terms of the quality and spaciousness of their physical surroundings. In fact, the move is very likely to be one of the negative tradeoffs being made to gain something that cannot be achieved by continuing to live in one's own home.

In markets where too much product becomes available simultaneously, marketing professionals warn against the dangers of numbing the prospects because of the deluge of direct mail solicitations and print ads to which they may be exposed. Information overload can obviate many of the benefits of an otherwise well-conceived marketing campaign. The support and referral infrastructure can also suffer from burnout when approached by too many seniors' housing representatives hoping for help in reaching their constituents. Representatives of a major national seniors' housing organization tell of a situation in Atlanta where one beleaguered church official finally told all area seniors' communities that he would be glad to hold one large meeting at which representatives could extol the virtues of their communities.

Marketing staff in areas where seniors' developments have had financial problems should expect that prospects will be very aware of these problems, particularly if they have been widely publicized. This situation can result in greater consumer scrutiny of the financial stability and history of a facility and the reliability, commitment, and experience of the management. Troubled facilities in a market do not necessarily have a negative impact on marketing of other communities, but new entrants, particularly those with no affiliation with a credible sponsor or other major organization or institution, may be subject to inquiries by potential residents about the financial and management support behind the community.

Filling New Communities

The impact of having many choices on the decision to move to a seniors' housing community varies from market to market. Although some experts have indicated that the decision-making process and resultant sales are more rapid in heavily developed markets, it frequently is not the case. Other experts suggest that, in markets where prospects have many facilities to consider, the decision process is delayed because the prospect knows that the choice is not limited or constrained by supply. Thus, although marketing activities may begin well before a community opens, results may not be strong until close to or after the community is operational. This statement clearly is less true for facilities charging entrance fees, particularly when substantial presales are required before the start of construction. In markets that have a number of rental properties, however, the delay in the decision process can create unplanned delays in filling the facility. This situation is also true for assisted living, where the decision is need-driven, shortening the time between considering and actually making the move. In addition, because of the limited tenure commitment required from a resident of a rental community (i.e., a monthly or yearly lease), moves from one rental community to another that may seem more appealing are not unusual in some markets. The combination of facility shopping and facility hopping can wreak havoc on achieving and maintaining stabilized full occupancy.

Some experts argue that time is not a critical factor for the mature consumer. David Wolfe describes seven principles for mature markets, the seventh of which is the *Timelessness Principle.* "Time is usually not of the essence in the decision-making process of the mature consumer; therefore, attempts to instill a sense of urgency in a purchase consideration generally are ineffective."[3]

Impact on Older Communities

The effect of market maturation and potential saturation on older facilities in an area varies depending on several factors, including reputation, operating philosophy, and the opportunities and/or limitations to make changes in the physical plant. A seniors' community that has operated for many years and has reached and maintained full occupancy can be in an excellent position to continue its success and withstand the effects of potential overbuilding. Communities such as Foulkeways, Kendal at Longwood, and the numerous facilities owned by ACTS Retirement-Life Communities in the Philadelphia area have lengthy waiting lists, filling vacancies without difficulty as units turn over. The excellent reputation that many older facilities have earned enhances their ability to continue to succeed in today's market. Another characteristic of communities that successfully continue to operate through changing market conditions is their attention to those changes and willingness to adapt their program or structure. On the other hand, some older facilities have difficulty maintaining their competitive edge. Unfortunate examples exist of facilities that have not kept abreast of the market's changing conditions and consumers' preferences. A long history of success can lead some managers to take that success for granted. Such communities may pay little or no attention to marketing and may even be unaware of what newer facilities are offering. This Rip Van Winkle effect can be devastating when an older facility is startled into wakeful scrutiny of new prevailing market conditions. Many older facilities in the case study markets indicated that they are becoming much more aggressive about marketing than they had been historically, responding to the newly discovered pressure of a more competitive marketplace.

Some older communities with antiquated physical plants or unit types that are no longer marketable may find that they have a diminishing waiting list or, in the worst instances, declining occupancy levels. Keeping up with the competition can be a particular problem for facilities dominated by studio apartments. Newer communities have responded to today's clear preference for larger units.

In some instances, facilities that were built on sites that at one time enjoyed the status of being in good neighborhoods find that changes in their neighborhoods can potentially be detrimental to their market positions. Strong facilities have been able to overcome this problem by virtue of their outstanding reputation for quality service and, pragmatically, by increasing the security around the community.

How Older Communities Remain Competitive

Older communities in markets with numerous new facilities work to sustain their success in many ways. The foundation for continued success may be the credibility that has long been established by providing excellent care and service. Residents of such communities become instrumental in the continuing ability of the facility to attract new residents through valuable word-of-mouth marketing. This method has certainly been the case in the numerous Quaker-affiliated life care facilities in the Philadelphia area and in the many facilities operated by ACTS in both the Philadelphia and south Florida markets. Some older facilities stay current with what is happening in their market through networking with others in the business. In Philadelphia, for instance, many of the Quaker and other nonprofit facilities have an ongoing tradition of sharing information. Others that become passive about marketing, lulled by years of 100 percent occupancy with a waiting list, are changing and increasing the extent and type of marketing they conduct.

In other cases, maintaining the competitive edge requires greater capital investment. Improving or changing the physical plant may be necessary in facilities built several decades ago when, for instance, the market for studio units was stronger. Many individuals interviewed at the older facilities for the case studies described building programs that incorporated such strategies as creating larger units by combining studios. Others have built new wings or additions, space permitting, or have moved to new locations.

Some troubled facilities in heavily developed markets have repositioned themselves to compete successfully. One assisted living facility in south Florida, Remington House (formerly Woodsetter Retirement Club), opened in 1987 and was originally licensed for 220 assisted living beds. The physical plant of the facility is shaped like spokes on a wheel, with four residential buildings housing residents and one centrally located building containing the main dining room and common and support areas. One of the four residential buildings is dedicated to residents with Alzheimer's disease and memory-related disorders; it has a self-contained dining room and accommodations for 30 residents. By 1997, occupancy had plateaued at 60 percent, and the staffing ratio was disproportionately high to the low number of residents. Having 102 employees resulted in expenses much greater than revenues and debt service coverage not being met. The tremendous amount of deferred maintenance meant the physical appearance of the facility was rapidly declining. Woodsetter was purchased in 1997 by a publicly traded company and renamed Remington House. Upon acquiring the property, the new owner implemented a plan of action in an effort to improve curb appeal and increase occupancy that included several renovations—new interior and exterior paint, new furniture for the common area and dining room, new carpet, and improved landscaping. To improve the facility operationally, licensed beds were reduced to 142, and staff was reduced to reflect current residency. From a marketing perspective, the strategy was to clearly define services by offering three levels of assisted living—basic, intermediate, and Alzheimer's care—with rates reflecting the level of care received. While the facility is still working toward achieving stabilized occupancy in the Alzheimer's wing, it should be understood that the Alzheimer's care market has increased tremendously, making it very competitive. This initiative has been successful for traditional assisted living occupancy, however, which reached and remains at 99 percent.

Case Studies of Three Regional Markets

The remainder of this chapter presents the history of the development and acceptance of seniors' housing in three geographic areas: Philadelphia,

Cincinnati, and south Florida. The Philadelphia study examines a large multicounty regional market, the Cincinnati study addresses a single-county market dominated by a metropolitan area, and the south Florida case study examines two small localized markets. The case studies are intended to illustrate the ways in which market development and maturation or saturation have occurred in each market. Each market has distinctive characteristics in terms of history, culture, and development. Although they share some similarities, the different experiences of each market area are striking and instructive for those who seek to better understand why different markets have had greater or lesser success in absorbing the seniors' housing communities that have been built.

Because the information used in each case study was compiled during the first quarter of 2001, the analysis represents conditions that prevailed at that time. Although the specific conditions of certain facilities in each market have undoubtedly changed, the overall history and trends that shaped the development and acceptance of seniors' housing have not.

The information presented for each market was obtained from highly knowledgeable local analysts familiar with the seniors' housing industry in general and the history of their particular market area. Specific data were collected on each major seniors' community and assisted living facility in each market area. Demographic data were obtained from the U.S. Census Bureau and Claritas.

Philadelphia

The Region and Its Submarkets

The Philadelphia area includes the Pennsylvania portion of a nine-county metropolitan statistical area that surrounds the Delaware River and incorporates portions of southern New Jersey. The analysis is limited to what is referred to as the Delaware Valley, encompassing five counties in Pennsylvania: Philadelphia (the city and county are the same), Montgomery, Bucks, Delaware, and Chester.

The region's geographic hub is Philadelphia, one of the nation's oldest cities, founded in 1681. The city of Philadelphia has many of the same characteristics as other old northeastern cities. Consisting of hundreds of small neighborhoods, Philadelphia is home to all economic sectors, from the affluent residents of Chestnut Hill and many neighborhoods in the downtown area to the working class and urban poor in south, west, and north Philadelphia.

Delaware County is characterized by a mix of extensive industrialization and residential communities that house workers. Movement between neighboring Philadelphia and Delaware County is common. Montgomery County, the wealthiest of the five counties, began to lose its rural character to commercial and residential development early in the 20th century. Both Bucks and Chester counties were largely agricultural before World War II, but development in both counties has accelerated since then. Lower Bucks County, which borders Philadelphia, is more densely developed than its outer portions.

The Philadelphia suburbs grew at a tremendous pace between 1950 and the 1970s in terms of both development and population. Between 1970 and 1990, although development continued to spread out quickly from the city deep into Bucks, Chester, Delaware, and Montgomery counties, population growth in the region increased only marginally overall because of a decrease in Philadelphia County and a marginal increase in Delaware County. According to 2000 Census data released by the U.S. Census Bureau, the four suburban counties grew steadily in population during the decade, with Chester County leading the way at 15 percent growth, followed by Montgomery, Bucks, and Delaware counties.[4]

Trends in Overall and Elderly Population

As might be expected, this region, which became home to nearly 4 million people during the 1980s and 1990s, has experienced population shifts away from the more densely developed urbanized areas in Philadelphia, lower Bucks, and eastern Delaware counties to the less developed portions of the region (see Figure 8-1). Chester County experienced the greatest growth during the 20-year period. While Bucks County followed with the second greatest growth rate between 1980 and 1990, Montgomery County experienced greater growth compared with Bucks County between 1990 and 2000.

Although Delaware and Philadelphia counties experienced overall losses of population, the elderly population increased substantially during the period in all counties except Philadelphia, where the population age 65 and older decreased as the population age 75 and older increased (see Figure 8-2). Between 1980 and 2000, the population older than 65 in the region increased from 456,496 to 535,959, and the number of those older than 75 increased from 178,088 to 264,185. Both in aggregate numbers and in proportion to the overall population, the elderly constituted a significant demographic segment of the region's population, exceeding the national averages in all but Bucks and Chester counties, which were growing primarily because of the influx of young families. The region was characterized by markets of substantial demographic potential for the development of seniors' housing.

Early History of Seniors' Housing Development

The tradition of facility-based care for the elderly in Philadelphia dates back more than two centuries; many of the facilities operating today trace their roots back to the 1800s. Although the early institutions differed in many respects from the communities found in the region today, the tradition of caring for the elderly in places outside one's home was well entrenched as a part of life in Philadelphia.

In the Philadelphia area, life care communities have traditionally been dominant. The emergence of

Figure 8-1 **Philadelphia Area Population Trends**

	Population			Percent Change	
County	**1980**	**1990**	**2000**	**1980–1990**	**1990–2000**
Bucks	479,211	541,174	597,635	13%	10%
Chester	316,660	376,396	433,501	19%	15%
Delaware	555,007	547,651	550,864	–1%	1%
Montgomery	643,621	678,111	750,097	5%	11%
Philadelphia	1,688,210	1,585,577	1,517,550	–6%	–4%
Total	3,682,709	3,728,909	3,849,647	1%	3%

Sources: U.S. Census Bureau and Claritas.

Figure 8-2 **Philadelphia Area Elderly Population Trends**

		Population			Percent Change	
County		**1980**	**1990**	**2000**	**1980–1990**	**1990–2000**
Bucks	65+	38,299	58,813	74,094	54%	26%
	75+	14,704	22,726	34,111	55%	50%
Chester	65+	28,686	40,860	50,677	42%	24%
	75+	11,219	16,079	23,549	43%	46%
Delaware	65+	71,322	84,685	85,669	19%	1%
	75+	28,088	34,248	43,616	22%	27%
Montgomery	65+	80,819	101,867	111,797	26%	10%
	75+	32,827	43,565	56,235	33%	29%
Philadelphia	65+	237,370	239,205	213,722	1%	–11%
	75+	91,250	101,806	106,674	12%	5%
Regional Total	65+	456,496	525,430	535,959	15%	2%
	75+	178,088	218,424	264,185	23%	21%

Sources: U.S. Census Bureau and Claritas.

the life care concept has always been identified with the Quakers (or Friends, as they are known) because of the numerous facilities associated with the Society of Friends. The life care model embodied by such facilities as Foulkeways and Kendal at Longwood represented the initiation of a steady and continuous phase of development from 1967 through today.

Changing terminology provides interesting insights into the way care for the elderly has been viewed. Evangelical Manor, a community that was chartered in 1888, describes its first 100 years in a special centennial edition of its annual report. When the German Home for the Aged (as it was formerly known) was opened in 1890, those who lived there were referred to as *inmates,* the common terminology of the late 19th century. By the 1920s, Evangelical Manor was caring for *guests* in its home in Philadelphia. By the early 1930s, references were made to the growth of the *home family,* which had by then moved to new and larger quarters. Another move occurred in the 1950s to accommodate the ever-growing *resident* population. The terminology reflects the changing philosophies of the management of care for the elderly, conveying with just a few words the transition from charitably motivated enforcement to paternalism to the encouragement of independence. A pamphlet published by Kendal-Crosslands and Kendal Management Services states this philosophy clearly: "Our communities are designed to be places where people 'live' rather than places where people are 'taken care of.'"[5]

In many ways, traditions begun in the 1800s set the stage for Philadelphia's successful evolution as a center of the life care continuing care industry today. This strong foundation of seniors' communities helped pave the way for the development of congregate housing and personal care facilities (assisted living) in the region. These types of communities became alternatives for those who did not want to or could not pay for the upfront entrance fees found in the predominant life care communities or who wished to delay a move until they became too frail to remain at home. Growth in these other forms of seniors' housing occurred primarily in the 1990s.

Development Trends

Independent Living. In many ways, the Philadelphia market is quite different from the other areas examined by the case studies. A striking and distinguishing feature of this market is the overwhelming dominance of a single concept, that of life care or continuing care. Of the 63 communities in operation (see Figure 8-3 for a list) as of this writing, 54 offer a continuum of care, including independent living units, assisted living, and nursing care beds. Of interest is the fact that ten new communities were opened since publication of the first edition of this book in 1991. The overwhelming majority of communities offer life care or continuing care contracts to their residents and are structured using a combination of upfront and monthly fees. Only a handful of communities offer a rental contract or option with no upfront entrance fee. While other areas of the country during the 1980s began extensive diversification into other models, particularly congregate housing, Philadelphia steadily produced communities that offered the full continuum of care.

Foulkeways at Gwynedd was the first life care community to open in the Delaware Valley. The development of this Quaker facility was fostered by the Gwynedd Friends Meeting. After visiting two such communities in California in 1964, Bill and Eleanor Clarke, members of the Gwynedd Friends Meeting, returned to Philadelphia convinced that this approach was the way to create the "active community of retired persons" that was the vision for the Beaumont site. A $300,000 grant from the Committee on Aging Friends helped to get the project started, and the first Quaker life care community in the Philadelphia area opened in Gwynedd in 1967.

Thus began development that resulted in three other Quaker-sponsored life care communities in the Delaware Valley (and two additional Quaker CCRCs in neighboring southern New Jersey). Although the Society of Friends looms as a major force in the area, each Quaker-sponsored life care community is owned and operated by a nonprofit corporation that is independent of the others.

Another significant force in the Philadelphia market has been the organization called Adult Communities Total Services, now ACTS Retirement-Life Communities, Inc. (ACTS). Pastor Richard Coons, leader of the radio ministry Church of the Open Door, became interested in life care in the late 1960s or early 1970s. Fort Washington Estates in Fort Washington, Pennsylvania, was ACTS's first life care facility. The organization developed six other life care facilities in the Delaware Valley between 1972 and 1993.

The continuing care model varies among the many facilities in the Philadelphia area. At Foulkeways, for instance, residents who must move to the nursing facility are assured, by their contract, that they will receive unlimited nursing care for the basic monthly fee charged for one of Foulkeways's studio apartments. Similar contractual arrangements, using a one-bedroom unit as the basis for the fee, allow residents unlimited nursing care at other facilities, such as Martin's Run. Some facilities base the nursing home accommodation fee on the type of unit the resident occupied before moving to the nursing home. Finally, certain communities, such as Rosemont Presbyterian Home, are structured on a fee-for-service basis, guaranteeing access to care in the nursing facility but requiring residents to pay the full daily nursing bed rate. Although management philosophies can be and frequently are quite different, elderly consumers appear to be satisfied that their needs and preferences are met by the varying options available to them.

The Philadelphia seniors' housing market has and continues to be dominated by nonprofit organizations. Eighty percent of the seniors' facilities in the Delaware Valley are owned by nonprofit organizations. At least 19 of these facilities are affiliated with one of ten religious denominations. Although few facilities are actually owned by churches themselves or their governing bodies, these associations have been influential factors in building the credibility that most facilities in this area enjoy today. As stated in the special centennial edition of Evangelical Manor's annual report, "We affirm our historical relationship to the United Methodist Church by adhering to the social principles of this Church, and by maintaining a strong identity with the United Methodist Church."

Although several facilities in the area have involved for-profit developers and owners, they continue to be in the minority. Before 1980, only two communities, Pine Run and Twining Village, were developed and owned by proprietary organizations. During the 1980s and 1990s, for-profit development increased yet accounted for only about one-third of all new independent living development.

Some of the for-profit communities have historical origins with nonprofit organizations, leading to greater acceptance in the Philadelphia market. For example, the Quadrangle, owned by Marriott's Senior Living Services division, has its roots in the nonprofit Quaker world. A group of Haverford College graduates, familiar with the Quaker life care communities, sought to build a similar community on the college grounds. Although that plan did not come to fruition, the Harrisons, a couple who were part of this group, began to promote plans for the new community to be built instead on the former Lloyd Estate, a mile from the college's campus. The Harrisons marketed the Quadrangle from their home, collecting small, refundable deposits from friends and acquaintances interested in moving to the community. In the early 1980s, Berwind Realty Services became involved as the developer. In 1986, after Berwind decided to discontinue its involvement in the seniors' housing field, Marriott bought the plans, the property, and the list of prospects. By that time, approximately 50 people had paid 10 percent deposits to reserve units at the Quadrangle, and another 150 had paid smaller deposits. Although the Quadrangle is a for-profit community, the Quaker influence continued. The original sponsoring group remained involved in planning and marketing the community, forming an early residents committee that worked on a voluntary basis in several capacities. The appearance of a Quaker endorsement helped the already credible and powerful Marriott to succeed with the project.

Just as for-profit communities began to evolve in the 1980s and 1990s, so did the emergence of a small number of varying types of independent living and congregate housing communities. Gloria Dei Manor opened in 1978 and could be considered the first community to offer freestanding independent living for seniors without providing assisted living or nursing care beds. Gloria Dei Manor still charges an upfront entrance fee yet features a very modest monthly fee. Although various common areas and amenities are available throughout the community, very limited services are available or provided in the monthly fee. The remaining independent living communities opened only after 1987. Despite growth in the independent living arena, it remains minimal, with only a few communities providing freestanding independent living in the Delaware Valley. Figure 8-3

Figure 8-3 **Philadelphia Market, Independent Living**

Year Opened	Name	Town (County)	Independent Living Units
1865	Simpson House	Philadelphia	160
1869	Deer Meadows	Philadelphia	146
1885	Bala Home	Philadelphia	30
1885	Masonic Retirement Home	Lafayette Hill (M)	70
1888	Evangelical Manor	Philadelphia	177
1890	Philadelphia Protestant Home	Philadelphia	277
1895	Frederick Mennonite Community	Frederick (M)	100
1896	Pilgrim Gardens (North American Baptist Home)	Philadelphia	90
1897	Friends Village	Newtown (B)	61
1904	Stapeley in Germantown	Philadelphia	43
1917	Souderton Mennonite Home	Souderton (B)	206
1923	Christ's Home	Warminster (B)	42
1937	Sacred Heart Manor	Philadelphia	48
1956	Rosemont Presbyterian Village	Rosemont (D)	151
1956	Tel Hai	Honey Brook (C)	193
1962	Harbinger Terrace and Luther Village (Lutheran Community at Telford)	Telford (B)	167
1967	Foulkeways at Gwynedd	Gwynedd (M)	243
1971	Peter Becker Community	Harleysville (B)	160
1972	Fort Washington Estates	Fort Washington (M)	91
1973	Kendal at Longwood	Kennett Square (C)	225
1973	Dock Woods Community, Inc.	Lansdale (M)	197
1974	Dunwoody Village	Newtown Square (D)	263
1974	Rydal Park	Rydal (M)	359
1975	Pine Run Community	Doylestown (B)	300
1976	Gwynedd Estates	Spring House (M)	161
1976	Ware Presbyterian Village	Oxford (C)	60
1977	Crosslands	Kennett Square (C)	250
1978	Rockhill Mennonite Community	Sellersville (B)	227
1978	Spring House Estates	Lower Gwynedd (M)	327
1978	Twining Village	Holland (B)	219
1978	Gloria Dei Manor	Huntington Valley (M)	131
1979	Lima Estates	Media (D)	300
1979	Cathedral Village	Philadelphia	277
1979	Southampton Estates	Southampton (B)	376
1980	Martins Run	Media (D)	189
1980	Pennswood Village	Newtown (B)	253
1981	Paul's Run Retirement Community	Philadelphia	243
1981	Heritage Towers	Doylestown (B)	238
1981	Elm Terrace Gardens	Lansdale (M)	134
1981	Wood River Village	Bensalem (B)	292
1983	Normandy Farms Estates	Blue Bell (M)	354
1984	Heatherwood	Honey Brook (C)	35

Figure 8-3 (continued)

Year Opened	Name	Town (County)	Independent Living Units
1984	Fountains at Logan Square East	Philadelphia	292
1985	Lafayette Redeemer	Philadelphia	247
1986	Quadrangle	Haverford (M)	349
1986	Waverly Heights	Gladwyne (M)	223
1986	Granite Farms Estates	Media (D)	359
1987	Attleboro Retirement Village	Langhorne (B)	136
1987	Harborview Towers	Philadelphia	125
1989	White Horse Village	Newtown Square (D)	333
1989	Bellingham	West Chester (C)	260
1989	Meadowood CCRC	Worcester (M)	270
1990	Beaumont at Bryn Mawr	Bryn Mawr (M)	200
1991	Gloria Dei Farms	Hatboro (M)	141
1993	Riddle Village	Media (D)	365
1993	Brittany Pointe Estates	Lansdale (M)	280
1994	Sanatoga Ridge	Pottstown (C)	130
1996	Jenner's Pond	West Grove (C)	214
1997	Sunrise	Abington (M)	60
1997	Maple Village	Hatboro (B)	114
1998	Freedom Village	West Brandywine (C)	292
1998	Gloria Dei Estates	Philadelphia	212
2000	Simpson Meadows	Downingtown (C)	66

Key
B = Bucks County D = Delaware County
C = Chester County M = Montgomery County

lists seniors' communities that offer independent living units. Only market-rate facilities with more than 30 units are included.

Assisted Living. Licensed as personal care homes in Pennsylvania at the writing of this book (but referred to throughout this section as *assisted living)*, assisted living also has a deep historical foundation in the Philadelphia region. As discussed earlier, many of the first seniors' communities in the area, founded in the late 19th century, were established to provide for the infirm or frail elderly, often indigent widows. Similar to the independent living market, these early communities were developed by nonprofit organizations, often religiously based. Quaker and Catholic influence is still evident in the names of the area's earliest personal care homes, including Barclay Friends and St. Joseph's Manor. Many of these early communities chose to maintain their original mission by providing only health care services in the form of assisted living and nursing care rather than expand to offer independent living or continuing care.

Although the number of freestanding assisted living facilities was limited before 1980, the majority of assisted living beds could be found as a component of the numerous continuing care communities. Fifty-eight of the region's 63 seniors' housing communities contained 3,247 assisted living units. Often, these beds were reserved exclusively for residents living in independent living apartments who were holding life care contracts, thereby guaranteeing a health care bed should the need arise.

As organizations began to realize the development opportunities for assisted living in the area, ten freestanding assisted living facilities were developed in the 1970s, half by for-profit owners. Growth in the 1980s was entirely dominated by for-profit developers, with another eight communities opening in the region. This gradual growth set the stage for an influx of new assisted living communities. Before 1990, the five-county Philadelphia area contained 35 assisted living facilities; by 2000, the number of assisted living communities had doubled. Unlike the independent living market, this surge of development was heavily dominated by for-profit organizations (90 percent). Major national for-profit companies like Alterra, Sunrise, and Atria and regional players like Brandywine Assisted Living and New Seasons Assisted Living seized the development opportunity in the area; each now owns several properties throughout the region. The first assisted living communities designated for those with Alzheimer's disease and related dementias also came to the region in the 1990s. National providers developed multiple communities, including Alterra's Clare Bridge, HCR Manor Care's Arden Courts, and Sunrise's memory unit, in suburban Philadelphia.

Figure 8-4 lists assisted living communities (in addition to those that are components of seniors' housing communities listed in Figure 8-3) with more than 30 beds. The number of beds designated for patients with Alzheimer's disease is shown in parentheses. The majority of these communities charge monthly fees greater than $1,500 and serve private pay seniors.

Development Pacing, Absorption, and Competition

Independent Living. A characteristic of the seniors' housing industry (in contrast to assisted living) in the Delaware Valley that has undoubtedly contributed to its continued success is the steady pace at which it emerged over nearly three decades. The rate at which new facilities were added did not place unusual stress on any one facility. Only rarely were more than a few facilities at a time attempting to reach initial fill-up. The geographic and socioeconomic target markets for facilities that opened simultaneously frequently differed, thus minimizing their directly competing for the same residents. Before 1970, there were 17 seniors' communities. During the period from 1970 to 1979, 17 more were built. Between 1980 and 1989, 18 more were constructed; during the 1990s, development slowed somewhat (particularly as construction of assisted living units escalated), and 11 more seniors' communities were built. During the 1970s and 1980s, approximately 4,000 independent living units per decade were built, whereas only half that amount was built during the 1990s (the actual number built per decade is not clear, as some communities may have expanded or contracted total independent living units later).

In contrast to many other markets, the facilities in the Philadelphia area have experienced lengthy preopening marketing campaigns, measured in years, not months. It was influenced in part by the trend toward lengthier presales periods by communities charging entrance fees than by those offered for rent. The passage of Pennsylvania's Continuing Care Provider Registration and Disclosure Act, which became effective in 1985, further contributed to the length of the preopening marketing campaigns. The act prohibited the release of escrowed entrance fees to the provider until 50 percent of the aggregate entrance fees anticipated under full occupancy had been received.[6] The use of tax-exempt financing frequently resulted in thresholds of 70 percent presales before the transaction took place. The pattern of lengthy and successful preleasing campaigns has facilitated smooth and relatively predictable fill periods for many seniors' housing communities in the Delaware Valley.

The extended preconstruction marketing period is characteristic of even the newest projects in the area. Four large CCRCs opened in the region in the 1990s: Jenner's Pond, Freedom Village, Brittany Pointe Estates, and Riddle Village. Marketing for and building awareness of these communities began several years before they opened.

The importance of boards of directors, residents committees, and residents referral networks cannot be underestimated, as they have helped many facilities in Philadelphia in the successful marketing and ongoing ability to maintain full occupancy and waiting lists—true of both older and newer facilities. Lloyd Lewis, founder and manager of Kendal at Longwood, indicated that he conducted few for-

Figure 8-4 **Philadelphia Market, Assisted Living**

Year Opened	Name	Town (County)	Assisted Living Beds (Alzheimer's Beds)
1848	Penn Home	Philadelphia	40 (4)
1886	Mary J. Drexel Home	Bala Cynwyd (M)	36
1886	Hayes Manor	Philadelphia	65
1891	The Hickman	West Chester (C)	75[a]
1893	Hutchinson House	Devon (C)	45
1893	Barclay Friends	West Chester (C)	48
1898	Friends Boarding Home	Kennett Square (C)	65
1900	Chalfont Care Group (formerly Victoria Manor)	Chalfont (B)	64
1936	St. Joseph's Manor	Meadowbrook (M)	89 (23)
1940s	Atria (formerly Chestnut Hill Residence)	Philadelphia	105 (11)
1949	Artman	Ambler (M)	110
1950	St. Mary's Manor	Lansdale (M)	90 (20)
1950	Devon Manor	Devon (C)	115[a]
1951	Harston Hall	Flourtown (M)	55
1959	St. Joseph Home	Holland (B)	38
1960	Cambridge Retirement	Philadelphia	92
1973	Chandler Hall	Newtown (B)	108
1974	Manatawny Manor	Pottstown (C)	122 (40)
1974	Masonic Eastern Star	Warminster (B)	34
1975	Springfield Retirement Residences	Wyndmoor (M)	122[a]
1977	Villa St. Teresa	Darby (D)	54
1978	Westminster Evangelical Home	Philadelphia	56
1978	Manorcare	Pottstown (M)	60
1979	Hill House	Bensalem (B)	144
1979	Willow Lake	Willow Grove (M)	110
1984	Nova Gardens	East Lansdowne (D)	35
1984	Harrison House	Coatesville (C)	120 (15)
1986	Bright Field	Lansdale (M)	168
1987	Mill Run	Bristol (B)	203 (85)
1987	Senior Suites	East Norriton (M)	206 (90)
1989	Summersgate	Jenkintown (M)	64
1989	Independence Court	Quakertown (B)	100
1989	Brighten Lakeside	Langhorne (B)	150 (47)
1990	D'Youville Manor	Yardley (B)	50
1990	Alterra Wynwood	Richboro (B)	113
1991	Luther Park	Hatboro (B)	60
1995	Arden Courts	King of Prussia (M)	(56)
1995	Highgate	Paoli (C)	124 (15)
1995	Arden Courts	Yardley (B)	(52)
1995	Spring Mill Presbyterian	Lafayette Hill (M)	67[a]
1996	Residence at Glen Riddle	Media (D)	116

Figure 8-4 (continued)

Year Opened	Name	Town (County)	Assisted Living Beds (Alzheimer's Beds)
1996	Alterra Clare Bridge	North Wales (M)	(48)
1996	Alterra Clare Bridge	Yardley (B)	(48)
1996	Woodbridge	Kimberton (C)	125 (15)
1997	Sunrise	Haverford (M)	63 (13)
1997	Alterra Wynwood	North Wales (M)	72
1997	Statesman Woods	Levittown (B)	28
1997	Alterra Sterling House	Bristol (B)	26
1997	Sunrise	Media (D)	77 (24)
1997	Sunrise	Blue Bell (M)	79 (18)
1997	Sunrise	Abington (M)	60
1998	The Colonnade	Schwenksville (M)	94 (30)
1998	Sunrise	Lafayette Hill (M)	70 (15)
1998	Alterra Cottage	Dublin (M)	(26)
1998	Residences at Chestnut Ridge	Chester (D)	105 (20)
1998	Columbia Cottage	Collegeville (M)	41
1998	New Seasons	New Britain (B)	100
1998	Sunrise	Malvern (C)	82 (15)
1999	The Oaks	Wyncote (M)	(48)
1999	Ridge Crest Gardens	Feasterville (B)	80
1999	Willow Crest Manor	Willow Grove (M)	65
1999	Chancellor Park	Philadelphia	135[a]
2000	Chancellor Park	Media (D)	100[a]
2000	Brandywine Assisted Living	Haverford (M)	94 (12)
2000	Sunrise	West Chester (C)	79 (15)
2000	New Seasons	Exton (C)	102
2000	Sunrise	Exton (C)	80
2001	New Seasons	Glen Mills (D)	103

Notes: Alzheimer's and related dementia beds, noted in parentheses, are included in the total assisted living bed count.
[a]All beds are licensed for assisted living, but a portion are considered "independent," according to marketing representatives.

Key
B = Bucks County
C = Chester County
D = Delaware County
M = Montgomery County

mal marketing activities since he sent letters to Swarthmore alumni and members of the Friends Yearly Meeting when Kendal was being planned. Lewis believed that the staff and board should be responsible for marketing and sales, emphasizing what it would be like to live at the community. Residents are also active in promoting Kendal and Crosslands, and many of the more than 900 deposits from future residents have come from relatives and friends of those who have resided in these communities. Resident referral programs have also been critical in marketing the seven ACTS communities, where residents who help refer new residents receive specific rewards.

Not every seniors' community in the area has met with initial or early success; however, the problems were not indications of a saturated market but rather of misunderstanding market conditions or mismanagement once facilities were in operation. Paul's Run, Pine Run, Heritage Towers, and Fiddler's Woods all have been through bankruptcy proceedings. The conditions that led to these problems vary.

Fiddler's Woods was the first, and perhaps best-known, bankruptcy in the Philadelphia area. The community, with 300 apartments and a 120-bed health care center, was developed by Sage Development on a tract of land in northeast Philadelphia. As discussed, the facility was to target the elderly Jewish market and was to be operated by Jewish Retirement Homes, Inc. The facility was financed through a tax-exempt bond issue of $33.1 million. Unfortunately, marketing did not yield the expected results, and funds were insufficient to make a required payment to Fidelity Bank, the trustee for the bondholders. The subsequent 1983 default and bankruptcy in the yet-to-be-opened facility were widely publicized. In 1985, the property was acquired by Forum Group, Inc., for approximately $11.5 million. This favorable price enabled Forum to open the facility and charge affordable rental fees (the endowment and life care programs were discontinued). The Lafayette, as it is now named, filled rapidly with older residents from the surrounding neighborhoods in northeast Philadelphia. In March 1992, the Lafayette (now known as Lafayette Redeemer) was acquired by Holy Redeemer Health System, which has successfully maintained its high occupancy level.

Paul's Run appears to have misjudged the interest in and ability of its local market to pay its upfront endowment fees. Inexperienced personnel were unable to successfully market the community's independent living units at a pace that enabled it to continue to keep up debt service payments. As mentioned earlier, however, increased support from its Lutheran sponsor, the addition of a highly experienced administrator, and its conversion to an affordable rental community yielded positive results, and the community has maintained close to full occupancy since that time.

Pine Run had been operated for ten years when Frank Elliott, the owner/operator, filed for protection from creditors in May 1986. Elliott indicated in newspaper reports that he had not anticipated how long residents would live at Pine Run. His actuarial misjudgment resulted in the inability to continue providing the same level of services as residents had been assured by their contracts. During the year before the bankruptcy filing, Elliott reduced services substantially, requested $10,000 in loans from the original residents, and ultimately sought to be able to evict residents who would not pay the increased fees. Elliott was eventually forced out by Horizon Financial, the community's mortgage holder. The highly publicized problems that had occurred at Pine Run over several years did not help the facility to increase its occupancy levels. In July 1988, management of the facility was taken over by Van Scoyoc Associates, and the knowledge and experience of the company's professionals, including President Gardner Van Scoyoc, enabled managers to consistently increase occupancy at the facility. In 1992, Doylestown Hospital purchased the community, and as of the late 1990s, it was successfully self-managed. The facility is fully occupied.

The experience and credibility of new management also enabled Heritage Towers to correct the problems that caused it to file for bankruptcy. Evangelical Manor became involved in managing the facility, taking the community from 33 percent occupancy to higher than 90 percent through the support and work of a knowledgeable board and marketing and management staff.

Springfield Residence (formerly Springfield Retirement Residence) was initially operated by Episcopal Community Services (ECS), the social service wing of the Episcopal Diocese. Early efforts to provide purely residential living at the community failed, and the facility was converted to life care with the addition of long-term health care. Springfield had mainly studio apartments with few kitchen facilities in the independent living units, however. Because Chestnut Hill and similar markets that it targeted were characterized by very large homes, the residents' transition to the facility was very difficult. Eventually, Chestnut Hill Hospital Healthcare acquired

Springfield. During negotiations, which lasted more than a year, no units were leased—a conscious decision by ECS because of the plan to discontinue the life care program. Subsequent to the sale, Springfield converted to a rental program, enlarged some of its units, added a personal care center, and increased its occupancy significantly. Now the community has 122 personal care units and considers approximately 30 percent of residents independent.

Philadelphia's "troubled" facilities all appear to have been able to correct their problems and achieve full occupancy with the benefit of stable and experienced management and marketing. The nonprofit status of many of these facilities also helped to provide an environment that facilitated their success.

An interesting by-product of Philadelphia's troubled facilities has been the restructuring of payment mechanisms that such facilities offered to residents. Each facility began under a life care program. Subsequent to bankruptcies and/or sales, each facility moved away from the life care concept. Heritage Towers, Lafayette, Paul's Run, Pine Run, and Springfield Residence converted to monthly rental programs, a strategy that in each case appears to have contributed to the successful workouts.

At the time this book was written, seniors' housing communities reported an overall average occupancy of 97 percent. Only seven communities reported occupancies below 95 percent, only four below 90 percent. Occupancy levels of these few communities fall short for a few specific reasons. Five of the communities are located in the city of Philadelphia, which is losing age- and income-qualified households. Two of the urban facilities are extremely old, with outdated rooms and community amenities. In addition, seniors' housing options in nearby suburban areas have increased tremendously. It is therefore not surprising that these urban facilities are experiencing vacancies. Moreover, another community in the suburbs recently added assisted living units to its campus and relocated a number of independent living residents.

Assisted Living. The rapid increase in the supply of assisted living communities not associated with a continuum of care during the late 1980s through the 1990s stands in contrast to the development of seniors' housing communities in the Philadelphia area. A total of 1,131 assisted living beds existed as of 1960, after which 810 were added in the 1970s and 1,046 in the 1980s. During the 1990s, however, the pace of development more than doubled over the previous decade, when 2,110 beds were built. During the late 1980s and early 1990s, temporary saturation conditions developed in the Bucks County portion of the region that took several years to work through. A combination of overbuilding, inexperienced developers, and an uneducated market contributed to these conditions in Bucks County. The sheer number of beds added to the Bucks County market during a short period and the difficulty of absorbing them all on a timely basis represented an early example of what was to occur nationwide in the mid- to late 1990s.

Approximately one-third of the freestanding assisted living facilities in the five-county area reported occupancy rates higher than 95 percent as of early 2001. Three-quarters of the facilities reported occupancies above 90 percent in this market. Another 11 percent had occupancy rates between 80 and 89 percent. The remaining facilities appear to be struggling to maintain acceptable occupancy rates, and four communities reported occupancies between 34 and 40 percent. While three of the four opened in 1999 or 2000, one facility, located in the city of Philadelphia, is older than 40 years.

Summary

Philadelphia is an example of a market in which the seniors' housing segment of the industry has matured over a lengthy period of time, one in which the steady pace of development increased awareness, understanding, and acceptance of seniors' housing, particularly CCRCs. The level of social acceptability of moving to life care and continuing care communities is also rather striking. A theme emerged during many conversations with representatives of facilities in the area: moving to a life care community was "the thing to do," an accepted way of life, in Philadelphia. Some who had been involved in marketing facilities in other areas of the country said they had never seen this acceptance so strongly entrenched elsewhere.

Many other factors have combined to enhance the overall success story in this market. The long tradition of providing and seeking care, the credibility of the sponsors, and their indigenous nature have been instrumental. The presence of an increasing number of professionals experienced in the development, marketing, and operation of continuing care facilities also contributes to the ongoing success of many communities. In some ways, this area has become the "University of Life Care," training individuals who have gone on to help create many new communities.

The Philadelphia area undoubtedly is an example of how much seniors' housing product can be absorbed over a lengthy period of time, giving the lie to the notion that, at least for communities offering a continuum of care, the market is saturated. What is interesting in the Philadelphia case study is the fact that both maturation and saturation have occurred, with Bucks County's experience with assisted living illustrating the notion that too much too fast equals saturation. This notion is further supported by the rapid development pace of assisted living communities in other parts of the Philadelphia market. Although many assisted living facilities exceed 90 percent occupancy rates, 25 percent languished below that level in early 2001. From a broader perspective, however, the combined number of communities and the units they comprise along with the high occupancy levels in the vast majority reflect a market that has accepted the various forms of seniors' housing as a way of life.

Cincinnati

The Region and Its Submarkets

Cincinnati and the areas of Hamilton County, Ohio, that surround and encompass it represent an amalgamation of many smaller neighborhoods and geopolitical subdivisions. (The case study does not include information on counties in Kentucky across the Ohio River from Cincinnati.) The tradition of neighborhood and community affiliation or identity is powerful and significant. Within the city limits are more than 40 discrete neighborhoods, each with an individual identity and socioeconomic mix. So strong is this pattern of neighborhood identity that it is not unusual to find that someone who has grown up on the city's east side may never have ventured to the western part of town. This pattern plays a significant role in the story of Cincinnati's seniors' housing industry.

Interstate-75 serves as a virtual demarcation line, running north/south and bisecting the city. The west side is home to white- and blue-collar middle-income segments of the population and tends to become more affluent as one moves northwest. The east side, with neighborhoods such as Hyde Park and Mt. Lookout, tends to be home to a much higher-income group. Areas north and farther east out Highway 125 grew rapidly in the 1990s. The central part of the city contains the majority of the lower-income residential neighborhoods.

The northeast and northern areas of Hamilton County also grew in the 1990s, with the fastest-growing corridor located along I-71 from the communities of Madeira and Kenwood north through Blue Ash and Montgomery into the surrounding counties. Newer suburban communities to the north and east of the city have experienced growth as well, prompted by the location of major employers such as General Electric and Ford and new construction of office buildings and parks along the northern and eastern sections of the I-275 beltway.

Trends in Overall and Elderly Population

Hamilton County and in particular its major population center, Cincinnati, have experienced overall population losses since 1980 (see Figure 8-5). The city has lost population to its suburbs as businesses relocated to sites outside the city limits. The population age 65 and older has also steadily decreased since 1980, losing a total of 15,088 persons between 1980 and 2000, and 20 percent of those age 65 and older.

Total population in Hamilton County decreased by 27,921 during the same time period. The elderly population has for the most part mirrored the patterns of the general population in terms of decreases in the city and increases in the suburbs. In contrast to the trend of overall population decreases in Hamilton County, however, the demographic data reflect an increasingly older population in Hamilton County since 1980. Most striking was the dramatic increase of the population 75 and older in Hamilton County between 1980 and 1990, reflecting the out-migration from Cincinnati to its suburbs during this period. Between 1990 and 2000, this segment was the only one to show an increase.

Figure 8-5 **Cincinnati/Hamilton County Population Trends**

	Population			Percent Change	
Age of Population	**1980**	**1990**	**2000**	**1980–1990**	**1990–2000**
City of Cincinnati					
Total	385,460	364,040	331,285	–6%	–9%
65+	55,742	50,763	40,654	–9%	–20%
75+	23,689	24,564	20,893	4%	–15%
Hamilton County					
Total	873,224	866,228	845,303	–1%	–2%
65+	104,459	115,466	113,898	11%	–1%
75+	42,123	51,108	55,596	21%	9%

Source: U.S. Census Bureau, *Census of Population, 1980, 1990, 2000.*

Early History of Seniors' Housing Development

Seniors' housing and care for the elderly in Cincinnati, like many areas of the United States, can be traced to the turn of the 19th century. The city's oldest community, Twin Towers Community, was founded in 1899, operating originally as the Methodist Home in Yellow Springs, Ohio. After a fire destroyed the home, it relocated to the 20-acre site presently occupied by Twin Towers. After opening its doors in 1908, Twin Towers went through a series of renovations and expansions, most significantly in the last half of the 1980s; today it offers 274 independent living units and 42 assisted living beds. From 1900 to 1980, nine facilities designed to serve the independent elderly were opened in the Cincinnati area (see Figure 8-6). Sponsors of these facilities included Baptist, Presbyterian, Catholic, and other religious institutions, as well as nondenominational and community-based organizations. All but one of the facilities developed during this period were owned by nonprofit organizations. All the facilities are still in operation today, pointing to the influence and importance of their sponsorship as instrumental in their ongoing success.

A somewhat unusual feature of the early seniors' communities to open in this market was the presence of both endowment and rental concepts. Most of the early facilities on the whole had relatively small independent living components compared with the 200 to 300 residential units found in many CCRCs in other parts of the country. Seniors' housing communities developed during the evolutionary period of Cincinnati's history in the industry were intended to respond to an unmet need that their sponsors perceived among their constituency.

Figure 8-6 lists seniors' housing communities that offer independent living units in chronological order of their opening; it includes only market-rate facilities with more than 30 units.

Development Trends

Independent Living. Twenty-nine seniors' housing communities were operating in the Cincinnati area (including Hamilton County and immediately contiguous portions of Butler, Clermont, and Warren counties) by 1990. Eighteen new facilities were developed between 1982 and 1989, and two existing facilities were expanded. Of these facilities, five communities containing 701 units were built in 1984 alone, and 13 containing 1,604 units were built during the four years from 1984 to 1987. Although nonprofit sponsorship characterized the facilities built before 1980, only three of those built during the 1980s were associated with nonprofit organizations. These new facilities added 2,042 independent living units to the existing supply of 1,447 market-rate units developed earlier in the 20th century. The 1990s saw a drop in development over the 1980s. Between 1990 and 1997, only three communities were built, adding another 191 independent living units. In 2000, two independent living communities were opened, adding 193 units.

Figure 8-6 **Cincinnati Market, Independent Living**

Year Opened	Name	Town (County)	Units
1899	Twin Towers	Cincinnati (H)	274
1909	Scarlet Oaks Retirement Community	Cincinnati (H)	141
1918	Westover Retirement Community	Hamilton (B)	42
1948	Judson Village Retirement Community	Cincinnati (H)	20
1950	Judson Village Retirement Community	Cincinnati (H)	20
1953	Mt. Pleasant Place	Monroe (B)	206
1956	Llanfair Retirement Community	Cincinnati (H)	116
1963	Marjorie P. Lee Retirement Community	Cincinnati (H)	108
1969	Beechknoll Community	Cincinnati (H)	88
1974	St. Paul Lutheran Village	Cincinnati (H)	191
1977	Maple Knoll Village	Cincinnati (H)	261
1982	DeuPree Community	Cincinnati (H)	83
1983	Amber Park Retirement Community	Cincinnati (H)	62
1984	The Franciscan at West Park	Cincinnati (H)	103
1984	New England Club	Cincinnati (H)	249
1984	Cottingham Retirement Community	Cincinnati (H)	118
1984	Evergreen Retirement Community	Cincinnati (H)	164
1984	HCR Manor Care Woodridge	Fairfield (B)	67
1985	Northgate Park	Cincinnati (H)	51
1985	Asbury Woods	Cincinnati (H)	50
1986	The Lodge at Montgomery	Cincinnati (H)	154
1986	Eastgate Retirement Community	Cincinnati (H)	153
1986	Western Hills Retirement Community	Cincinnati (H)	79
1987	Seasons Retirement Community	Cincinnati (H)	216
1987	Mallard Cove	Cincinnati (H)	72
1987	Brookwood Retirement Community	Cincinnati (H)	128
1989	Sutton Grove Retirement Community	Cincinnati (H)	75
1989	Berkeley Square Retirement Community	Hamilton (B)	147
1989	Valley Creek	Cincinnati (H)	71
1990	Mason Christian Village	Mason (W)	62
1993	Mercy St. Theresa Center	Cincinnati (H)	32
1997	Cedar Village	Mason (W)	97
2000	Mercy Community at Winton Woods	Cincinnati (H)	73
2000	The Waterford	Fairfield (B)	120

Key
B = Butler County
H = Hamilton County
W = Warren County

As far as seniors' housing is concerned, Cincinnati might well be described as the city that HUD built. A review of the April 1990 "Multi-Region Audit of the Insured Retirement Service Centers Program" (221(d)(4)) provides substantial insights on the overbuilding of this market. Nine retirement service centers (ReSCs) were approved by HUD's Cincinnati area office while the program was in operation, more project approvals than were issued by any other HUD area office. Six of these ReSCs were located in or adjacent to Hamilton County.

One of the HUD projects was foreclosed, and the mortgages for three others were assigned back to HUD by the banks holding them. The information in the audit reveals myriad problems that demonstrate a substantial lack of understanding of the fundamental market and operational issues of seniors' housing.

Overstatement of income and absorption and underestimation of operating costs characterized many of the ReSCs. Concern about market issues was evident even while the loans were being underwritten. As shown in Figure 8-7, the audit reveals that during loan underwriting, unresolved concerns regarding five projects included such issues as too many units being proposed, mistargeting of the population to be served, and "saturated market/ demand problems."[7] According to the audit report:

> The Cincinnati Office approved at least five HUD fully insured ReSC projects with substantially more units than recommended by the field economists. Units approved for loan insurance ranged from 17 to 133 percent above the number of units recommended by the economists. All five projects were experiencing rent-up problems, and three of the projects' mortgages were in default at the time of the audit. The Cincinnati Office's project files did not contain any documentation to explain why the economists' recommendations on project size were either invalid or were not critical to the potential success of the projects involved.[8]

Comparing the average number of independent living units per facility further underscores this problem. The average number of these units in facilities developed before 1980 was 116. Facilities that opened during the 1980s averaged 138 units. HUD ReSC facilities in this market averaged 199 independent living units, however.

A conversation with a local HUD official confirmed much of what the audit report documented. Market studies done for many of the ReSCs often described much broader geographic market areas than were reasonable in this city of neighborhoods. Demographic analysis targeting the population age 62 and older overstated the market for facilities that would ultimately serve the population 80 and older.

Figure 8-7 **Unresolved Market Concerns**

	Beechknoll/ Northgate	Eastgate	Evergreen	Lodge of Montgomery	New England Village
Insured Mortgage Amount	$5,042,200	$7,201,800	$15,689,500	$9,608,700	$11,922,000
Status	Assigned	Foreclosed	Assigned	Assigned	Assigned
Too Many Units	X	X			X
Mistargeted Population	X				X
Saturated Market/ Demand Problems	X	X			
Percent Rental Income Overstated		197	28	155	315
Percent Actual Operation Costs Exceed Estimated		34	59	N/A	6
Percent Estimated Units Absorbed per Month Overstated		167	131	158	393

Source: U.S. Department of Housing and Urban Development, "Multi-Region Audit of the Insured Retirement Service Centers Program" (90-TS-1 11/112-0008), April 1990.

The education of everyone involved—from the lenders to the developers to the government—proved costly in this highly overbuilt market.

The problems encountered by many of these facilities were well publicized in the local press. Extensive coverage in the August 27, 1989, *Cincinnati Enquirer* focused on the involvement of HUD, the inexperience of the developers, and the massive misjudgment of the market that led to Cincinnati's saturated conditions. One article pointed to other related factors that helped create this troubled story:

> Ohio's construction industry needed a boost[;] Ohio's elderly needed affordable housing. And Ohio needed to make sure that retirees and their assets stayed in Ohio—and Ohio's tax base. The answer to all three problems: state bonds backed by federal guarantees that could raise money to build upscale apartment complexes.... The combination of available money from the bonds and a risk-free investment fueled a building boom.[9]

An interesting footnote is the story of Mason Christian Village, a facility that applied to HUD's 221(d)(4) program, only to be turned down. The rejection was appealed but without success. Mason Christian Village's 62 independent living units (the smallest project to apply to the Cincinnati area office) were built without the HUD loan guarantee.

Several Cincinnati-area facilities struggled with occupancy problems throughout the 1980s. Troubled facilities included the Lodge of Montgomery, Evergreen, New England Club, Northgate Park, Eastgate Senior Village, and West Park II. All had great difficulties filling their units. The substantial publicity about the troubled seniors' housing communities resulted in greater uncertainty among buyers and a fair amount of price slashing in the hope of enhancing the competitive edge. As of early 2001, however, all these facilities were reporting high occupancy rates, most over 95 percent, demonstrating that the relatively lengthy period of saturation had finally ended. Among all the seniors' communities, the majority report occupancies of greater than 95 percent. Two older facilities, opened before 1970, reported that their independent living units are only half occupied. Both communities offer a large number of assisted living beds, and their outdated independent living apartments and physical building may not be appealing to independent retirees who have abundant options to choose from in the area. Three facilities have occupancy rates between 81 and 92 percent for independent living units.

Assisted Living. Assisted living units are licensed as *residential care facilities* in Ohio. Similar to the Philadelphia market, the origin of assisted living is found in the early seniors' housing, including Twin Towers, Westover Retirement Community, and Judson Retirement Community, among the first in the area. The first freestanding communities were developed by nonprofit religious organizations to care for the frail elderly. They included Mt. Healthy Christian Home (opened in 1966), the Franciscan at St. Clare (1970), and Mercy Franciscan Terrace (1971). It was another 11 years before the next assisted living community, Camargo Manor, was developed, this time by a for-profit organization. Four assisted living communities were developed in the late 1980s, one specializing in care for those with Alzheimer's disease and dementia. National for-profit companies, including Alterra, Sunrise, and Marriott dominated new development between 1997 and 2000. During this four-year period, eight communities were built, adding 369 standard assisted living beds and 158 specialized Alzheimer's beds (including two Arden Courts facilities dedicated exclusively to care of Alzheimer's). This surge of development almost doubled the number of existing assisted living beds and increased the number of Alzheimer's beds sixfold.

Before 1997, there were 455 assisted living beds and 24 Alzheimer's beds in facilities without independent living components. The majority of beds (1,389) were found in 23 seniors' communities offering independent living and other levels of care.

Figure 8-8 lists assisted living communities (in addition to those listed on Figure 8-6) that have more than 30 beds, with the majority charging monthly fees higher than $1,500 and serving private pay seniors.

Development Pacing, Absorption, and Competition

Independent Living. As indicated earlier, 18 new or expanded seniors' communities were added to the supply in the Cincinnati area during an eight-year period. By far, the heaviest development activity occurred between 1984 and 1987, when 16 facilities were opened, adding more

Figure 8-8 **Cincinnati Market, Assisted Living**

Year Opened	Name	Town/County	Assisted Living Beds (Alzheimer's Beds)
1966	Mt. Healthy Christian Home	Cincinnati (H)	123
1970	The Franciscan at St. Clare	Cincinnati (H)	50
1971	Mercy Franciscan Terrace	Cincinnati (H)	49
1982	Camargo Manor	Cincinnati (H)	33
1986	Terrace at West Side	Cincinnati (H)	41
1987	Alois Alzheimer's Center	Cincinnati (H)	(82)
1989	The Victoria	Cincinnati (H)	98
1989	Bayley Place	Cincinnati (H)	85 (24)
1997	Alterra Sterling House	Springdale (H)	42 (12)
1997	Alterra Sterling House	Fairfield (B)	42 (12)
1997	Sunrise at Kenwood	Cincinnati (H)	46
1999	Brighton Gardens	Cincinnati (H)	120 (26)
2000	Arden Courts Anderson	Cincinnati (H)	(60)
2000	Sunrise at Finneytown	Cincinnati (H)	55
2000	Bridgeway Pointe	Cincinnati (H)	102
2000	Arden Courts Kenwood	Cincinnati (H)	(60)

Note: Alzheimer's and related dementia beds, noted in parentheses, are included in the total assisted living bed count.

Key
B = Butler County
H = Hamilton County
W = Warren County

than two-thirds of the 2,042 independent living units built during the 1980s. As mentioned earlier, at least five facilities built during that four-year period struggled to reach full occupancy. As of early 1990, New England Club and Eastgate had achieved occupancy levels of 45 and 55 percent, respectively. Four of the five troubled facilities were insured under the ReSC program: Eastgate Senior Village, Lodge of Montgomery, Evergreen, and New England Village. The audit report on the ReSC program revealed that overestimation of absorption for three of these four facilities (not including Eastgate Senior Village) ranged from 131 to 393 percent, naturally resulting in overestimated income. Those factors, combined with a tendency toward underestimating expenses, laid the path for trouble. Although the actual absorption pace for the ReSC properties was not significantly different from the industry norms, unrealistic expectations contributed to the problems.

Preopening marketing activities for many of the facilities built during the 1980s began approximately six months before opening, a pattern typical of rental facilities. Because of the number of new facilities introduced to the market during a short period of time, however, many communities were unable to achieve substantial preleasing and also experienced extended leaseup periods. There were exceptions, however. The Seasons, which opened in 1987, had achieved 94 percent occupancy by early 1990. The facility, owned by American Tectonics, was located on an excellent site in Kenwood, in the I-71 growth corridor. The Seasons targeted an upscale market, differentiating itself from nearly all its potential competitors. Although the Seasons opened later than many of the facilities built in the 1980s that were trying to fill during the same period, it succeeded, at least in part, because it differentiated itself from its competitors.

The problems of the Cincinnati seniors' housing market appear to have settled during the 1990s, with all these facilities reaching stable occupancies. Three communities opened between 1990 and 1997, and all are considered fully occupied. Two freestanding independent living communities opened in 2000; one has reached 85 percent occupancy, while the other is filling at just over one unit per month.

Assisted Living. As of early 2001, the assisted living communities in this market reported a wide range of occupancy rates. Among freestanding communities opened before 2000 that were willing to share information, occupancies ranged from 60 to 100 percent, with an average of 85 percent. Of nine facilities reporting occupancy, only four are 95 percent occupied or better. Three report vacancies greater than 20 percent. The four freestanding communities opened during 2000 are struggling to fill, with occupancies of 42 to 80 percent.

Summary

The Cincinnati story in many ways epitomizes market saturation, that is, too much product introduced during too short a time period. The development of seniors' communities during the 1980s took place despite clear indications that the market could not support it. History repeated itself during the 1990s in the assisted living segment of the market. Although 158 of the 565 assisted living units built between 1997 and 2000 were specifically designed to serve those with Alzheimer's disease, the addition of eight properties during that relatively short period created a substantial number of units to be absorbed. The supply of freestanding assisted living units doubled during that four-year period.

On the most fundamental level, the demographic characteristics of the market simply did not warrant the level of development that took place. Cincinnati has been plagued by population losses, not only among its population in general but also among the elderly. Although those losses were more modest among the young elderly (those age 65 to 74), the target market for seniors' housing facilities had declined dramatically between 1970 and 1980 and had achieved only modest gains between 1980 and 1990. Between 1990 and 2000, the city of Cincinnati continued to lose total and elderly population, and Hamilton County continued to experience overall population declines, although the segment age 75 and older did increase modestly. Even the suburban areas, however, despite growth in the elderly population, were unable to support the level of development that occurred.

The inexperience and the ill-conceived expectations of many organizations that entered the seniors' housing industry in Cincinnati in the 1980s further contributed to the problems. Expectations of drawing from a wide-ranging market area proved to be unfounded. Most facilities drew residents from a radius of about five miles, reflecting the strong local neighborhood orientation. Lack of awareness of the true age of the target market led to further overestimation of the pool from which facilities expected to draw. In contrast, most of the organizations that developed assisted living facilities were national, publicly held corporations. Despite this fact, another period of overbuilding (this time assisted living) has led to unsatisfactory performance for many communities as they struggle to attain full occupancy. The experience of the seniors' housing communities in the 1980s suggests that eventually these newer facilities will stabilize, but it will require an investment of time, financial resources, and marketing effort.

South Florida

The Region and Its Submarkets

The study of south Florida focuses on portions of two adjacent counties along the East Coast: Palm Beach and Broward. The study area includes four key cities forming two major population hubs along Route 1, Florida's major coastal highway: Delray Beach and Boca Raton in southern Palm Beach County, and Deerfield Beach and Pompano Beach in northern Broward County. Although these four cities are clustered where the two counties meet, they represent somewhat different submarkets. The areas evaluated in Palm Beach County, for instance, are more affluent than those in neighboring Broward County.

Much of Palm Beach County was developed in the early 1970s with planned unit developments

(PUDs). The low cost of this land and the high density achieved through PUDs provided an affordable housing base that became quite attractive to the elderly. Development in Delray Beach was extensive during the early to mid-1980s but has since slowed because the area is nearly built out. Delray Beach is characterized by single-family and multifamily residential developments, which have traditionally served retirees but have begun to attract young professionals. West Boca and West Delray are both centers for retirees in Palm Beach County, with Boca Raton representing one of the most prestigious areas in the county.

The majority of Broward County's growth also occurred in the 1970s, reflecting, in large part, inmigration from Dade County to the south. In addition, Broward also experienced a substantial wave of retirees moving to Florida from the northeast part of the country, specifically New York. Deerfield Beach is made up predominantly of single-family housing, except for beachfront multifamily condominiums and apartments. Pompano Beach, which is less affluent, is characterized by multifamily housing.

The major north/south highways in both these submarkets are U.S. Route 1 and I-95, which run parallel to each other in the eastern portions of the counties. Much of the development in the two areas emanated from the coast west to I-95 in the 1960s and early 1970s, and extended west of I-95 to the Florida Turnpike during the late 1970s and the 1980s. U.S. 441 is west of the turnpike and is the farthest major north/south roadway in that portion of the counties. Some of the area between the turnpike and U.S. 441 saw development in the 1980s, although it was scattered. Throughout the 1990s, this area was a growth corridor for planned developments, specifically in Boca Raton, attracting young families more than young retirees.

Trends in Overall and Elderly Population

Broward County's population nearly doubled between 1960 and 1970, increasing from 333,946 to 620,100; it grew to more than 1.62 million in 2000. Growth in Palm Beach County was slower during the 1960s, when it increased from 228,106 to 348,753; however, heavy growth occurred in the 1970s through 2000, reaching 1.13 million by 2000.

The case study communities in Palm Beach County demonstrated significantly greater population growth between 1990 and 2000 than those in Broward County. The most distinctive characteristic of these communities is the proportion of the population that is elderly (see Figure 8-9). Approximately one-fourth to more than one-third of the population was age 65 or older in 1990 in these areas, which is more than four times the national norm. Another notable trend is the tremendous growth of the population age 75 and older in Delray Beach, which nearly doubled between 1980 and 1990 and gained another 27 percent during the 1990s. With the exception of Boca Raton, the areas experienced overall population decreases or minimal growth between 1980 and 1990. Despite this trend, the elderly population age 75 and older grew in number in all areas except Pompano Beach. Between 1990 and 2000, all areas experienced steady growth, with the population 75 and older growing at the fastest rate. The demographic depth of these unusual markets fueled the growth of the area's seniors' housing industry.

Early History of Seniors' Housing Development

The seniors' housing industry began in this study area in 1967, when the nonprofit Gulfstream Baptist Association (which became First Baptist Church of Margate, Florida) began development of a life care community with two cottages containing six units in Pompano Beach. Significant expansions included the acquisition of land and the addition of more cottages and apartments. By 1972, the campus included 59 cottages housing 159 residential units, 249 apartments in two buildings, a 60-bed health center, and kitchen and dining facilities attached to the health center. Although demand for this facility was strong and the community remained full, inadequate revenues from the fees and poor financial planning resulted in bankruptcy in 1973. The seniors' housing community was operated under the jurisdiction of the bankruptcy court until 1976, when it was sold to a nonprofit corporation, John Knox Communities, Inc., with a subsequent sale in 1978 to John Knox Village of Florida, Inc.[10] Only two communities were developed in the 1970s: St. Andrews Estates North opened in 1978 and Abbey Delray North in 1979, adding 644 independent living units. In the 1980s, ten additional facilities were constructed, including five

Figure 8-9 **South Florida Area Total and Elderly Population Trends**

Age	Population 1980	Population 1990	Population 2000	Percent Change 1980–1990	Percent Change 1990–2000
Boca Raton					
Total	48,767	61,492	74,764	26%	22%
65+	11,782	13,163	14,830	12%	13%
75+	4,647	6,377	7,481	37%	17%
Delray Beach					
Total	47,109	47,181	60,020	0%	27%
65+	15,154	14,881	15,551	–2%	5%
75+	3,953	7,099	9,050	80%	27%
Deerfield Beach					
Total	71,522	46,325	64,583	–35%	39%
65+	24,400	16,760	18,943	–31%	13%
75+	8,111	9,535	11,975	18%	26%
Pompano Beach					
Total	87,842	72,411	78,191	–18%	8%
65+	23,868	18,207	18,264	–24%	0%
75+	9,982	8,990	10,533	–10%	17%

Source: U.S. Census Bureau, *Census of Population, 1980, 1990, 2000.*

freestanding independent living communities with 1,045 units, and five communities offering assisted living. Four communities provided a continuum of care, including nursing care.

During this period, John Knox Village was able to withstand and overcome the negative impact of the bankruptcy and, through reorganization and sale, was able to stabilize and maintain its high occupancy levels, developing additional facilities as the continuing demand was perceived. John Knox Village today operates as a successful life care community, which it has been since its sale by the bankruptcy court. From 1967 to 1978, it was the only seniors' housing facility in the Palm Beach/Broward County study area, and in many ways its highly publicized problems shaped the perceptions of future consumers in the market.

In 1977, Florida passed legislation regulating life care communities in the state. Governed under Chapter 651, the State Department of Insurance and its nine-member advisory board are responsible for ensuring that facilities meeting their definition of continuing care abide by the regulations. The regulations require that both a provisional Certificate of Authority and a Certificate of Authority be obtained. The provisional certificate requires disclosure regarding the applicant, organization, construction, and financial data, as well as preliminary market and economic feasibility studies. The actual Certificate of Authority is not issued unless the applicant presells 50 percent of the units, as evidenced by the receipt of 10 percent of the entrance fees. Chapter 651 also places stringent requirements on the use of the entrance fees. The formalization of the requirement to presell 50 percent of the units and stricter escrow requirements that came into effect in the mid-1980s has had a substantial impact on the development of CCRCs in Florida. The result was a cessation of development of CCRCs between 1982 and 1988.

Development Trends

Independent Living. Although no further development occurred in Pompano Beach/Deerfield Beach until 1985, activity did begin in the markets in south Palm Beach County and, once again, in the form of life care communities owned by nonprofit organizations. In 1979, Abbey Delray North opened in Delray Beach. Originally initiated by Krauss Company, a local developer, the life care concept to be offered at Abbey Delray North was very new to the south Palm Beach County area. After struggling to market the new community for about a year, Life Care Services (LCS), a nationally known and widely experienced company, was hired to develop, market, and manage the life care facility. At that point, the property was acquired by Lifecare Retirement Communities, Inc., a nonprofit corporation created by LCS to own and hold this and other seniors' housing facilities. Its success in this effort led to the immediate initiation of a second facility, Abbey Delray South, which opened in 1982. A 90-bed skilled nursing facility is also located on the south campus.

A second organization experienced in life care, Adult Communities Total Services (now ACTS Retirement-Life Communities, a Philadelphia-based nonprofit organization), came to Boca Raton and developed St. Andrews North in 1978 and South in 1980. ACTS closely allied itself with Bible Town/Community Church, which was founded in 1950 and had a nondenominational membership of approximately 2,000. Each winter between January and March, Bible Town held conferences attended by people from all over the county. Bible Town's pastor, Tori Johnson, had maintained a friendship with Pastor Richard Coons, president of ACTS, and was instrumental in supporting the marketing of St. Andrews North through the church's membership.

Although nonprofit life care communities dominated the south Palm Beach market until the mid-1980s, the rental concept began to take hold in both Deerfield Beach/Pompano Beach and Boca Raton/Delray Beach during the second half of the decade. Heritage Park East was the first rental facility to open in the Palm Beach area, while the Court at Palm Aire, the first new facility to be developed in Pompano Beach since John Knox Village, originally offered prospects an option to rent a unit or pay an entrance fee. Numerous other rental facilities followed during this period, including the Horizon Club and the Forum at Deer Creek in Broward County and Heritage Park West and the Veranda Club in south Palm Beach County.

The popularity of developing rental facilities rather than CCRCs continued throughout the 1990s. Three rental facilities opened in Broward and Palm Beach counties in the 1990s. All of them were developed by for-profit providers that recognized the desire for this type of seniors' housing.

One factor that has been influential in shaping seniors' housing development in the case study area has been the strong elderly Jewish market. In-migration from the Northeast, including New York, New Jersey, and Pennsylvania, has resulted in large concentrations of Jewish population in Delray Beach, in particular, and portions of Deerfield Beach and Pompano Beach. This population has shown a distinct preference for rental seniors' communities rather than the life care/entrance fee model. Communities such as Horizon Club, which offers only rentals, and the Court at Palm Aire, which offers a rental option, have traditionally attracted large numbers of Jewish residents.

Many facilities developed during the latter part of the decade, particularly in the Palm Beach County market, were owned and operated by local Florida-based organizations entering the seniors' housing industry for the first time. Both the Boca Raton/Delray Beach and Deerfield Beach/Pompano Beach markets, however, have been dominated by large, experienced for-profit seniors' housing organizations. Of the 15 communities in operation in 2001, nine are operated by for-profit providers, including Hyatt and Marriott.

Figure 8-10 lists seniors' housing communities that offer independent living units in chronological order of their opening. It includes only market-rate facilities with more than 30 units.

Assisted Living. Florida began licensing assisted living facilities in 1975 and has since amended the original legislation several times. The current amendment (1997) transferred authority for assisted living from the Department of Health and Rehabilitative Services to the Department of Elderly Affairs and also renamed adult congregate living facilities *assisted living facilities.*

In addition to the assisted living components located in ten independent living facilities (containing 674 units), numerous freestanding assisted living facilities were developed in the latter half of the 1980s and during the 1990s in Delray Beach and Boca Raton in Palm Beach County and in Deerfield Beach and Pompano Beach in Broward County.

Nine assisted living facilities were opened between 1985 and 1988, and all but one were developed by

Figure 8-10 **South Florida Market, Independent Living**

Year Opened	Name	Town/County	Units
1967	John Knox Village	Pompano Beach (B)	602
1978	St. Andrews Estates North	Boca Raton (P)	284
1979	Abbey Delray North	Delray Beach (P)	360
1980	St. Andrews Estates South	Boca Raton (P)	321
1982	Abbey Delray South	Delray Beach (P)	288
1984	Edgewater Pointe Estates	Boca Raton (P)	350
1985	The Court at Palm Aire	Pompano Beach (B)	200
1986	Marriott's Horizon Club	Deerfield Beach (B)	228
1987	Harbour's Edge	Delray Beach (P)	271
1987	Seasons Retirement Community	Pompano Beach (B)	110
1987	The Veranda Club	Boca Raton (P)	189
1988	Heritage Park West	Delray Beach (P)	98
1989	Forum at Deer Creek	Deerfield Beach (B)	198
1990	Casa del Mar	Boca Raton (P)	154
1994	Marriott Stratford Court and Brighton Gardens	Boca Raton (P)	312
1998	Preserve at Palm Aire	Pompano Beach (B)	258

Key
B = Broward County
P = Palm Beach County

for-profit providers who no doubt recognized the need for this type of seniors' housing. Delray Beach is home to three of these facilities, including the first freestanding assisted living facility designed specifically for those with Alzheimer's disease and related dementia, opened in 1986. The 1990s brought a surge of assisted living development in the region, similar to many areas across the nation. From 1992 through 2000, 13 facilities were opened, six of which were developed in Pompano Beach. Only one of these entrants, Miami Jewish Homes, is affiliated with a nonprofit organization, and it is targeted to those with dementia.

Assisted living facilities designated for those with Alzheimer's disease and related dementia also became more popular in the region in the 1990s. Two facilities were developed exclusively for this population, and another six facilities included designated units within the assisted living facilities.

Figure 8-11 lists assisted living communities (in addition to those listed on Figure 8-10) that have more than 30 beds, with the majority charging monthly fees higher than $1,500 and serving private pay residents.

Development Pacing, Absorption, and Competition

Independent Living. Since 1979, the south Florida seniors' community markets have been characterized by steady development. As illustrated in Figure 8-10, new facilities were opened almost yearly throughout the 1980s.

One of the most interesting aspects of the ongoing development in these markets has been that it is based largely on expansion by existing providers. This expansion has occurred in response to the strong demand that they were unable to meet with a single facility. This pattern was set, in fact, by John Knox Village, which expanded during an earlier period (1967 to 1980) from a few cottages and apartments to a community that now offers 602 residential units, 177 nursing beds, and 62 assisted living beds. As population exploded in these areas, the demand among the elderly population was demonstrated by the continuing success of organizations such as ACTS,

Figure 8-11 **South Florida Market, Assisted Living**

Year Opened	Name	Town/County	Assisted Living Beds (Alzheimer's Beds)
1985	Living Legends Retirement Center	Deerfield Beach (B)	130
1985	Heritage Park East	Delray Beach (P)	145
1985	The Grand Court	Pompano Beach (B)	205 (80)
1986	Liberty Inn	Delray Beach (P)	(66)
1986	Remington House	Pompano Beach (B)	99 (30)
1987	Colonial Inn at Heritage Park	Delray Beach (P)	60
1987	Avante Terrace	Boca Raton (P)	53
1988	Sunrise Atrium	Boca Raton (P)	220
1988	Avondale Manors	Pompano Beach (B)	55 (26)
1992	The Elysium of Boca Raton	Boca Raton (P)	144
1993	Meri-Lee Retirement Home	Pompano Beach (B)	40
1994	Dehoernle Alzheimer's Pavilion	Deerfield Beach (B)	(46)
1994	Atlantic Shores	Pompano Beach (B)	30
1994	The Lighthouse Inn	Pompano Beach (B)	50
1996	The Renaissance	Deerfield Beach (B)	167 (32)
1996	Belair by the Sea	Pompano Beach (B)	30
1996	Nova Vizcaya Retirement Residence	Pompano Beach (B)	96
1998	The Plaza at Deer Creek	Deerfield Beach (B)	127 (30)
1998	Arden Courts	Delray Beach (P)	(56)
1999	Bristol Park of Coral Springs	Pompano Beach (B)	120
2000	Homewood Residence	Delray Beach (P)	86 (24)
2000	Homewood Residence	Boca Raton (P)	78 (18)

Note: Alzheimer's and related dementia beds, noted in parentheses, are included in the total assisted living bed count.

Key
B = Broward County
P = Palm Beach County

with St. Andrews and Edgewater Pointe Estates communities, and Life Care Services, with the two Abbey Delrays and Harbour's Edge. Other organizations, such as the locally based Heritage Park Retirement Centers and Forum also benefited from the strong, ongoing demand for seniors' housing.

Not all organizations and communities, however, experienced success. The Court at Palm Aire in Pompano Beach was developed by Life Care Communities Corporation (LCCC) and taken over by the Kaplan Organization, which bought LCCC in 1987. The Court at Palm Aire suffered from inception from management problems and a pricing approach that confused and ultimately angered some residents and prospects. The community originally offered both a life care/entrance fee arrangement and a straight rental option to prospective residents, a mixture that is believed to have created confusion in marketing the community. In fact, facility representatives also indicated that many early prospects were unfamiliar with the life care concept and needed much education. Unfortunately, the fees set by the original management team at LCCC were determined to be too low by the team that followed, which, in 1987, implemented rate increases of 12 to 18 percent. Many residents moved out, lowering the overall occupancy rate from 84 percent to a low of 45 to 50 percent in 1988. In 2001, the facility provided 200 independent living units and 60 assisted living beds and offered only monthly rentals. The Court at Palm Aire has slowly built its occupancy level to about 90 percent (as of early 2001), but it suffered during its early years while other communities flourished.

The Horizon Club, a facility consisting of both independent living and assisted living units, was opened in late 1986 by the Radice Corporation, a Florida real estate development firm that entered the seniors' housing industry during the mid-1980s. Although Horizon Club appeared to be a viable community, its parent corporation suffered from other significant problems and ultimately went bankrupt. Unfortunately, the reputation and perception of this property were negatively impacted by the frequent turnover in ownership, management, and marketing companies. Although it had reached approximately 82 percent occupancy two years after it opened, the Horizon Club's occupancy actually decreased after that period. Marriott acquired the property in 1990, which appears to have been a stabilizing influence that increased credibility, and the community has now stabilized at an average occupancy rate of 90 percent. While the occupancy has stabilized, marketing the facility to potential residents and their families is an ongoing challenge in this heavily saturated market. This facility, like many others in the market, has had to spend more marketing dollars on high-quality brochures and advertising and to be more aggressive in marketing to attract residents and maintain acceptable occupancy levels.

For some of these troubled facilities, the problems were primarily a reflection of marketing and management teams' inexperience in seniors' housing. Some of the problems experienced may have been a result of the limitations of a concept that did not embrace either health care or personal care. Such communities in other parts of the country have experienced rapid and heavy turnover problems resulting from the age and level of frailty of the residents they attract and the communities' inability to continue to serve these residents once additional care is required.

With the exception of three facilities with occupancies ranging from 87 and 90 percent, all independent living facilities reported occupancies higher than 95 percent at the time this book was written.

Assisted Living. In the south Florida market, ten of the 15 communities offering independent living also offered assisted living (674 units). As in many other markets, the majority of the freestanding assisted living communities were developed during the 1990s. During the period from 1990 to 2000, the number of units doubled in the overall markets being analyzed. Interestingly, the majority (nine of 13) of them were in the Pompano/Deerfield Beach submarket, with six in Pompano Beach. Despite the greater number of actual facilities in Pompano Beach, the number of beds opened in Pompano and Deerfield during the period were nearly the same (366 in Pompano and 340 in Deerfield). Most of this development took place in 1994 and 1996, when three facilities opened in each year.

Occupancy rates ranged widely among assisted living communities in this market. Occupancies ranged from 50 to 100 percent for assisted living communities with no independent living components that opened before 2000. The majority had occupancies between 82 and 91 percent (13 facilities). The average occupancy rate was 83 percent. Of the 20 facilities opened before 2000, only three reported occupancies of 95 percent or more. The remaining four freestanding communities had occupancies of 50 to 72 percent. Two communities opened in October 2000 and after seven months had filled approximately one-third of their units (four units monthly).

It is also interesting to note that occupancy rates for assisted living facilities vary according to where they are located. Pompano Beach experienced the greatest development of assisted living facilities in the 1990s, with six facilities opened over a six-year period. Occupancies in these six facilities range from 50 to 90 percent, with the average 76.5 percent. In contrast, assisted living facilities located along with independent living in Pompano Beach all report occupancies greater than 90 percent.

The experience in Deerfield Beach is quite similar. Two large assisted living facilities, each with beds for patients with Alzheimer's disease and related dementia (AZ/RD), and a freestanding AZ/RD facility opened in Deerfield Beach between 1994 and 1998, adding 340 assisted living units (62 designated for AZ/RD beds) and 46 freestanding AZ/RD beds. The two assisted living facilities reported occupancies of 72 and 84 percent, while the AZ/RD facility reported 90 percent occupancy. All the older assisted living facilities, the majority existing along with independent living, reported occupancies ranging from 91 to 100 percent.

While the occupancy problems of the late 1980s and 1990s seem to have stabilized, a new problem faces the assisted living industry in this area. Assisted living facilities are having difficulty securing professional liability insurance as well as affording it.

The Renaissance of Deerfield Beach is an assisted living facility with a separate Alzheimer's wing that was originally built in 1987. An expansion of 32 Alzheimer's beds and 15 assisted living beds was completed in 1997. The biggest problem this facility recently encountered, like many assisted living facilities, is the inability to secure professional liability insurance. This problem was exacerbated at the Renaissance because it had an extended congregate housing license, which allowed it to accept Medicaid-eligible residents. The extended license enabled the facility to provide more extensive care and allow residents to age in place, thus creating greater liability for the facility. To deal with this situation, the facility had to place 25 residents in other facilities and relinquish its extended license while maintaining the standard license for an assisted living facility. Doing so resulted in a dramatic decrease in population. In an effort to recoup the loss in population and ultimately income, the facility began accepting independent residents who required little to no additional services for a rental rate of $1,200 per month, a typical rate for independent living in south Florida but low in the assisted living industry. While the Renaissance continues to work toward increasing its assisted living population, it is also making operational improvements in an effort to help increase revenue.

Summary

Absorption of all the south Florida study area's life care/CCRCs has been steady, allowing them to reach full stabilized occupancy levels. Some rental facilities, unfortunately, have not met with the same degree of success. Lengthy premarketing periods have been characteristic of all the life care/CCRCs, but not of most rental facilities (with the exception of Forum's Deer Creek). While premarketing periods before opening for entrance fee facilities are measured in years (usually 1.5 to 2.5 years), premarketing periods for rental communities are measured in months (typically six to nine months).

As mentioned, Florida's Chapter 651 legislation had many effects on the life care/continuing care industry in the state. Perhaps one of the more salutary effects has resulted from the requirement that facilities must demonstrate at least 50 percent presales before receiving a Certificate of Authority. This requirement may have prevented a number of facilities from entering the market that would have had difficulty in filling units. It also, in effect, forces a much lengthier premarketing period to reach necessary presale levels than might otherwise have occurred.

The independent living market is now dominated by rental facilities rather than continuing care communities. Harbour's Edge, opened in 1987, was the last CCRC to be developed in this area. Rental independent living facilities have emerged as a popular housing option, with 1,319 units developed since 1987. Most of these facilities also provide assisted living on their campuses.

The south Florida assisted living market endured a substantial amount of growth during the early 1990s. First and foremost, the greater total number of assisted living facilities in the market results in a greatly saturated market. Further, new entrants did not properly analyze the market to identify existing and potential competition, and demand and penetration rates. Ultimately, too many products entered the market at the same time. While many of the facilities offer a variety of services and amenities, they are competing in an extremely diluted market. As a result, performance for many facilities, particularly those that are not part of a continuum of care, has been below acceptable levels. In an effort to increase occupancy, properties offered incentives and discounts to potential residents during the early part of the 1990s, but this practice ended by the late 1990s. The market stabilized somewhat in the latter part of the 1990s, and in the past two years, several facilities even experienced slight improvements in occupancy levels. These improvements for some facilities are in part the result of intense marketing, which facilities appear to be continuing in an effort to remain competitive in the south Florida market. Further, the entry of newcomers into the market has slowed tremendously, which is having a positive effect on the occupancy levels of existing facilities.

Case Study Comparisons

These case studies of three different seniors' housing markets demonstrate that, although they share some features, the ways in which various areas respond to the development of seniors' housing can differ greatly. It is interesting to consider what elements appear to have fostered the successful ongoing absorption of new seniors' housing communities, both independent and assisted living. Although each market presented in the case studies differs in many ways from the others, certain common elements may have been critical to continued successful absorption or market maturation. Not all these elements, however, are necessarily prominent in each market.

Independent Living Facilities

The first factor is the early introduction and entrenchment of the continuing care model of seniors' housing. As would be expected, this approach, which dominated the formative years in the seniors' housing industry throughout much of the country, was prominent in each market examined. In Philadelphia, it was practically the only model that existed until the 1980s. Even today, the Philadelphia area has only a handful of freestanding independent living communities. Throughout the 1960s and 1970s, continuing care proliferated in the south Florida market. In the late 1980s and throughout the 1990s, rental freestanding independent living began to take hold in south Florida. In Cincinnati, seniors' housing has historical roots dating back to the late 19th century. Historically, Cincinnati has had a greater mixture of continuing care and congregate rental projects than the other two case study markets.

Related to this characteristic, and perhaps more significant, is the presence of the very strong nonprofit sponsors who initiated, dominated, and have remained prominent in the seniors' housing market in all three geographic areas. The Quaker facilities and other nonprofit sponsors in the Philadelphia area, some with very long histories of providing care, contributed to the successful establishment of a seniors' community model—the CCRC—that still dominates this market. Other major nonprofit players include ACTS, which became prominent in both Philadelphia and south Florida, and Life Care Services's subsidiary, Lifecare Retirement Communities, in south Florida.

Perhaps the most critical feature, however, is that most of these providers were associated with more than one facility in their respective markets. In Philadelphia, four facilities are associated with the Quakers. ACTS has seven facilities in the Philadelphia area. The south Florida markets also illustrate the principle of success through expansion by existing providers, as demonstrated by ACTS's St. Andrews and Edgewater Pointe Estates facilities and by Life Care Services's Harbour's Edge and Abbey Delray North and South, John Knox Village, and the two Heritage Park Retirement Centers. In effect, all these organizations successfully leveraged the market strength and credibility that they developed with their first facilities and thus were able to continue to satisfy market demand for more of what they offered. The marketing base for each was strong, and each had the advantage of being able to show the market an existing facility to demonstrate what elderly consumers could expect. The quality of the experience of living in each facility became evident from a growing reputation in the market, which enhanced the credibility of the providers. Finally, each was able to benefit from one of the greatest marketing resources a seniors' housing community can have: satisfied residents, who became a strong source of referral for new prospects. Building from these strengths, the market base for seniors' housing in Philadelphia and south Florida continued to expand.

Expansion was accomplished despite problems that occurred in Philadelphia and south Florida. ACTS maintained the ability to fill each community successfully, and it continues to represent a dominant force in both the Philadelphia area and south Florida. Other well-publicized bankruptcies in Philadelphia did not deter expansion in that market. John Knox Village survived a bankruptcy and became highly successful. Starting with only a handful of units in 1967, John Knox Village eventually expanded in response to market demand until it encompassed 650 independent living units, 120 nursing beds, and 28 assisted living beds.

Another important factor in successful markets is the consistency in managing and marketing facilities. For instance, it has been the case at many Quaker continuing care communities (and others) in the Philadelphia area. In contrast, several facilities that experienced difficulties in each market had been unable to present a consistent image to the public because of frequent changes in the management team, marketing approach, and in some cases ownership.

Perhaps one of the most outstanding characteristics of markets in which maturation rather than saturation occurred was the pace at which facilities entered the market. The actual quantity of facilities and units was less a factor than the time period during which the initial absorption for each occurred. The south Florida and Philadelphia markets have experienced a steadier introduction of seniors' housing communities. The overwhelming majority of south Florida's growth occurred after 1980, whereas in Philadelphia, it occurred over a long period of time, a trait that has contributed to its ability to continue to absorb new communities.

In contrast, 13 new communities containing 1,604 independent living units were built between 1984 and 1987, representing two-thirds of total units in Cincinnati at that time and causing a glut that took years to absorb. During the entire decade between 1990 and 2000, only five new communities opened, adding 384 total new independent living units. On average, the communities built between 1983 and 1987 had 119 independent living units, whereas those built in the 1990s averaged 77 units. For comparison, during the period between 1983 and 1987, 333 new units needed to be absorbed annually in the Cincinnati area versus only 38 annually between 1990 and 2000. The Cincinnati area had more troubled facilities than did the south Florida markets in the late 1980s and early 1990s. As mentioned, expansion in the south Florida markets was in large part the result of existing providers' adding new facilities to capitalize on the continuing market demand for the first facilities. Additionally, many facilities in the south Florida markets may have been more responsive to the demands and needs of the market than have been some of the newer facilities in the Cincinnati area. Organizations with existing track records in other parts of the country as well as in the local Florida markets were able to refine their communities based on what they learned from their own residents. On the other hand, many facilities built in the Cincinnati area in the 1980s were developed by organizations inexperienced in seniors' housing, and this lack of knowledge was reflected in the facilities' marketing, management, and possibly even design.

With the exception of a small number of facilities in each of the three markets, occupancy rates are now reported to be higher than 95 percent, demonstrating that the independent living units were eventually absorbed in those markets despite what might be construed as high market penetration rates.

Assisted Living Units

The assisted living story is new, particularly when compared with the long history of independent living development in these case study markets. In all three cases, freestanding assisted living development burgeoned throughout the 1990s, reflecting what might be construed as saturation (too many units in too short a time) as compared with market maturation. Numerous assisted living facilities in these markets are maintaining optimum occupancies, while others are struggling. It is simply too soon to tell what the outcome of this surge of assisted living development will produce. If anything can be learned from the independent living studies, it may be that over time the assisted living arena will mature and move from what resembles market saturation to market maturation.

Comparison of Case Study Statistics

Figure 8-12 illustrates the differences among the three case study areas as reflected by a simple analysis of demographics, unit counts, and market penetration in 1990 and 2000. The assumptions used in the analysis were selected to reflect generally applicable conditions across all markets to carry out the comparison. It assumes that households age 75 and older, rather than those 65 and older, form the eligible pool. It also assumes an annual household income level of $25,000 in 1990 and 2000. Data on households by age and income were provided by Claritas. In its "Demographic Update Methodology," Claritas explains that the "1990 census income distributions are advanced to the estimated and projected means through a process that estimates the movement of households or families from one income category to the next based on [a] specific area's estimated rate of income growth."[11] For this reason, the analysis assumes a household income of $25,000 in both 1990 and 2000 to illustrate an accurate comparison.

The analysis includes 100 percent of all units in all facilities in the geographic area defined for each case study. Therefore, the market penetration rates illustrated are considered extremely conservative, because most communities draw a certain percentage (frequently 20 to 30 percent) of their residents from outside the local market.

As illustrated in Figure 8-12, all three case study markets experienced significant increases in the number of age- and income-eligible households. The Philadelphia case study examined a region, while the Cincinnati and south Florida studies looked at more narrowly defined markets. In terms of the rate of growth in eligible households, however, Cincinnati led the three areas during the period from 1990 to 2000. As for the growth in seniors' housing, the independent living segment of the Philadelphia and south Florida markets grew at a similar pace—approximately 20 percent during the decade—while Cincinnati's growth rate slowed to 10 percent, a response no doubt to the overbuilding during the 1980s that led to the problem of absorption experienced in that area. The real story reflected by the numbers in Figure 8-12 is the growth in the number of freestanding assisted living units (not associated with communities offering a continuum of care). While south Florida and Cincinnati basically doubled their supply between 1990 and 2000, the Philadelphia area experienced an increase of a slightly lower magnitude than either of the other markets.

Because of the changes related to eligible households and total units in the three case study markets, penetration rates also changed. Penetration rates for independent living units decreased in all three markets as a result of the comparative slowing of growth in this product compared with the significant increase in the number of qualified households. The greatest decrease in market penetration for independent living occurred in Cincinnati, where the smallest number of new independent living units was

Figure 8-12 **Market Penetration in Case Study Markets**

	Philadelphia		**Cincinnati**		**South Florida**	
	Independent Living	*Assisted Living*	*Independent Living*	*Assisted Living*	*Independent Living*	*Assisted Living*
1990						
Eligible Households	44,009		9,523		9,608	
Total Units	10,459	3,148	3,509	585	3,525	1,169
Market Penetration Rate	23.8%	7.2%	36.8%	6.1%	36.7%	12.2%
2000						
Eligible Households	70,653		15,794		14,662	
Total Units	12,533	5,948	3,893	1,162	4,249	2,343
Market Penetration Rate	17.7%	8.4%	24.6%	7.4%	29.0%	16.0%
Percentage Change 1990–2000						
Eligible Households	60.5%		65.9%		52.6%	
Total Units	19.8%	88.9%	10.9%	98.6%	20.5%	100.4%
Market Penetration Rate	–25.6%	16.7%	–33.1%	21.3%	–21.0%	31.2%

Note: Cincinnati analysis includes only 50 percent of units in facilities outside Hamilton County. Alzheimer's units are not included in the analysis of assisted living units.

added during the 1990s. In contrast, because of the tremendous surge in the development of assisted living in all three areas, penetration rates increased in all three case study markets. Philadelphia experienced the lowest increase, reflecting in part its sizable population and the fact that the number of freestanding assisted living units increased more slowly than in the other two markets, which helps to explain why the product appears to be doing somewhat better in the Philadelphia area than in the other two markets.

As mentioned, many of the independent living facilities that were considered "troubled" in the 1980s have stabilized and are now fully occupied and have waiting lists. Again, this factor is attributed to the increase in eligible households and the relatively stable growth of new units during the 1990s. Several submarkets in these case study areas represent areas with high concentrations of seniors' housing (lower Bucks County/northeast Philadelphia, for example) that are maintaining reasonably full occupancies despite market penetration rates nearing 30 percent.

With the boom in assisted living development that occurred during the 1990s, it is not surprising that the increase in the total number of freestanding assisted living units in each market was close to or exceeded 100 percent during the last decade. Cincinnati appears to be re-creating its independent living troubles of the 1980s in the assisted living arena. Eight new assisted living communities were opened between 1997 and 2000, adding 527 beds in just four years (an annual absorption of 132 new units). As explained in the Cincinnati case study, these facilities are struggling to fill, some reporting occupancies as low as 42 percent. The Philadelphia market has also seen tremendous growth of new assisted living facilities opened during the 1990s, yet the majority of assisted living facilities in the Philadelphia area are maintaining occupancies of more than 90 percent. Three of the newest communities to open in this market are struggling to fill, and some of the older communities continue to struggle to maintain acceptable occupancy rates. No doubt it can be attributed in part to the lack of physical appeal compared with the numerous modern choices in the market. South Florida has also seen tremendous growth in assisted living, nearly doubling the number of beds between 1990 and 2000. The number of assisted living units nearly doubled between 1990 and 2000. Very few facilities reported occupancies higher than 95 percent, and the majority reported occupancies between 82 and 91 percent. At the time this book was written, four new facilities were still struggling to fill.

If any certainty is illustrated by the case studies, it is that each market has a different history and pattern of development and differs in the way consumers respond to the types of seniors' housing communities developed. Expectations that market response will be the same from one to another can lead to a cookie-cutter approach to market analysis, rather than one that takes into consideration the potential differences.

Notes

1. Herbert J. Sims & Co. and American Association of Homes and Services for the Aging, "From Start-Up to Success: A Statistical Analysis of Emerging Continuing Care Retirement Communities," 1999.

2. R.C. Wetzler and R. Lageman, "Measuring Demand for Senior Housing," Fitch, Duff & Phelps, 2000, p. 6.

3. David Wolfe, *Serving the Ageless Market: Strategies for Selling to the Fifty-Plus Market* (New York: McGraw-Hill, 1990), p. 10.

4. U.S. Census Bureau, unpublished data.

5. "Values and Standards of Kendal-Crosslands and Kendal Management Services," 1987, p. 6.

6. Continuing Care Provider Registration and Disclosure Act, P.L. 391, No. 82, §3212 (1984).

7. Ibid., p. 12.

8. M.A.J. McKenna, "HUD Housing Sinks in a Flooded Market," *Cincinnati Enquirer,* August 27, 1989.

9. "John Knox Village of Florida, Inc., Information for New Board Members," 1988.

10. Claritas/NDS, "Demographic Update Methodology," May 1999.

Michael Mathers; courtesy AIA

The University Retirement Center at Davis in Davis, California, is set on a ten-acre campus. It offers a full spectrum of retirement living and health care options, including cottages, garden apartments, independent living apartments, assisted living units, and a health center with an Alzheimer's wing. Architect: Ankrom Moisan Associated Architects

9 The Use of Market Studies

Tools for Each Team Member

The market study conducted for a planned seniors' housing community traditionally has been considered an evaluative tool that is commissioned and used by the developer, sponsor, and/or owner. Historically, market feasibility studies were considered a necessity primarily for obtaining financing; however, market studies can be an influential planning document that has practical applications for all the major team members.

Long before a third party such as a regulatory agency or lender requires a market study, market analysis provides the first indications of whether to proceed with a project. Information contained in the market analysis provides guidance to the developer as to how to shape the project to meet the target market's needs and preferences. The architects look to market analysis to determine how to program space and design buildings to match the tastes and functional capacity of prospective residents. Marketing professionals use the market analysis to plan their budgets, develop targeted marketing strategies, and determine where and how to spend marketing dollars. Finally, lenders use market studies as an internal decision-making tool, as a catalyst to bring together key team members to resolve issues, and as a sales tool for obtaining investors.

Developers and Owners

Determining Feasibility

One of the most critical uses of a market study is to reach the first key decision in project planning: whether to proceed with the development. The high degree of specialization of seniors' housing and the resulting restrictions on its marketability warrant a preliminary determination of potential market viability before spending the substantial dollars required to develop a project.

Several key factors addressed in market analysis are considered important in determining whether to pursue a development opportunity. The first is potential depth of the target market in the specific geographic area. Analysis of demographic data for the proposed market area yields a profile and quantification of age- and income-eligible households that are designed to provide a measure of market depth (see Chapters 2 and 3). The relative volume of households that meet specific criteria for eligibility for a project is one way to determine whether to proceed with a project. As described in Chapter 3, low market penetration levels (typically below 4 or 5 percent) of age- and income-qualified households are considered acceptable levels of comfort for market depth.

A second and a related indicator is the competitive environment. Market analysis helps to identify competitive facilities in the market and delineate their characteristics. Information on occupancy and fill rates for competitive facilities can be instrumental in determining how a market is responding to various options for seniors' housing. On the most simplistic level, long fill periods, empty units, and difficulty in reaching full occupancy are considered troublesome warning signs. Future competition is also a factor in reaching a go/no go decision. The number of projects coming online and the nature of their sponsors/owners are considered when determining how much a market can absorb (see Chapters 2, 3, and 7).

A developer/owner can initially assess a project's potential market viability before either a formal or an independent market analysis has been conducted. Some organizations, particularly those that undertake multiple seniors' housing projects, have developed the in-house capability to conduct market analyses to determine development opportunities. Many of these same organizations, however, should obtain an independent opinion of market feasibility as part of the decision-making process. Organizations planning to develop seniors' communities may look to outside market analysts to provide the initial and only determination of feasibility, to confirm or refute internally reached conclusions, or to assess feasibility and help plan the project.

Determining Project Characteristics

Market analysis provides information that is useful in determining and refining project characteristics. The overall size of the community being planned (i.e., number of units and/or beds) is assessed based on depth of the qualified market and number of competitive units that exist, remain to be sold, and are likely to open during the next several years. Information on competitive product volume and timing is an important tool in determining how much a market can absorb.

Market studies in areas that have existing competitive seniors' communities provide localized market parameters for determining unit mix, unit sizes, payment methods, and pricing levels. By evaluating characteristics of local competitive seniors' communities, the developer/owner can reach an informed decision about whether to replicate already successful features or to define niche opportunities that are not currently being addressed in the market. Feedback on market response to existing seniors' facilities enables the developer to assess which features, such as unit types and payment programs, are more or less successful in a specific market.

In using local competitor data to reach decisions about project characteristics, however, one must consider when competitive facilities were built and make adjustments, as appropriate, to account for more current trends in seniors' housing development. For instance, a market such as the Philadelphia metropolitan area is dominated by many communities developed many years ago. These facilities tend to have a high proportion of studio and one-bedroom units, which by today's standards are small. In the northeast section of the city of Philadelphia, several communities date back to the late 1800s and early 1900s.

Two of these facilities, Deer Meadows and Evangelical Manor, offer primarily studio apartments (approximately 75 percent) and only a few two-bedroom units. Another early community, the Philadelphia Protestant Home built in 1890, offers 34 percent studio units, 60 percent one-bedroom apartments, and a few two-bedroom units. The proportion of studio units was significantly decreased in communities developed in this market in the 1980s. The Lafayette Redeemer, opened in 1985 in northeast Philadelphia, does not have any studio units; approximately 60 percent of the units have one bedroom, and 40 percent have two bedrooms. Similarly, four CCRCs were opened in nearby Bucks County between 1978 and 1981, each with fewer than 20 percent studio units. Pennswood Village has an equal number of one- and two-bedroom units with only 10 percent studios. Southampton Estates, an ACTS facility, offers mostly one-bedroom units, an equal number of studios and two-bedroom units, and even has 15 three-bedroom apartments. These changes to unit mix and sizes over time reflect the market's desires. An understanding of industry trends is necessary to place local market information into the proper context. Today's preference for larger units suggests that local competitor information in the northeast Philadelphia/lower Bucks County market reflects a somewhat dated approach to seniors' housing development, and decisions regarding new projects in this market must be made accordingly.

Understanding Consumers' Attitudes And Preferences

The inclusion of consumer research in market analysis and market studies should be a much more common occurrence than it is. Although consumer research can form a bridge between project planning and project marketing, many organizations that have experience in this industry—developers, owners, architects, lenders, and marketing firms—point to its usefulness as an analytical tool.

One of the most important ways in which consumer research can assist developers/owners is by educating them about their prospects—elderly consumers. The use of various forms of direct consumer research (see Chapter 4), including focus groups, mail surveys, and telephone surveys, enables the developer/owner to gain a better understanding of how consumers might respond to the seniors' community planned.

On the most basic level, consumer research enables one to gauge the public's level of familiarity with and understanding of the type of community proposed, which becomes a factor in developing the marketing program. Information about whether the specific elderly target market is interested in moving to the proposed community and when such a move is contemplated or planned, and an evaluation of the services and programs offered are extremely important in assessing the overall viability of a potential seniors' housing development. For instance, a project that is being designed to reach a highly affluent group of seniors that on average will be in their early 70s when they move must test that specific group's interest. Consumer research should be used to help evaluate whether that target market will be attracted to the project planned. This type of research is, however, much more likely to be successful when it addresses independent living, given the increased frailty and memory impairment of those who are candidates for assisted living.

Other, more specific features can be tested, including acceptability of the proposed site and its impact on market area draw, perception of a sponsor or developer/owner, and its influence on project acceptability. Consumer research can also provide guidance in developing and refining the project's characteristics. Testing a project concept through direct contact with prospective elderly consumers provides a developer/owner an opportunity to evaluate current preferences on methods of fee payments. It allows one to fine-tune assumptions about unit types and mix, design features, services, and amenities. With regard to services and amenities, consumer research can be used to assess not only which services should be offered at a seniors' community but also which ones are considered most important and which should be included in the fee structure or offered on a pay-for-service basis.

Finally, consumer research may be structured as an initial task in project marketing. Focus groups and surveys can be used to attract a local advisory group. Such a group can be extremely helpful in providing ongoing reactions to project plans as they develop and can also be useful in a marketing campaign. Local advisory groups comprising prominent older members of the community may become strong advocates for a seniors' housing community, acting as a valuable source of referrals.

Direct mail surveys, in addition to obtaining data, can be used as a source of initial leads for project marketing. By incorporating a separate reply card that allows the recipient to provide name, address, and phone number only if interested in being kept informed about the project, a survey can be a successful early marketing tool without requiring that all those who are interested actually complete the survey.

Determining the Fill Period

One very critical factor in planning a seniors' housing community is accurately estimating the period of time it will take to reach stabilized occupancy. Although no formulas exist for projecting fill periods, information derived from the market analysis is helpful in developing a reasonable estimate. Factors considered in market analysis that provide guidance include the extent of consumers' familiarity with and acceptance of seniors' housing models, the fill-up experience of recently developed comparable facilities, the number of units a market must try to absorb concurrently, the strength or softness of the traditional housing resale market, and the depth of the target market. All this information should be developed and available through market analysis.

Other critical elements also have an impact on a given seniors' community's fill period. The quality of the marketing program and the experience of marketing professionals are clearly important. For independent living communities in particular, the potential requirement and successful ability to reach high levels of presales before construction are likely to result in a larger number of move-ins during the early months after the community has opened. The strength and reputation of the organization that owns, operates, and/or sponsors a community and its ability to reach a related affinity group also can have a positive or negative impact on a project's fill period.

Satisfying Third-Party Requirements

The more commonly observed use for market feasibility studies is to satisfy requirements set forth by lenders and regulatory authorities. Traditionally, sources of both debt and equity financing have required that an independent feasibility study be conducted for a planned seniors' housing community. Local lending authorities and underwriters of bonds issued by authorities such as industrial development, hospital and health care, and even local redevelopment authorities require that a feasibility study be completed; typically, that study is included in the official statement used to sell the bonds. Many direct lenders, such as commercial banks, have continued to require their borrowers to present independently prepared market and/or full financial feasibility studies (see "Lenders" on p. 178).

An increasing number of states have passed legislation governing the development of life care facilities and CCRCs. Currently, 34 states have some form of legislation pertaining to these communities, some of which requires submission of a market or financial feasibility study. Figure 9-1 lists the states and their regulatory agencies that require feasibility studies before approving construction and operation of a continuing care retirement community.

Architects

Before Design

Information in the market analysis is considered so valuable that many architects experienced in designing seniors' housing will not begin design until a market study has been completed. Increasingly, architects use the market study to translate market needs and preferences into an appropriate design and architectural program. Although an architectural firm may occasionally take on a client before the completion of a market study to assist in obtaining the

Figure 9-1 **States Requiring Feasibility Studies for CCRCs**

State	Responsible Agency
Arizona	Department of Insurance
Connecticut	Department of Social Services
Florida	Department of Insurance
Iowa	Commissioner of Insurance
Maine	Department of Human Services
Maryland	Office of Aging
Michigan	Corporation and Securities Bureau of Consumer and Industry Services Department
New York	Department of Health
North Carolina	Department of Insurance
South Carolina	Department of Consumer Affairs
Washington	Department of Social and Health Services

necessary zoning approvals, architectural firms experienced in seniors' housing often require that a prospective client conduct or obtain a market study before initiating design.

Space Programming

The contribution of a market analysis to architectural programming may be more influential in designing functional space for a seniors' community than in its actual look or external design. Information contained in a market study provides a locally derived basis for making decisions about how large a project should be, what types of units and how many of each should be planned, what kinds of services are to be provided, and what functional capabilities the target market expects. In programming the space in a seniors' housing community, the architect uses this information to develop a plan for the amount of each type of space, the functional plan for the space, and layout and adjacency requirements.

Architects are able to translate information about lifestyles into the way the space will function. For instance, learning from a study that the target market is affluent and represents the country club set will affect the design and layout of dining facilities. The room can be designed to accommodate table service and may be sized to promote leisurely rather than regimented dining, and one or more private dining rooms might be included for residents' private parties.

Understanding the Target Market's Tastes and Preferences

Architects look for information in market studies that provides insights into values, lifestyle, tastes, and preferences of the target market. Such information, which is best derived from direct consumer research, enables the design team to create a building concept that will respond to the specific local target market. Information about consumers' preferences, combined with an understanding of their background and socioeconomic characteristics, can be applied to the development of the architectural program and specific design features.

In some cases, architectural firms conduct their own consumer research on a project's design and functionality. When a market analysis or consumer survey has been conducted before the architect's involvement in a project, the information derived can be useful in preparing for brainstorming sessions with prospective residents. Once architects have conducted brainstorming sessions or focus groups with consumers, they are better able to evaluate responses to earlier surveys, because they have gained insights from their own in-depth discussions with consumers.

A Catalyst for Team Planning

The market analysis can serve as a catalyst for ongoing project planning in the area of design. In some cases, a study generates information on design issues and raises questions that must be resolved by bringing the team together. Some architects have noted that developers tend to keep design and market analysis professionals separate. This approach can be deleterious to project planning, because it limits the potential opportunity for creativity and problem solving derived from the team's synergy.

When the professionals who have conducted market analysis are also involved in financial analysis and planning, team planning continues to be interactive. Having responded with programming and design to the input from market analysis, the architect in turn provides the financial consultant with information on the costs of building the facility that are necessary to develop an appropriate pricing structure and determine financial feasibility. This information is tied back to the market analysis, because it must be determined whether the market can support the prices required for the project to be financially feasible. This set of interactions underscores the iterative nature of planning.

Marketing Professionals

Gaining Clients' Acceptance

A project's success depends to a large extent on the quality of its marketing program and activities. Marketing professionals with substantial experience in this industry agree that a market analysis must be conducted before they can plan and implement a well-structured, targeted marketing program. In some cases, marketing firms have the expertise to carry out their own market analysis, but when they do not, marketing professionals may require the prospective client to obtain a market study before they will enter into a contract with that client.

Developing the Marketing Budget

Marketing plans frequently show long-range month-by-month activities that occur both before and after a facility opens. It is critical for the marketing professional to obtain information on how long a project will take to fill, information that is normally provided by a market study. It is most useful to marketing professionals if a study has plotted a monthly fill projection. Marketing professionals also look at information on how competitive projects have fared, particularly those that opened recently.

Information on market area definition and the location of substantial numbers of the elderly target market in that area can also contribute to the development of a marketing budget. These data enable the marketing professional to identify appropriate media sources that are likely to reach the target market. Localized media costs are an important component of the marketing budget.

Developing Marketing Strategies

The market analysis provides the requisite context for the creation of a project's marketing strategy. Information on who the competitors are, what they offer, how they package and price their services, and how they position their products is essential in planning the best strategy for a new community. All this information is typically incorporated in a market study. By becoming familiar with competitor data and socioeconomic characteristics of the target market, the marketing professional is able to develop a project's marketing mix. The marketing mix consists of product, place, promotion, and price, a four-factor classification system for what are considered "controllable variables" that can influence the market.[1] A given project's marketing mix may attempt to replicate or emulate successful features of competitive facilities in the market area, or it may seek to establish a differentiated market niche for the community.

Familiarity with the competitive environment is also useful in determining the orientation of a marketing campaign. In markets with little or no competition, the marketing effort must encompass a significant educational role, increasing elderly consumers' familiarity and understanding of the seniors' housing concept. In more mature markets that contain a number of existing communities of varying types, the marketing campaign might be more oriented toward advantageously positioning a project against its competitors and may emphasize less educating potential buyers.

The results of direct consumer research, which is part of some market studies, can be extremely useful to the marketing professional. It helps the professional to determine the extent to which education in the market will be required and to assess the market's familiarity and understanding. The marketing program, like the design, needs to be informed and shaped by knowledge of consumers' preferences: what they will buy, what services and amenities are important to them, and how much they are willing to spend. Finally, consumer research surveys and focus groups can provide invaluable insights about how the market perceives competitive facilities and the organization that will develop the new project.

Lenders

Internal Decision Making

A market and/or financial feasibility study is one of a number of tools lenders use to decide whether to become involved in a proposed seniors' housing development. Frequently, the study is part of the underwriting criteria established by a lending source considering financing the development. Because of the complexity of this business, many experienced lenders are convinced of the importance of understanding the specific market environment where a project will be marketed and operated. Lenders look to the study to provide them with information on the depth of the target market and the nature, extent, and track record of existing and planned competition; they are increasingly interested in seeing a study incorporate direct consumer research.

Feasibility studies must present the basis for assumptions, which lenders then evaluate for reasonableness. A supporting basis must be provided for assumptions about the level and compensation of staff for the facility as well as nonstaff operating expenses. Information developed from the market study provides support for many of the key assumptions that drive financial forecasts. For instance, the forecast fill rate is based on information taken from the market analysis, particularly with regard to how competitive projects are filling and the level of the market's familiarity with the concept of seniors' housing communities. Although it may not be incorporated in final feasibility documents, the sensitivity of the project to potential changes in projected absorption must be evaluated.

In addition to absorption, market-related assumptions critical to project feasibility include the appropriateness of pricing structure and levels. Market analysis provides information on the type or types of payment mechanisms with which the market may be familiar. For instance, in markets such as Philadelphia that are dominated by the use of entrance fees, this information is considered when developing the appropriate pricing approach. Information from the market study on the ranges of prices being charged and their relative acceptance in the market is also used for decisions about project pricing. In their review of feasibility documents, lenders look at the proposed pricing scheme to assess whether it conforms to market norms. Information contained in market and financial feasibility studies enhances lenders' ability to determine whether a project meets the institution's underwriting criteria and helps to facilitate an informed lending decision. Therefore, the study is an important component of an institution's deliberation as it weighs the risk of taking part in the financial transaction.

Team Decision Tool

The market and financial feasibility study can serve as a catalyst to bring the project team together to resolve issues. In its review of these studies, the lender notes both the rationale and support for the assumptions being made. Experienced lenders often go back to the feasibility consultant to challenge and question assumptions to increase their understanding and comfort with the proposed project. In highlighting particular strengths and weaknesses of a project, the study allows the lender to draw all the parties in the transaction together to discuss areas that may be sensitive and that need further work and resolution. For instance, if operating expenses appear to be higher than might be expected, the lender can bring the team together to discuss the issue and determine whether changes can reasonably be made to bring expenses into line. The study thus becomes a source for reaching greater comfort and consensus on key project assumptions.

Obtaining Investors

One of the most traditional uses of the market or financial feasibility study is the provision of an independent assessment of a project's potential viability for securing investors. In cases where debt financing involves the sale of bonds or equity financing involves the selling of partnership shares to investors, this independent study has long been a requirement of institutions handling the transaction. The study is a tool that legitimizes the investment to a prospective investor and provides information that will enhance the investor's ability to make an informed decision.

In summary, while the market feasibility study is a critical component in the due diligence process required in financing a seniors' housing community, it plays a major role in planning. Many continue to feel that they can simply wait until it is time to finance a project before having a market study conducted, but this line of thought is a critical mistake. By the time financing is imminent, it is too late to significantly adjust the community's characteristics, including overall size, unit size, mix and pricing, and services and amenities. A good market study will help to shape these elements to meet market needs—the reason a market analysis should be considered one of the most important tools in planning and financing a seniors' housing community.

Note

1. E.J. McCarthy, *Basic Marketing: A Managerial Approach,* 6th ed. (Homewood, Ill.: Richard D. Irwin, 1978), p. 39.

Glossary

AAHSA. American Association of Homes and Services for the Aging.

ACLF (adult congregate living facility). An arrangement offering housing and support services but no skilled or intermediate nursing care.

ADL. Activity of daily living, such as bathing, dressing, or walking.

AHCA. American Health Care Association.

ALF. Assisted living facility.

ALFA. Assisted Living Federation of America.

All-inclusive (extensive) contract. An upfront entry fee and monthly charges that remain the same regardless of the resident's level of care.

ASHA. American Seniors Housing Association.

Assisted living. A special combination of housing, supportive services, personalized assistance, and health care designed to respond to the individual needs of those who need help with ADLs and instrumental ADLs (IADLs). Support services are available 24 hours a day. Assisted living beds are designed for frail seniors who need assistance with ADLs but who do not require continuous skilled nursing care. Such beds can also be located in a separate wing or floor of a congregate residence or in a freestanding assisted living building. They typically have more stringent licensing requirements than congregate or independent living units.

CARF. Rehabilitation Accreditation Commission, formerly the Commission on Accreditation of Rehabilitation Facilities.

CCAC. Continuing Care Accreditation Commission.

CCRC (continuing care retirement community). A living arrangement that provides for or arranges for the provision of housing and health-related services for an older person under an agreement effective for the life of the person or for a specified period greater than one year.

Condominium ownership. An opportunity to share in the ownership of a continuing care or life care community by holding fee simple title.

Congregate housing. Designed for seniors who pay for some congregate services (housekeeping, transportation, meals, for example) as part of a monthly fee or rental rate and who require little, if any, assistance with ADLs. Residents of congregate living/independent living units may or may not receive some home health care services provided by in-house staff or an outside agency. Some congregate housing communities also include a designated assisted living component.

Cooperative ownership. An opportunity to share in the ownership of a continuing care or life care community through shares in the corporation.

Effective buying income (EBI). Money income less personal tax and nontax payments, a number often referred to as *disposable* or *after-tax* income.

Endowment fee. See *entrance fee.*

Entrance fee. An upfront fee designed to cover the development costs or to retire construction debt associated with a unit, or possibly to build up reserves for future medical or other variable expenditures.

Fill period. The time it takes to reach full occupancy after a facility opens.

Focus group. A small group used to determine what people in a target market think about a product.

Independent living. See *congregate housing.*

JCAHO. Joint Commission on Accreditation of Healthcare Organizations.

Modified contract. A living arrangement with an upfront entry fee and monthly charges that remain the same regardless of the resident's level of care for only a specified period of time (e.g., 30 days per year), or increased monthly charges for the resident as the level of care increases but at a discount from the market value of the services (e.g., a 10 percent discount on the daily nursing rate for residents).

Monthly fee. Fees tied to the cost of operating a community.

NCAL. National Center for Assisted Living.

NCOSH. National Council on Seniors Housing.

NIC. National Investment Center.

PUMS. Public Use Microdata Sample.

Refundable entrance fee. Return-of-capital program.

Rental contract. An arrangement in which no upfront entry fee is charged. The resident's monthly charges increase directly with the level of care provided.

Retirement Service Center. A HUD-sponsored mortgage insurance program.

Index